SO-DJY-801

UMPTEEN WAYS OF LOOKING
AT A POSSUM

Everette Maddox
photo courtesy of Nancy Harris, used with her permission

To Bill Daniel,

With hopes that you
like Everette and his
poems —

UMPTEEN WAYS OF LOOKING
AT A POSSUM:
CRITICAL AND CREATIVE RESPONSES
TO EVERETTE MADDOX

edited by
Grace Bauer and Julie Kane

Julie Kane

New Orleans ❧ 2006

XAVIER REVIEW PRESS

For permission to use copyrighted material, grateful acknowledgment is made to the copyright holders on pp. 305-307, which are hereby made part of this copyright page.

Library of Congress Cataloguing-in-Publication Data
© 2006 by Grace Bauer and Julie Kane
ISBN 1-883275-16-4

Xavier University of Louisiana
1 Drexel Drive
New Orleans
LA 70125-1098

Contents

Front Matter

Nonfiction

Poetry & Song Lyrics

Back Matter

R. S. Gwynn

Preface

I knew Everette Maddox only slightly and thus can't add very much to the wealth of reminiscences, anecdotes, and tributes collected in *Umpteen Ways of Looking at a Possum*. We met on only a couple of occasions, and, while the meetings were all too brief, two things—both of them often remarked on by others—stand out for me. One was Everette's unique appearance. One December in the mid 1970s, my first wife and I were traveling from Texas to North Carolina for a family Christmas, and we decided to stop in New Orleans to visit my friend Ralph Adamo, a fellow graduate of the University of Arkansas MFA program. I was in my first teaching job and only a step or two removed from grad-school penury, so I asked Ralph if he could put us up for the night. He couldn't, as he was living in fairly Raskolnikovian circumstances himself, but he arranged for us to stay at the apartment of a poet named Everette Maddox, a few poems of whose I'd read and admired shortly before. The apartment, as it turned out, was the one that Everette shared with his then-wife, and one of its previous occupants, I later learned, had been F. Scott Fitzgerald (O fateful omen!). Everette and his wife were leaving for a few days and had generously turned over their place to a couple of total strangers, though I guess Ralph had shown him some of my own poems and vouched that I wouldn't lift the flatware.

Another Arkansas friend, Leon Stokesbury, had described Maddox to me as the skinniest guy he had ever seen, and when we met him on the street as we approached the apartment we weren't disappointed. Like the thin man in Donald Justice's poem, when he lay down he must have become the horizon. Everette was on his way out of town and had dressed for the chilly day. He was wearing a black wool overcoat, a dark fedora, and a muffler, carrying, I seem to recall, a heavy briefcase. Even wrapped in all of these insulating layers—and there must have been a three-piece suit underneath—he still could have concealed himself behind a telephone pole. There wasn't much more than a quick exchange of pleasantries and thanks, but the memory of him is still vivid. He must have been about thirty and was still more or less solvent and employed. I can still see the darkness of his hair and beard (neatly trimmed then) and the depth of his eyes. He looked distinguished, elegant, alien, doomed. The apartment itself had high ceilings, lots of books, a couple of cheery gas space heaters, and a large, sunny kitchen where Ralph, my wife, and I spent the better part of the next afternoon drinking Jax and picking apart a huge pile of spicy boiled crabs. It was my first visit to New Orleans, and I felt that it had lived up to at least part of its reputation as a place where good things were to be had easily, maybe a bit too easily.

The next time I saw Everette must have been at least ten years later, and things, I had heard, had been going downhill for him for a good while. I was in town for an academic conference, and Ralph and I went out for drinks one evening. At a bar—I don't think it was the Maple Leaf—we ran into Everette. I don't think that he was officially homeless then, but he was thinner than before (if such were possible!) and was obviously working full evening shifts cadging drinks. Still, his appearance, for a poet who was by all reports on the skids, was remarkable; he wore a red plaid shirt, a knitted wool tie, a Brooks Brothers tweed jacket—somewhat the worse for wear but reasonably clean—and held in either hand the ever-present pipe and glass of bar scotch. We talked a good while—about exactly what I couldn't say now—but this time I was struck by another thing about Everette—his voice. Even in that busy bar, with the jukebox blaring and dozens of conversations swimming against the tide, his voice was deep and clear. Coming as it did from the face of that bearded Russian mystic (google up a photograph of Dostoyevsky and you'll see what I mean) with the long-neglected teeth and the far-seeing blue eyes, it was very striking. I never heard Everette read his own poems, but I am sure that the accounts of his stage presence and performing voice given here are accurate.
It should be clear from the pages that follow that Everette had a large circle of friends, admirers, enablers, muses, and hangers-on. That none of them was capable of saving him from himself is no discredit to anyone, for I suspect that saving himself was the last

thing on Everette Maddox's mind. He wrote the poems, he generously sponsored other poets at the Maple Leaf, and he provided the source of a thousand memories, some of them wryly funny and many of them poignantly sad—but none of them tragic. Most importantly, he was the center around which a teeming, vibrant literary scene revolved. Grace Bauer and Julie Kane have done an admirable job of assembling this testament to Everette's life and writing, and may their efforts serve to introduce his work to the wider audience it deserves. Heretofore, Everette was the kind of poet whom, if you weren't in New Orleans, you heard about only from those who were. Well, they are all here now and are ready to tell you his story.

Acknowledgments

The editors wish to thank Susan Belasco, Sherry Harris, Amelia Montes, Linda Pratt, and Hilda Raz for their advice in the early stages of this project. Also Lester Sullivan at the Xavier University Library and the staff of the Historic New Orleans Collection, for their support of our archival research. Thanks to JC Reilly, for her technical assistance, and to John Anderson, for his help in securing our cover image. Special thanks to the University of Nebraska Research Council and the Maude Hammond Fling Research Fellowship, whose generous support helped us see this project through to publication. Thanks to all of our contributors. And special thanks to Thomas Bonner and Robert Skinner of Xavier Review Press, who made this project happen despite the personal and professional hardships they endured as the result of Hurricane Katrina.

Grace Bauer and Julie Kane

Introduction

400 HONOR HOMELESS POET WHO DIED, proclaims the headline from February 1989. The story, which went out on the Associated Press wire service and was carried in newspapers around the country, details the jazz funeral of Everette Hawthorne Maddox, who died at Charity Hospital in New Orleans on February 13th at the age of forty-four. After the infamous funeral, which was a party Maddox himself would have enjoyed, most of his ashes were thrown into his beloved Mississippi River by his friends. Some were buried on the patio of his equally loved Maple Leaf Bar, marked by a plaque inscribed with the self-composed epitaph, HE WAS A MESS.

Everette Maddox, known to some as "Rette," was born and raised in Prattville, Alabama, and attended the University of Alabama at Tuscaloosa, where he published his first poem in *The New Yorker* while still in his twenties. He left Tuscaloosa without finishing his Ph.D. and moved to New Orleans in 1975 to teach, first at Xavier University, then at the University of New Orleans, and finally as a poet in the public schools. While he was acknowledged by many colleagues as a brilliant teacher of both writing and literature, his prodigious drinking habits interfered with his ability to hold a job, resulting in the dissolution of his marriage, homelessness, and eventually his untimely death from esophageal cancer.

Maddox was a man of contradictions. Though he was of average height and weighed little more than a hundred pounds fully clothed in the three-piece suits he favored, he was, nonetheless, a monumental presence—especially when reading poetry. His voice was so resonant, one wondered how it could emanate from a man his size. He was homeless, but never, ever, seen in public without a tie. He was once spotted sleeping on a park bench covered with the society pages of the *New Orleans Times-Picayune*, in which he appeared that day. He was widely read and famous for impromptu recitations of poems and lengthy prose passages he'd learned by heart—John

Berryman, Alan Dugan, Dylan Thomas, Wallace Stevens, Thomas Wolfe, F. Scott Fitzgerald, Flannery O'Connor, James Joyce, Mark Twain, and many more—yet he could be hopelessly absent-minded about present, practical matters. Renowned for his wit, he also battled bouts of depression, moods so dark they often frightened those who knew him.

Those moods, along with poor health, seemed to run in Maddox's family. Both his parents were by all reports solitary people who died, as he did, young and from cancer. His younger brother, Bill, who published numerous works on political science and one novel, died in 1998 at the age of forty-eight from complications related to alcoholism. Perhaps the family shared a genetic predisposition to doom, or perhaps it was the dark side of his Romantic sensibility that caused Everette Maddox to doom himself.

While Maddox published only three volumes of poetry in his lifetime—*The Thirteen Original Poems* (1976), *The Everette Maddox Song Book* (1982), and *Bar Scotch* (1988)—his legend and his influence loom larger than that modest output might suggest. Many writers who knew him cite him as an influence on their writing and reading lives, though also, as Rodney Jones acknowledges in the poem "Elegy for a Bad Example," a cautionary tale. He was a central figure in the New Orleans literary scene, especially beginning in 1979, when he helped inaugurate a weekly reading series at the Maple Leaf Bar on Oak Street. Those readings, which have continued since his death, featured most of the poets and writers who lived in New Orleans during that period—Andrei Codrescu, Peter and Nicole Cooley, Ellen Gilchrist, Yusef Komunyakaa, and countless others—and many who passed through. In 1980, the first *Maple Leaf Rag* anthology, featuring work by readers in the series, was edited by Maddox, Maxine Cassin, and Yorke Corbin and published by Cassin's New Orleans Poetry Journal Press.

Maddox's reputation has continued to grow since his death. In 1993, a posthumous volume, *American Waste*—composed of poems written on bar napkins, beer coasters, and the backs of envelopes during the last months of the poet's life—was edited by friends and published by Portals Press. That same year, the journal

Negative Capability, under the guest editorship of Dale Edmonds, published a selection of Maddox's poems and a group of elegies written about him. The following year, 1994, brought three significant publications. Portals Press published a fifteenth anniversary issue of the *Maple Leaf Rag* which was dedicated to Maddox and contained several tribute poems. *The New Orleans Review* produced a special double issue dedicated to Maddox with his color portrait on the cover and critical articles on his work by William Matthews, Rodney Jones, and William Lavender. And that year's *Oxford Companion to Twentieth-Century Poetry* contained a 250-word critical and biographical entry on Maddox, describing him as "the literary equivalent of Charlie Chaplin's little tramp," whose poems "present a persona aware of and vulnerable to the inhumanities of man but still hoping for the best."

As the twenty-first century unfolds, the Maddox legend continues to grow, attracting a new generation of fans who encountered his work only after his death. One such example is David Kunian's 2002 Public Radio documentary, *He Was a Mess: The Short Life of New Orleans Poet Everette Maddox.* In 2004, Tensaw Press in Mobile, Alabama, brought out the second posthumous collection of poems by Maddox, *Rette's Last Stand.* And a play based on Maddox's life was staged in spring 2006 by the Mondo Bizarro Theater Company of New Orleans. Meanwhile, personal tributes to Maddox continue to appear in literary journals and in works by individual artists.

This volume represents an attempt to collect the best of the work that has been written about Maddox to date. The tributes take the form of nonfiction essays, poems and song lyrics, fictional stories with a character obviously based upon Maddox, and journalism articles—each with its own section. Included in this volume are National Book Award winner Ellen Gilchrist, National Book Critics Circle Award winners William Matthews and Rodney Jones, Lamont Poetry Prize winner William Harmon, and many other distinguished names from American letters. Here, too, are the voices of art critic Doug MacCash, blues bassist Spike Perkins, and jazz deejay Fred Kasten—friends of Maddox who can approach his life and works with an artist's eye or a musician's ear, not just a writerly or academic sensibility.

In verse, in prose, in the direct language of memoir, in the controlled language of academic criticism, these critical and creative responses to Maddox strive to make sense of the dualities and contradictions embodied in his life and works. In these pages, Maddox comes across as a poet of platonic love and a poet of boorish lust; as a populist and an elitist snob; as a deeply Southern poet and as one filled with anger at his native Alabama. To some, he defied the Puritan work ethic and dedicated his life to poetry; to others, he exemplified the consequences of a string of bad choices. He was both the British-tradition poet of painstakingly crafted lines and the spontaneous poet of blunt American speech—jotting down his late poems on bar napkins and coasters as William Carlos Williams had once jotted his on little medical prescription pads. The brilliant classroom and barroom teacher of literature was a man deeply suspicious of academia. He drank "for the pain" and for communion with others; or he drank because he had a disease that would not let him stop drinking, even when alcohol robbed him of his wife, job, home, and health. He was, as William Matthews summarized, "both homeless and widely beloved . . . formal and informal, destitute and dignified . . . street poet and prosodist, Rhett Butler and Rette Maddox."

The dualities and contradictions embodied by Maddox continue to resonate for other writers. They are the dualities and contradictions of the human condition and of the artist's vocation. The need to write about Maddox, to wrestle with his ghost, is the need to make sense of those contrary impulses, those clashing American myths, as much as it is to honor his influence and his body of work.

In a letter to his longtime friend Robert Woolf, Maddox once described his life as a "museum of consolation prizes." His poems continue to console those who knew him and delight readers who discover the work that survives. It is our hope that this collection helps to further his poetic reputation.

Everette Maddox Chronology

Oct. 9, 1944   Born in Montgomery, Alabama, to Everette Hawthorne Maddox, Sr., and Dorothy Stuckey Maddox

Apr. 25, 1949   Brother William Stuckey Maddox born

June 1963   Graduates from Autauga County High School in Prattville, Alabama; earns a City of Prattville scholarship to college

Sept. 1963   Enters the University of Alabama at Tuscaloosa

Dec. 5, 1966   Father dies of lung cancer in Autauga County Hospital in Prattville, aged 50

June 1967   Earns a B.A. in English, with a minor in Latin, from the University of Alabama

Sept. 1967   Begins graduate studies in English at the University of Alabama under a National Defense Education Act Fellowship

Aug. 1968   Earns an M.A. in English from the University of Alabama

Sept. 1968   Begins doctoral coursework; employed as a Teaching Assistant in the University of Alabama English Department

1968   Wins Hallmark Honor Prize of Kansas City State poetry contest

Mar. 14, 1969   Mother dies of lung cancer in St. Jude's

Hospital, Montgomery, aged 51

Fall 1970   Abandons doctoral studies; employed as a
                 Temporary Instructor in the University of
                 Alabama English Department

1971   Attends the Hollins College Writers'
                 Conference in Virginia

Fall 1971   Publishes poems in *The New Yorker,
                 Kansas Quarterly,* and *Western Humanities
                 Review*

Spring 1972   Organizes a visiting reading series which
                 brings poets Mark Strand, Michael
                 Benedikt, and Charles Simic to the Univer-
                 sity of Alabama campus

1972   Publishes poems in *Shenandoah, kayak,* and
                 Intro 4

Summer 1974   Publishes two poems, including "Thirteen
                 Ways of Being Looked at by a Possum," in
                 The Paris Review

Sept. 1974   Begins working as a part-time tutor in the
                 Writing Lab of The University of Alabama
                 English Department; has ceased to teach in
                 the department

Nov. 1974   Teaches at Lucille Sanders Elementary
                 School in Fayetteville, NC, under the
                 Fayetteville Poets-in-the- Schools Program

1975   Marries wife Celia at the University Club in
                 Tuscaloosa, Alabama.

Sept. 1975	Hired as Poet-in-Residence at Xavier University of Louisiana; moves into the house at 2900 Prytania Street where F. Scott Fitzgerald once lived; Celia and her daughter accompany him
Winter 1975	Publishes a poem in *Carolina Quarterly*
1976	Chapbook, *The Thirteen Original Poems*, published by Xavier University
June 1976	Let go from Xavier University position
Aug. 1976	Begins teaching as an Instructor in the University of New Orleans English Department; lives with Celia and her daughter in a house on Constance Street
Feb. 4, 1977	Everette's niece, Shellie Jessica Maddox, born to William Maddox and his wife, the former Alice Kay Williams; William Maddox is finishing a doctorate in political science at the University of Tennessee
Summer 1977	Travels with Celia to Germany, England, France, and Holland
June 1978	Let go from his instructorship at the University of New Orleans; separates from Celia; becomes romantically involved with Eileen Hutchinson
June 1979	With poet Robert Stock and painter Franz Heldner, founds the Maple Leaf Bar Sunday afternoon literary reading series
July 1979	Relationship with Eileen Hutchinson ends

Sept. 1979	Leaves New Orleans for Mobile, Alabama
Jan. 1980	Returns to New Orleans from Mobile; moves in with poets Ken Fontenot and Robert Stock at 8418 Freret Street
1980	With Maxine Cassin and Yorke Corbin, edits *The Maple Leaf Rag: An Anthology of New Orleans Poetry*
Fall 1980	Begins teaching in the New Orleans Poet-in-the- Schools Program, under the auspices of the Children's Arts Council
1981	Begins working part time at the Maritime Museum in the International Trade Center Building
Fall 1981	Having divorced Alice in February, William Maddox takes a one-year leave from the University of Central Florida to be a Visiting Assistant Professor of Political Science at the University of New Orleans; he and Everette move into an apartment at 7326 Green Street
1982	*The Everette Maddox Song Book* is published by Maxine Cassin's New Orleans Poetry Journal Press
Dec. 1982	Evicted from his apartment on Green Street for nonpayment of rent
Mid 1980s	Homelessness and unemployment become permanent conditions

June 20, 1986	William Maddox marries Laurie Ann Robert in New Orleans
Aug. 1986	William Maddox is employed as a Visiting Associate Professor at the University of New Orleans; does not return to Florida when his term ends in June 1987, preferring to try his luck as a fiction writer in New Orleans
May 1988	*Bar Scotch,* Everette's second collection of poems, is published by Bill Roberts and Hank Staples's Pirogue Publishing
Jan. 1989	Travels with Bill Roberts and Julie Kane to read poetry at Chris's Restaurant in Montgomery, Alabama, and the Fort Walton (Florida) Art Museum
Feb. 13, 1989	Dies of esophageal cancer at Charity Hospital in New Orleans
Feb. 19, 1989	Memorial service is held at the Maple Leaf Bar; jazz band, The Riverside Ramblers, leads a parade of 400 mourners through the streets of Carrollton

Everette Maddox

Thirteen Ways of Being Looked at by a Possum

1
I awake, three in the morning, sweating
from a dream of possums.
I put my head under the fuzzy swamp of cover.
At the foot of darkness two small eyes glitter.

2
Rain falls all day: I remain indoors.
For comfort I take down a favorite volume.
Inside, something slimy, like a tail, wraps around my finger.

3
Hear the bells clang at the fire station:
not hoses, but the damp noses of possums issue forth.

4
Passing the graveyard at night
I wish the dead would remain dead,
but there is something queer and shaggy about these mounds.

5
From the grey pouch of a cloud
the moon hangs by its tail.

6
At the cafeteria they tell me they are out of persimmons.
I am furious. Who is that grey delegation
munching yellow fruit at the long table?

7
I reach deep into my warm pocket
to scratch my balls; but I find, instead,
another pocket there; and inside, a small possum.

8
My friend's false teeth clatter in the darkness
on a glass shelf;
around them a ghostly possum forms.

9
At an art gallery the portraits seem to threaten me;
tails droop down out of the frames.

10
I screech to a stop at the red light.
Three o'clock, school's out:
eight or ten juvenile possums fill the crosswalk.

11
Midnight at Pasquale's. I lift my fork,
and the hard tails looped there
look curiously unlike spaghetti.

12
When I go to the closet to hang my shirt on the rack,
I have to persuade several possums to move over.

13
Drunk, crawling across a country road tonight,
I hear a shriek, look up, and am paralyzed
by fierce headlights and a grinning grill.
I am as good as gone!

NONFICTION

Ralph Adamo

Introduction to *American Waste*

For seven years, no poems, but the poems were incubating. When the work started to pour gleefully and painfully out, it was work that had taken the print of the increasingly hard life the poet lived. In place of the mannered (one might say "well-mannered"), wry, and humorous poet of the first books was a gnarled spirit, bawdy, unwilling and maybe unable to mask feeling in detachment. Lust and the bite of concrete are chunked at the reader. Sleep is desired, a square meal, a fuck, but one with lights and violins, for the street incubated an ultimate romantic, not just a learned one, a man still wearing his heart on his sleeve, a lover of insatiably ambitious longings.

When our friend Everette Maddox died in the chill Lenten season of 1989, he was easily the best-loved poet in the city of New Orleans, for his resonant, funny, and exquisitely crafted poems, yes, and for his vivid reading of them on the many occasions when he held his audiences in a delighted thrall, but he was beloved as much for the grace and courage with which he "lived the life"—having made an absolute commitment to the creation of poetry, his own and others', and to the pursuit of an ideal of romantic love that even many of his friends found baffling, and to the poet's wine (Scotch, in Everette's case)—and for the generosity that opened up to his brilliant intellect the kernel of truth and beauty in even the most humble poet's work. (As founding host of the Maple Leaf Bar's Sunday afternoon poetry reading series, Everette introduced and encouraged hundreds of local and traveling poets over a period of ten years.)

This is not the forum for biography. Yet in coming together to edit, order, argue about and finally publish this last manuscript (a literal term in this instance) of his, we have thought it useful to preface the work with some notes on the reality from which it springs.

Everette died at forty-four, in "Big" Charity Hospital in New Orleans, on Monday, February 13, eight days after hosting the annual Mardi Gras Poetry extravaganza open mike reading, of advanced esophageal cancer, after a stay in a ward of only a week. During this time no medical procedures—beyond one to ascertain the stage of his illness—were or could be performed, due to the disastrously poor state of his general health, including the fact that even by his own standard of elegant thinness, Everette was emaciated, jaundiced, and virtually starving from his recent inability to swallow food.

For most of the previous five years he had been homeless, though not always without a place to stay (he had a wide network of friends, many of whom were more connected to bar life and the streets than to poetry); for several years before that, his dwelling place—and his attention to such matters—had been minimal. Though he had a few more-or-less standard house-sharing situations in the couple of years immediately following it, Everette had been without a home almost since the breakup of his marriage in the late seventies.

Everette was not the kind of homeless person who is adept at survival skills, beyond having a true and generous heart. He claimed not to know how to boil water. He once watched in amazement while I made tuna fish sandwiches for both of us. He was always cold, except in the steamiest depth of the city's tropical summer. For Everette, New Orleans had a long winter. And yet there were nights when he slept curled on a bench in the back of the Maple Leaf Bar, or in the marginal shelter of the library façade or the church steps on Carrollton Avenue. The image of Everette huddling into this thin coat and puffing away at his pipe to stay warm can still make his friends feel a deep, slashing chill.

He tried to work. When he had teaching jobs, he was a great teacher. He was a great teacher over drinks too, a scholar of Joyce and of the liveliest, most difficult writers in general. In the bars he was called "professor," respectfully, maybe as much for his coat-and-tie as his learning. But work gradually ceased to seem, then to be, possible, even the work of writing poetry.

Maxine Cassin's press, The New Orleans Poetry Journal Press, published his first book, *The Everette Maddox Song Book*, in 1982; it was a collection gleaned from several earlier book-length manuscripts. In 1988, Bill Roberts' and Hank Staples' Pirogue Publishing put out a book called *Bar Scotch*, which was made up largely of work that had not gone into the earlier collection. Everette had begun his long dry period by the early eighties; a sonnet sequence, partially represented in *Bar Scotch*, and dedicated to one of his most enduring romantic crushes, was nearly his last wave of writing.

But when *Bar Scotch* was published, little more than a year before his death, it kicked over some weight that had held him down, and Everette began to write again, this time a steady stream of poems from the lowest down places you could get in America in the 1980s, combined with powerful elements of a new imagining of lust, and new arrows of nostalgia. The title of this book he had had in mind at least since the mid-eighties, when, sitting on a corner near the Maple Leaf's street window, Everette read over and over again the name on a dumpster that was a nearly permanent part of the landscape then: American Waste. It made him laugh. He thought it would be the perfect title for the next book of poems he would write, whenever that miracle was going to happen.

The milieu of *American Waste* then is, on one level, the bars and public places on Oak Street and that tiny area of Carrollton in which he moved. Besides the Maple Leaf, the bars include one lately called Muddy Waters (Jed's of an earlier era) and owned by a family of Australians, and another around the corner called the Carrollton Station.

His pals with square jobs and houses and straight, or straightening-out lives don't figure too prominently in this book. Instead, it is the bartenders (like Brent and Terri) and the bar buddies like Dusty and the women who work or sing or just drink in bars who create the magic that breaks Everette's cranky, breakable heart there at the end. Or who make him laugh, or converse at cross purposes with him, or help him up, or fuel in him bursts of longing.

Much of this work has a mirthful bitterness and a directness that is startling. It reminds me of the work of certain Chinese poets who have renounced the world and gone to live (with apparently undiminishing supplies of wine) up some rocky mountain. One in particular, in fact, who lived up his mountain for years and when he died, his friends went around from stone to stone copying down the poems he had composed and left there in the elements. Everette's last book is a little like that. It has the feel of plain-speech, unimpressed and uninterested in impressing. It has that terrible feel of verisimilitude.

A note then on the methodology. Because he had no place to go and because his belongings were scattered among several friends' households, Everette needed someplace to put his poems as he finished them. He would write in longhand, wherever he was, then revise and rewrite, and finally on whatever paper (sometimes a napkin, or the back of a flyer, or a beer coaster) was handy, he would compose a final draft in block print. This he brought upstairs to the apartment Hank Staples lived in over the Maple Leaf, and Hank would put each new poem in a brown paper bag he kept lying flat on his dresser. After something less than a year, the bag bulged with more than ninety poems (and pieces of still more, like the fragments from coasters that we have arranged as a poem in numbered sections), most of which are published here. In a very few cases, Everette had left incomplete or unclear drafts. Generally, remarkably, his final drafts and his intentions were very clear. In the case of perhaps a dozen poems, the consensus of the group was that Everette himself would have considered the poem unfinished or unsuccessful, and we have omitted those. Some poems were controversial among us; but if a poem had the support of more than one person (or the cantankerous support of just one)—it was included.

The other editors of this book were Everette's brother Bill, who writes novels; Nancy Harris, who (along with Helen Toye, another editor and keeper of the Maddox wardrobe) took up the responsibility for continuing the Sunday reading series, unbroken for thirteen years; Patrick Travis, the publisher of this book and the one who gave final shape to the table of contents; poet Ken Fontenot; and Fred Kasten, WWNO radio personality and Everette's old friend from Alabama where, together with Bob Woolf, they wrote under the name "Buck Potatox."

We have not taken the liberty of dedicating *American Waste*, but the people who live in these poems, and the people still living on the streets know it is for them.

New Orleans, December 3, 1992

Randolph Bates

"Even Odd": On Everette Maddox's Teaching

Not long after I met Everette Maddox, I saw him teach. This was in late summer in New Orleans. I believe the year was 1980. He, several others, and I—all of us scrambling for work—had been hired to teach poetry-in-the-schools. We were gathered in the old LaSalle Elementary school on Perrier Street, then home to the New Orleans Center for Creative Arts (NOCCA). There, Loyola professor John Biguenet and NOCCA writing director Tom Whalen observed each of us teach a poetry-writing lesson and offered some critique before sending us on for assignment to middle and high schools in the metropolitan area. Each poetry-in-the-schools teacher also observed others. The training session is now a haze to me, but I remember Everette. Not that I can summon the specifics of what he taught, only that his lesson was the most interesting.

A year or two later, I had the opportunity to observe him in a teaching situation again: He was one in a series of writers I paid to visit a class of adults enrolled in a Tulane non-credit course called Living Authors, which I moderated. Initially Everette's presentation seemed formal, like his tie and jacket and the tradition of his sonnets; but also, like most of his poems and like Everette himself, his was with us soon became immediate, funny, and very natural. The part that remains clearest to me across the years was simply his talk—specifically the kind of story fragment that we commonly tell each other in relaxed conversation. In response to someone's question that I have forgotten, Everette told us about his weekend job at the Maritime Museum in the International Trade Center. Saying it was work he liked, he spoke of idle Saturday afternoons when no one came in and when, after dusting a brass ship fitting or two with his sleeve, he read some of the paper or a page in a book, or dozed and dreamed, or just looked out the big windows and thought. I've never seen the setting he conjured for us, but as he spoke I understood and envisioned him there inside the Maritime Museum in a way that reminds me of the atmosphere in a poem. I doubt I'll forget it.

I don't know if I was even aware then of the university teaching that originally brought Everette to New Orleans. My sense of him in those days was more a matter of running into him in the Maple Leaf and Muddy Waters', of hearing his welcoming introductions of other poets on Sundays, and of sighting him having meager after-noon coffee breakfasts among retirees at the lunch counter of the Woolworth's that stood on Oak Street. My son Richard recently reminded me we once happened to meet Everette around the corner from Woolworth's when Richard was a boy. Richard remembers, though I don't, my introducing him to the poet. At some point, probably in the early nineties, Richard began reading Everette's poems with an attention he gave to few other poets. My slender Maddox collections gravitated into his room, went away to college, and stayed with him after he graduated. He still has my copy of *The Everette Maddox Song Book*, in which Everette scrawled, "Hold your ear." Richard writes and performs his own music now, and last week when I telephoned to talk with him about his continuing appreciation of Everette's poems, he said it's because "they read like jokes or song lyrics, but they're not" and because "they're short and sweet and feel fresh off the bar coasters." Before we hung up he spontaneously quoted whole poems into the receiver: "Here's to Falling" ("not failing"), "What I Said to the Sky" ("fuck you and the clouds you rolled in on"), "Things I'd Like to Do Preferably Before I Die" ("one more/ summer storm/ would be nice"). As Richard bucked along through his recollection of the lines, it became obvious from the recitation itself that he's learned something lasting from Everette about how to value poetry and possibly about more.

When I knew I was going to write this, I also called my wife Cheryl's cousin and close friend, Alexis Roux Roser. Alexis once had Everette as a teacher. Through the spring of 1982 when she was a student at Grace King High School in Metairie, he visited her English class and taught poetry. She remembers there were "no poetic entrances and exits" associated with his visits. "He was very simple, very humble. He would look right into our eyes, and some-

34

times his eyes seemed to jump to catch our attention. . . . He sipped a lot of coffee. . . . His hand stroked his whiskers, and when he read poetry to us—this was a small thing, but many of us noticed it—he would stretch on his toes. We liked that. . . . There was a wonderful quietness about him, but he knew when to be loud and when to be quiet. Sometimes when he talked, his voice became . . . *majestic!* He was able to make us have fun, . . . but there was something sad about him too. . . . The class really liked him.

"He loved poetry and wanted so much for us to love it too. . . . When he showed us some of his work, he let it stand on its own. . . . His classes were mostly quiet listening, then writing. Afterwards he'd leave quietly, no fanfare. Quick. The last day he left quietly too, and he was quicker than usual when he left that day. . . . I loved him, I loved Mister Everette. . . . I don't know if he knew how much he inspired us."

I can imagine Everette being an exacting teacher of students who aspired to become his peers in the practice of poetry. But toward students beginning to appreciate the vocation, those in the schools, his method must have been gentle, even tender. In this poem, for instance:

Even Odd

*For my poetry students at McMain-Spectrum
Junior High School, New Orleans, October 1980*

There go the days
Like a stick on a fence:
even odd, even odd
into winter.
When were you born?
I was born in October.
Is your birthday a banner
in the summer sky?
Where do you fall?
Are you the odd one in line?
If you told a kid that
he'd laugh.

But that's the language
doing that. That's
the language
making you laugh.
Put a hand over
your shirt pocket.
Can you feel that?
That's your heart
doing that.
That's your heart
laughing at the language.
The language wants
to love you: let it.

Grace Bauer

Museum of Consolation Prizes

> *My life = a museum of consolation prizes.*
> —Everette Maddox

I first laid eyes on Everette Maddox at a reading at The People's Playhouse over on Apple Street. I remember thinking he looked like D. H. Lawrence (though others have insisted he favored Poe) with his dark hair, full beard and the beautiful deep blue eyes that would be one of the things that made me fall in love, nearly at first sight, years later, with his younger brother, Bill.

But this was summer, maybe early fall, in the mid 1970s, and I had just moved to New Orleans, living with a man who had picked me up hitchhiking in Key West and brought me back to his home town. I was fresh out of college in Philadelphia, with no job prospects and no idea of what I wanted to do with my life, beyond scribbling in notebooks (which up to that point I rarely showed to anyone) and having a few adventures. New Orleans seemed like a good place for both, and besides, despite the peculiar circumstances of our meeting, I was in love. So there I was—in The City That Care Forgot, living behind a fledgling photography gallery, working in a mental hospital, writing freelance articles for a feminist newspaper called *Distaff*, and venturing timidly into the lively local poetry scene, mostly via The New Orleans Poetry Forum, a loosely organized (what organization in New Orleans wasn't "loose"?) group of poets who got together weekly to drink wine and talk about each other's poems.

Rette was one of the smallest, thinnest men I'd ever seen, and yet he always loomed, somehow, large. He had the commanding voice of a Southern preacher (which I later heard his daddy had once been) and a laugh—more like a cackle—that always reminded me of a cross between Walter Brennan in *The Real McCoys* and some cartoon version of the devil.

My immediate impressions of Rette, and everything else I

encountered, were tinged with the stereotypical perceptions of a Yankee. But I was a Yankee thoroughly enthralled with my newly chosen home in the deep South. New Orleans seemed like another country, perhaps another universe, but one I was anxious to claim citizenship in. I'd wander the streets, sniffing the heady scents of gardenias, magnolias, jasmine, and sweet olive that thrived in people's gardens. Beads that had been tossed from floats during Mardi Gras, which I'd yet to experience, still festooned the branches of the trees along the neutral ground. People actually called that strip of grass down the middle of the avenues *the neutral ground*! The streetcar seemed more like a Disneyland attraction than public transportation; I'd ride it down to the French Quarter to sip coffee at the Cafe Du Monde or grab a po-boy at Mena's, check out the sleaze on Bourbon Street and the endless sideshows in Jackson Square, feeling superior to the throngs of tourists— though I was, of course, still gawking like one—because this was now my town.

It was several years from that first meeting before I got to the point where I could say I actually *knew* Everette. He had, I eventually learned, moved to New Orleans around the same time I had— though he came with somewhat better prospects—a temporary teaching position at Xavier University. We traveled in some of the same circles, attended the same readings, got sloshed at many of the same parties, but each time we encountered each other, I had the feeling he didn't really remember me from the times before. This was probably the case, since I was, as I said, a bit timid about my own poetic attempts (perhaps, looking back at some of those early poems, not timid enough) and I was certainly not one of the ethereally beautiful women Everette would notice and worship from afar till his dying day.

What finally initiated our friendship was, appropriately enough, another poet. John Berryman, to be exact. By this time, I had gone through a series of jobs—waitressing, cooking in a natural foods restaurant, serving drinks to tourists on the paddleboat Natchez, tallying forms for the census bureau, teaching poetry workshops in neighborhood senior centers through an Artists in the City Program. For two years I commuted back and forth to Montana, where my lover and I worked the summer season in Yellowstone. But then that relationship fell apart and I returned to New Orleans on my own and got a job working at the main branch of the New Orleans Public Library. I did not know, when I found the letter to Everette tucked inside the copy of the *Dream Songs* I pulled off the shelf one day, that Berryman was one of his favorite poets. I only knew that the note intrigued me, as did the man I had known at a distance for several years. And so I wrote a poem for the occasion, called "On Finding a Note to Everette Maddox in my Library Book, New Orleans, 1979," and mailed it, along with the misplaced letter, to Everette.

Looking at the poem now, I can't say it's a very good one, but, defying Auden's proclamation that "poetry makes nothing happen," it opened the door to a friendship that, while often cantankerous, became in the next few years a deep and abiding one, so I consider that brief lyric, which appeared in the first *Maple Leaf Rag*, one of the few poems I was ever well paid for. As fate would have it, it was around this time that Everette, along with sculptor Franz Heldner and poet Robert Stock, hatched the idea for a poetry reading series at the Maple Leaf Bar—where they, and many of us, spent far too much time.

The Leaf was—and is—a neighborhood dive so authentically New Orleans it's been used as a set in several movies. It has pressed tin walls and ceilings, a spacious back patio, and some of the grungiest bathrooms in the developed world. The bar featured a diverse lineup of great music seven nights a week: Buckwheat Zydeco, BeauSoleil, Marcia Ball, Charles Neville's jazz band, L'il Queenie and the Percolators, the Radiators, the Rhapsodizers, and the inimitable James Booker, who, much like a musical version of Everette, remains a legend who left the world too soon. For a time, there was chamber music on Sunday afternoons or performances by the New Leviathan Oriental Foxtrot Orchestra. But then the readings began. They were held on Sunday afternoons, and Everette was the host par excellence. His introductions were enthusiastic, generous, and often displayed Rette's legendary wit—e.g., his dubbing writer and painter Helen Toye "the face that launched a thousand sips" or poet Ken Fontenot "the Cajun Keats." Everette was central to the success of the readings, though he never hogged the limelight—except on those occasions when he himself read in either the ironic, self-deprecating public persona of his own poems or as the more bombastic Buck Potatox, a sort of alter ego created by Everette with two old friends from Alabama, Fred Kasten and Bob Woolf. Buck was, I think, their version of Berryman's Henry Pussycat.

One could never predict what a Maple Leaf reading might be like. There could be a packed room of people paying rapt attention, or there could be half a dozen loyal souls trying to hear over the shouts of sports fans drinking at the outer bar. There were usually two featured readers per week, though occasionally there would be "theme" events—or the infamous Mardi Gras open readings, where some people came in costume. I recall one in particular, where a local painter, in his cups, heckled a poet who responded with a right hook that relieved the painter of one or two of his teeth. I myself was once featured, along with my friend Nancy Harris, at a reading that was postponed a good two hours due to flash floods that stranded a crowd in the bar, while the scheduled readers were stranded across town on Freret Street. Said readers, while up to their elbows in river water, had a stash of cheap champagne— purchased to celebrate my birthday—in the back seat of their stalled Honda, which we imbibed with gusto till the waters receded and we made our way to the captive audience on Oak Street, who gladly listened to us read our poems while drinking the rest of our champagne.

Whatever the crowd, Everette would be there prepared to offi- ciate, dressed, as always, in a suit and tie. In the many years I knew him, there was only one time—a morning after a night when Everette helped himself to about half the bottle of bourbon intended for the sole consumption of Walker Percy at a book signing in the French Quarter and somehow ended up in my apart- ment on Napoleon Avenue and eventually passed out in my bed— that I caught a glimpse of him without the tie.

I think the readings gave Rette a sense of purpose as well as a community. Plus the bar paid him—twenty bucks a week, I think it was, which to him, was real money—and threw in a few free scotches. People often hung around after the readings to drink and talk, sometimes staying till nighttime when whatever band was playing started up, and then all bets were off. It was in the hours after the readings that Everette sometimes gave his best literary performances. Though he often forgot where he'd left his hat, his pipe, even the notebook with his most recent poems, he had an impressive memory for things he'd read and learned by heart, and would break into a recitation, sometimes at surprising moments.

I remember one sweltering Sunday, sitting around with a few people sipping something cool, while Everette was curled up like a cat on a bench, seemingly asleep, which was nothing out of the ordinary. What was extraordinary was the way he bolted upright when someone mentioned Berryman, leapt to his feet, and gave a spirited recital of *Dream Song #14* (*Life, friends, is boring. . .*), then promptly lay back down and went back to sleep. There are dozens of stories like this. Most of them, I believe, true.

But there are equally true stories of Everette's darker moods. While he could be erudite, entertaining, charming as all get-out and downright hilarious, he could also sink into depressions so dark they were frightening. They could be set off by anything—large or small—and could last anywhere from minutes, to hours, to days, weeks, months. I once witnessed such a plunge that was caused by nothing more than the fact that a po-boy he'd had delivered to the Maple Leaf arrived dressed with mayonnaise. Everette exploded, said it looked like the delivery guy had jerked off on his French bread. He hated mayonnaise, and because it was on his sandwich, he suddenly hated the world and everything in it, including himself. Though someone whose sandwich had arrived sans mayo gladly offered to trade, Everette could not, or would not, let go of whatever demon had taken over.

Many such depressions were caused by his desperation over the women he fell in love with—most often, at least in the time I knew him, from very much afar. I was never sure if these women even knew the extent of his adoration, or if they did, what they made of it. Though Rette swore it was true love each time, it seemed to me more like fixation—though I was not about to tell him that. He would choose his latest Laura, his most current muse, and being unobtainable was part of her job description. It was, I think, longing he was really in love with. It was longing that led him to poems.

When it came to poems, Everette could be critical, but he refused to be a critic. He told me once about a junior high school teacher who'd noted his interest in verse and lent him a huge anthology. She'd meant for him to keep it for a while, but he took it home and stayed up all night reading it cover to cover. When he brought it back to her the next day, carrying it as reverently as a Baptist would his Bible, she was surprised, and asked him which poems he'd liked. "I liked 'em all," he told her, and in the retelling chortled. "Hell," he said, "I was so amazed at all those poems in one book, it never occurred to me I was supposed to like some of them more than others. I was just so damn happy to know such a book existed."

For a while in the early eighties, some of the poets who lived uptown started getting together now and then for informal workshops, accompanied sometimes by potluck dinners and, of course, copious amounts of wine. Everette dubbed the group The Oyster Loaf Conference, his pun on Bread Loaf and a favorite local poboy (served, God willing, without mayonnaise), and while he read and listened intently during these workshops, he rarely offered much in the way of comment. He might laugh or not, he might shake his head or not, he might stroke his beard and give an approving or disapproving *hmn*, but little in the way of practical nuts and bolts advice on revision, as others did. I think he wanted to be there to observe his friends' creative processes, but not to interfere with them.

Friends were important to Everette. Both his parents had died quite young—while he was still in college—so his only surviving family was his brother Bill, who moved to New Orleans in 1981 to spend a year as a Visiting Professor of Political Science at the University of New Orleans.

I met Bill his first night in town at Borsodi's Coffeehouse, over on Freret Street. This was another venue for poetry readings, these held on Wednesday nights. While Borsodi's did not serve alcohol, Robert Borsodi, who'd been involved with coffeehouses since the old Beat days in California, didn't mind if people snuck in a bottle of wine or two, which my friends and I did that night. Everette showed up with Bill, delighted to have him in town, where they were going to rent a house together. He seemed proud to be showing him around New Orleans and introducing him to his many friends. Bill struck me as a little shy, and as possessing a more stable temperament than Everette. And then there were those blue eyes, which I took note of as I poured him a coffee cupful of my cabernet.

It may have been Berryman that brought Everette and me together; with Bill and me, it was the Rolling Stones. Soon after we met, it was announced that they would be coming to the Super-dome. We both admitted that we'd been Stones fans since we were kids but had never seen them in concert, and I admitted to him that I thought I'd had my first orgasm while watching Mick Jagger on *Hullabaloo*—or was it *Shindig*? I'm not sure what possessed me to share that particular bit of information, but he responded by suggesting we go to the concert together. "Okay," I said, "it's a date." I reached my hand out to shake on it, but instead, Bill leaned over and kissed me. I paused to catch my breath, then looked him squarely in the eye, and said, "This is going to be a disaster." But I kissed him back.

For a while then, everything was idyllic. I was happy with Bill, who seemed happy with me. Everette was happy living in the little house on Green Street, which was not only a more domestic accommodation than anything he'd had for a while, but also included his brother. And he seemed thrilled that Bill and I had gotten together—at least most of the time. I remember one late night when the three of us, and a few other friends, were sitting around on Bill and Everette's living room floor (the living situation *was* relatively domestic, but the furniture was minimal), Rette looked at us and said, "Watching you two makes me so happy, I forget how miserable I am." It was typical Everette wit. But not long after that, one of his depressions struck again, and looking at us only made things worse. "My brother's in town for less than two months," he bemoaned, "and he's not only got a girlfriend, but a girlfriend who's a poet. I've been here for years, and I ain't got shit."

I asked Bill then if Everette had always been subject to these moods, and he said yes, he had been, even when they were kids. When I suggested that alcohol probably exacerbated things, he said, "No, actually, he used to be much *worse.*"

I'm not sure how reliable that information was. When it came to their childhoods, both Everette's and Bill's versions of the story contained contradictions that were hard to sort out. They both undoubtedly loved their parents deeply, and saw them as rather Romantic characters. Both versions included a kind of poverty, or near poverty, that may or may not have been genteel. The family was, from what I could gather, isolated from friends and other extended family, both geographically and by choice, though Bill also described times when his mother did not leave her room, suggesting she was incapable (mentally, not physically) of doing so. Sometimes Bill's description of the red clay hills surrounding their little house was tinged with nostalgia, other times with disgust. Everette regularly referred to his home state as *Ala-god-damn-bama,* but was also known to break into a chorus of "Stars Fell on Alabama" with tears in his eyes.

Their father was the first to pass away. Everette was in college, and this left Bill, still in high school, living alone with his mother, who kept more and more to herself. Bill told me of coming home one day and looking into the refrigerator, as any teenage boy might, to find nothing but a carton of cigarettes and a bottle of Pepsi. Somehow—he declined to go into detail, though I know he was writing about it in a novel he never got to finish—he managed to fend for himself. It was not long before his mother also died. She made it only one year past fifty, the age at which his father had died.

Whatever their parents may or may not have done right, it is clear that they instilled and encouraged a love of books that verged on reverence in both their sons from a very early age. Books were magic to Everette and Bill. It was books, I believe, that nourished them, their creativity and their inner lives, but also an insatiable longing for *something else* that they shared—to the bitter end. I don't think the real world ever quite measured up for either one of them.

As for my idyllic relationship with Bill, though I wasn't sure why I had predicted disaster, my initial assessment of the situation proved prescient. My sense that Bill possessed a more stable temperament than Everette did not. He was subject to the same radical shifts in mood, the same reliance on alcohol as a crutch that only crippled him further—though, God knows, none of us were exactly teetotalers in those days. This was New Orleans, after all—home of go-cups in bars and drive-in daiquiri stands.

It did not help that Bill was recently divorced and had a young daughter still living in Florida, whom he missed terribly. For a while, he continued with visitation, bringing her to New Orleans a couple of times. I never met her, though I offered to cook dinner for them one weekend when I knew she was coming. He demurred, preferring to keep these aspects of his life separate and feed her Happy Meals.

A string of events soon sent things spiraling downward. Bill's ex-wife was going to remarry, there were disagreements about visitation, Bill totaled his car, and piling debts led him to file for bankruptcy. So much for relatively stable. There were fights, flamboyant break-ups, passionate reconciliations, then Bill would just disappear from sight for a week or two at a time. He'd reappear to tell me I was one of the best human beings on the planet, then disappear again. When his year at UNO was up and he returned to Florida and his teaching job in Orlando, I admit I was relieved.

Bill's exodus left Everette at loose ends again, though their relationship was a bit strained by this time. When they had moved in together, I think they both expected to relive the best parts of their childhoods—the parts that were magical. But that didn't happen. They shared the propensity for mood swings, but their timing was not always mutual. If Bill was in an up mood while Everette was in a down, Bill had little patience for it and absolutely no idea how to pull Everette out of it—or perhaps no inclination to. I think it was pretty much vice versa.

My memory of where Everette was living gets spotty at this point, though he was not yet, as he later became, truly homeless. I became involved with someone else, and in addition to working full time was taking classes at UNO and had vowed to clean up my act and focus more on my writing. It left less time for hanging out in bars, though I'd still show up if the music was particularly good, which was often enough. I still attended the readings at the Maple Leaf, but not quite as faithfully. When I did, Everette was still his usual self—or selves.

In 1982, Maxine Cassin, editor of the New Orleans Poetry Journal Press, published *The Everette Maddox Song Book*, Rette's first full-length collection of poems. The book signing party, held in February at the Maple Leaf, was a grand event featuring free hot dogs and cold beer—Everette's choice of menu—plus potluck contributions from his friends. The book lifted his spirits for a while. He gave numerous readings in New Orleans and several back in Alabama.

Somehow, this led to a number of other New Orleans poets heading over to Mobile to read at a place called The Lumberyard. The readers were Nancy Harris, Chris Munford, Helen Toye, and me—though another carful or two of our friends decided to come along. The entire weekend was such a bacchanalia, I remember only snatches after the reading—which drew a large and attentive audience. Though we were mostly unknown poets, we were friends of Everette's, which I take it was recommendation enough for the locals.

Everette seemed proud to be showing us off to them, and Mobile to us. I recall walking along the river, seeing some famous battleship, eating dinner at a nice restaurant, but also being taken to some dingy stripper bar where a woman humped a pole. I believe we were asked to leave, though I can't remember why. I do remember driving around searching for the house where someone had arranged for the lot of us to crash for the night, Robert Williams jumping out of the car and playing an accordion in the middle of an intersection, a hungover breakfast at another nice restaurant before the drive back to New Orleans.

Fond, albeit foggy, memories of this weekend in Alabama were something Everette would bring up for years afterward, though his darker moods seemed to come more often and last longer. Having a book published did not make the difference in Everette's life he had expected it to make. Though he would not have admitted it, I think he was hoping the book might receive more critical attention than any small press book is likely to get. I know he hoped it would impress the lady love it was dedicated to more than it probably did. Plagued with pain from his seriously rotted teeth, he seemed to drink more, eat less, and as a result, grow even thinner, till he was, as my friend Martha McFerren put it in a poem, "hardly wider than his tie."

As 1984 was rolling into view, change was on a lot of people's minds. A World's Fair was coming to New Orleans, and the changes along the riverfront seemed Orwellian enough to some of us. Rents in the city were skyrocketing, as was the crime rate. I was doing my part to contribute to those statistics. Within a one-year period, I'd been stalked by a flasher, robbed at gunpoint and subsequently taken on a police chase, and had my apartment broken into in broad daylight. Yet another relationship had come to a particularly painful ending—though chance encounters and surreptitious late-night phone calls made any kind of real emotional closure impossible for me. My job at the library, which had seemed ideal with its comparative lack of stress and constant access to books, was starting to bore me. The thrill of being paid to read *The New York Times* was wearing off, as was my patience with the kids who filed in every afternoon to work on their term papers. Besides, computers were starting to replace card catalogues and *Readers Guides*, which scared the hell out of me.

In 1984 I was accepted into the MFA Program at the University of Massachusetts in Amherst, and after much soul-searching, long walks around the city I'd loved for a decade, and many late-night conversations with friends, I decided to go.

Everette had mixed reactions to my decision. On the one hand, he was proud that I'd gotten accepted; on the other hand, he didn't want to see another friend leave town. He distrusted academia in general and creative writing programs in particular, but was excited that I'd have the chance to work with Jim Tate, who was one of the poets of his own generation that he greatly admired. Of course, before I left, I had to read one more time at the Maple Leaf. Almost everyone I'd known in New Orleans over the last decade showed up at the reading. One of the bartenders was throwing a World's Unfair party at the bar the same afternoon, and we all ended up second lining down Oak Street in one of the spontaneous parades that sometimes happen in New Orleans—a town that loves to throw beads and stop traffic. Everette was in great spirits, doing his distinctive little two-step shuffle as we headed toward the batture.

I was presented with a book of photographs and a few goodbye poems. Everette's, which was addressed to me and our friend Linda Spence, who was leaving around the same time to move back to California, was one of my favorites:

A Parting Shot

A big black cloud chugged in
over the Crescent City.
A fat tear slid
down the side of the Superdome.
Books wept. Plants pined.
Freret Street was awash in woe.
And, over on Oak,
an old poet's heart
cracked like a rock in Scotch.
Dis-spenced! Dis-graced!
O double grief to drown!
The world's unfair!
What consolation? None
but the bar's bad booze,
his pal's good work,
and a half-assed hope
that friendship's arc, somehow, sometime,
curves back.

I only saw Everette a few times after I left New Orleans. He sent me one brief note—a few scribbled sentences he'd managed to find an envelope and stamp for—during my first year in Massachusetts. For spring break of my second year, I visited New Orleans and read at the Maple Leaf. Everette liked my new poems—especially the ones about how much I missed New Orleans. My homesickness appealed to him.

In 1987 I received my M.F.A. and got a more or less permanent adjunct job at Virginia Tech. It was about this time that I began to hear from Bill again, out of the blue. After publishing a well-received book on political science and being granted tenure, Bill had promptly resigned from his position, saying academia was killing his soul. He moved back to New Orleans, got a job as a bartender, and dove into writing fiction. I would hear reports on Everette from him and other friends—one time they'd say he was doing much better, the next time they'd say he was worse off than ever. In 1988, *Bar Scotch* was published by Pirogue Publishing. Rette made sure our friend Nancy sent me a copy, and I sent back a note—addressed to the Maple Leaf—telling him how much I liked it.

The last time I saw Everette was New Year's Eve of 1988. I was in New Orleans for just a few days, and ran into him—at the Maple Leaf, of course. The friends I was ringing in the new year with were splitting our time that evening between the Maple Leaf and Muddy Waters across the street. I'd brought a few friends from Virginia along, and sensed they found both places way too seedy for their tastes. Everette was morose. He was in a suit and tie, as always, but seemed downright dirty, instead of just the rumpled I was used to. When I hugged him, it was like embracing a skeleton. He complained of a sore throat that wouldn't go away. I don't know where he was by midnight.

Though there had long been reports of declining health, I think many of us told ourselves Everette would outlast us all out of sheer orneriness, but that was not to be. Six weeks later, Nancy Harris called to tell me the news of Everette's death, which was, in retrospect, a shock—though not a surprise. As an adjunct, I was both too busy and too poor to make it back to New Orleans on short notice for the funeral, though I heard all about it. It sounded like a shindig Everette would have enjoyed.

I kept hearing from Bill a few times a year, though he never said much about his reaction to Everette's passing. Bill remarried and divorced within a few months. He published a novel called *Scacciato* with Portals Press, and also started publishing poems—mostly prose poems—in various little magazines. He'd send me copies and let me know how he was doing. In one letter, he'd tell me he was drinking very little, then he'd write to let me know he'd checked himself into Charity Hospital to dry out. He spent some time in a halfway house on the Gulf Coast in Mississippi and said he was glad to be away from the craziness of New Orleans, then he'd be back in New Orleans, relieved to have survived the doldrums of the Gulf Coast. He was happy when I finally got a tenure-track job at the University of Nebraska, but kept warning me not to let academia steal my soul.

In 1996, John Travis of Portals Press published my book of poems, *The Women at the Well*, and I headed back to New Orleans for a book party at—where else?—the Maple Leaf. I'd come to town with a man I was seeing, and Bill kept his distance. We talked, but only briefly. Though his letters had been telling me how well he was doing, he looked, I thought, like hell. At a Saturday night party, he read a recent prose poem that sounded like his typically witty self. He promised to be at my reading the next day, but never showed. A letter later explained he'd overslept—though the reading was at three in the afternoon.

I was in my office at the university when Nancy Harris called to tell me that Bill had been rushed to the hospital and was on his deathbed as we spoke. He'd drunk himself into irreparable liver failure. Like Everette, he died in a place called Charity.

There is, of course, a familiar template to this story—*artistic genius self-destructs*. We can look at the history of writers, painters, musicians, other artists, and find, unfortunately, many similar tales. I wish I could say I have come to understand why that is, but I have not. Perhaps whatever synapses in the brain fire the creative spark, for some people, snap off intermittently, leaving them in an impenetrable darkness. Maybe stories that romanticize such self-destruction convince some that this is what real artists and writers are *supposed* to do. I do think, in Everette's case, that he was determined to live an extraordinary life, even if it killed him. That what he wanted most was for his life to make a great story. Of course, some of the greatest, most enduring stories, are tragedies... Maybe I'm complicating something more basic—and it was the ravages of alcoholism, plain and simple, that destroyed both the Maddox boys.

They were among the brightest, funniest, most charming men I have ever known, but also the darkest and most possessed by demons. What the true source of those demons was remains a mystery to me. Though they both had what most people might rightly call a death-wish, I still think of them both as also having, at least at times, an absolute zest for life. If that sounds like I contradict myself—well, you know what Whitman said. Very well.

When he signed my copy of *Bar Scotch*, Everette alluded to the Berryman lines I'd quoted in the poem I had written for him almost a decade before. *More misunderstandings*, he wrote, and then added in parentheses, *thanks for finding me.*

Despite all the misunderstandings and all the loss, despite the contradictions, I, too, remain thankful for what I found in the man and keep finding in the poems he left behind.

Thomas Bonner, Jr.

Everette Maddox Comes to New Orleans

In the late 1970s, as chair of the Department of English at Xavier University of Louisiana, I was running a small creative writing program, supported by the National Endowment for the Arts, that included the appointment of a writer-in-residence. During the early summer we had lost our visiting writer, Carl Senna, to a northeastern college, and the fall semester was rapidly approaching. In New Orleans the number of active writers with MFAs or the equivalent was low, and the only MFA degree-granting institution in proximity was the University of Alabama-Tuscaloosa. I called Donald Kay, the chair of English there, to ask if he could recommend an available graduate from his department. He recommended Everette Maddox, although he indicated some concern about the writer's drinking habits. Everette had a good reputation at Alabama for both his writing and teaching. Initially, he had been studying in the Ph.D. program in English, and subsequently he transferred to the MFA courses. His first published poem appeared in *The New Yorker*; it included the word "career" as a verb, "careering around a mountain." The need, the recommendation, and the magic of the language in his writing made him an appealing prospect.

Everette came down to New Orleans for an interview and we hired him. Charming and almost courtly, he had the appearance of Edgar Allan Poe in some ways—slender, dark hair, piercing eyes, and moderate beard. He displayed an interest in teaching and got along easily with faculty and students—nearly all of whom were African American. In general he spoke softly and bore himself patiently. I don't recall a harsh word or moment. His students responded well to his quiet sense of humor, his irony, and his obvious interest in them. He was happy to be in New Orleans and on our campus.

When Everette came to Xavier, he was still married and his wife actually did the cover drawing for *The Thirteen Original Poems*, a chapbook by Everette that we published. His poems appeared in several occasional publications of the university. Soon afterwards, his marriage ended, but he was always gracious and restrained when speaking of his former wife. There was every indication that he maintained a friendship with her.

His life at Xavier came to an end with the close of the funding for the writer-in-residence position. A place on the faculty existed, but his drinking had increased as well as his eccentric behavior on campus. On one occasion he had walked across campus with a glass of scotch and thought someone had reported that to the university dean. So he went to the office to apologize to the nun who held that position. She was not in, so he knelt down before her secretary and apologized to her. No one had reported the scotch incident, for the campus was rather laid back on such matters. The cumulative effect of this behavior suggested that he would not continue to do well academically. Everette actually told me that his life was becoming more difficult and that he was concerned about his being effective in his teaching and writing. When he left Xavier, he taught briefly at the University of New Orleans and later as a poet-in-the-schools, and then as curator-guard at the Maritime Museum downtown. Afterwards, he became almost a legendary fixture at the Maple Leaf Bar on Oak Street.

At Xavier and in the subsequent years, Everette continued to publish his poems in literary magazines and locally published collections. He found considerable support both for himself and his writings among the friends he made in the city. His poetry drew on his own experiences and observations. He was a keen observer. The poems were frequently infused with a quiet, ironic humor. One that comes to mind often is set in Palmer Park, in which a man clothed in a suit of artificial fibers incinerates. Drinking and allusions to it permeated his poems, almost like that in Edward Arlington Robinson's poetry. At the Maple Leaf, Everette expanded his work with poetry to include sponsoring Sunday readings, a legacy that continues today with the inspiration and leadership of Nancy Harris. I remember Everette's reading his own work in a manner that suited his personality and character: gentle manner, humble presence, ironic perspective, and quiet humor. He often had a glass of scotch with him if the venue permitted. *That,* as the title of his penultimate book indicates, was his favorite drink.

I saw less of him in the later years. Friends would say they had seen him at the Maple Leaf or in the Riverbend neighborhood and that he was not looking physically well. The last time I saw him, he appeared very thin and frail, almost brittle. I heard that he sometimes slept in a dumpster close by the bar. Friends tried to help him, but he seemed to have his own direction despite its dangers. I do not know if he had a woman in his life toward the end, nor do I know about his funeral. When he died, I was away from New Orleans.

Everette will be remembered for his poetry and his life in New Orleans. As a poet, he had a keen sense of the music and power of language with little escaping his eyes and ears. He brought readers and listeners into the core of an experience where the universals begin to emerge from the particulars. His life in New Orleans suggested the romantic image of a poet who has failed to cope with the traffic of his surroundings but who has found in truth and beauty a power that, as he distilled it, could sustain others but not himself.

Ken Fontenot

Bar Scotch, Lost Loves, and New Orleans: Some Notes on a Southern Poet

He was a Southern poet if only because he mostly belonged to Alabama and New Orleans, never having lived anywhere else for any length of time. Once, in the summer of 1977, he and his wife of that time (he was married and divorced but once) took a trip to Germany to visit her relatives. They also saw France, England, and Holland. In the early 80s, to me, in the soft lights of our nightlife, he spoke beamingly of that trip.

Everette Hawthorne Maddox was born on October 9, 1944, in Montgomery, Alabama. He was the eldest of two sons, brother Bill being born in 1949. Ah, October: the birth month of John Lennon and Dylan Thomas, two artists who also died young and at the height of their powers. Rette's parents, Dorothy and Everette Maddox, Sr., raised him outside Prattville, a small town only a short drive from the capital. Is it perhaps a coincidence that his father, a sign painter, passed his love of printing words on to his son? After all, during Rette's final days he resorted to printing his poems on napkins and coasters because his handwriting had become unreadable.

In addition to his own work—poems of an impeccable quality—his great contribution to literary entertainment was to showcase writers of promising (and not so promising) talent at readings which he hosted. During the nearly ten-year existence of his weekly poetry reading series at the Maple Leaf Bar in New Orleans (it was billed as the longest of its kind in the South) I don't believe Everette ever missed a Sunday as host and moderator. I mean not even a priest could be counted on for such perfect attendance. *O!* if only there had been a job for him so relevant to his life! And he was willing to listen to everyone's poetry, no matter what the excellence or lack of it.

Although he was a critic of the first order, it's not that he barely tolerated shoddy poetry in some. Rather, he possessed an egalitarian philosophy about readers of their own poetry whereby everyone was given an equal chance. Almost never did he screen readers before a performance; he sought them out, and they sought him out. It was a case of "anything goes," especially during the Mardi Gras readings when throngs of people would step up to the microphone. I believe such personal democracy reflected the former teacher in him, for likewise in his classes all students had a chance, not just a talented few.

He drank, as Faulkner did, "for the pain." His triumph is that the pain didn't shortchange a remarkable sense of humor, though he could be extremely cranky at times. Walter Boswell, an ex-Maddox buddy from their days together in Tuscaloosa, recalls wanting to talk to the bard about an early poem called "A Girl Playing an Oboe." Rette turned away, got defensive, and said, "To hell with it, let's not even discuss it." Still, talking was his gift, one which he denied almost no one he took a shine to.

His major preoccupation—unrequited love—is an old theme, but he manages to do such new and funny things with it. And his has been largely (also) a humor of self-deprecation. Everybody identifies with the underdog. One has only to think of the success of Charlie Chaplin, Woody Allen, Rodney Dangerfield, and even, at times, Sylvester the cat.

The fact is, he was born in no century to survive in, given his idiosyncrasies. Had he been a young man in 1830 England—the year when drinking among the general populace was at its peak—he would have been respected for his individuality and perhaps given a job, even if a modest one. As it is now in Korea, for example, men who drink excessively might still hold their jobs. The reason: drinking has been part of the social tradition, almost perhaps a ritual. This is not to condone alcoholism. It is just to say that in many ways Everette was in the wrong place at the wrong time.

He told me once that in high school he took first place in a talent show for his stand-up comedy routine which he said brought down the house. Thus it was no accident that in his prime he could utter forth just one sentence and have any listener bent over with laughter.

We can understand his lyrical mind better if we look at the literature he loved most and which most influenced him, if not always directly, then by their very subjects and tones. His two favorite novels were Twain's *Huckleberry Finn* and Fitzgerald's *The Great Gatsby*. Joyce's *Ulysses* ran a close third—perhaps he admired Joyce's complex and brilliant syntax, which the latter pulled, like Rette, as if a magician, from a hat. Rette *was*, in a way, Huck Finn: poor, but honest to the core—someone who could spot a phony a mile away. Both too possessed a child-like innocence at odds with those of us who always seem a bit too serious. Like Gatsby, also, Rette was a romantic, as evidenced by the shy manner he courted women, as well as by his love of finely tailored Brooks Brothers' clothes. Add to that this country boy's fascination with the big lights and glamour of the city life. Moreover, he was fond of quoting Fitzgerald's Daisy to me, the part where she says, "Rich girls don't ever marry poor boys." Alas, it was a quote that most hit home.

As for favorite poets, he most identified with John Berryman and Alan Dugan. He wrote much like them, too, although he worked hard at being the original he was, with his own unmistakable voice. Berryman's gloom and humor were both Rette's. Also his tragedy. Think of the tragicomedy in Berryman's fourth "Dream Song," where only his civility keeps him from pouncing on this beautiful woman at the dinner table, a woman, incidentally, he is unable to win over to his side. However, what Rette saw in Dugan was the masterfully controlled short line and the low-brow humor. He frequently praised Dugan in my presence. In January of 1989 in Austin, in fact, I bought for him a copy of Dugan's new and collected poems. I planned it as a gift to be given the next time we met. Alas, however, it was too late.

Before I conclude with a personal reminiscence, I would just like to mention a note on his personality. He had a curious predilection for attracting people the way a magnet attracts filings. (Many of his friends—and there were hundreds—paid tribute to him at a traditional jazz funeral in February of 1989.) Gregarious perhaps to a fault, he would often get angry sitting on his bar stool, a trait which, oddly, only served to enhance his individualism, his professor-like tenacity, lending credence and charm to his laughter that followed later.

I lived in the same house with him for several months in early 1980 in New Orleans, a few blocks behind the Maple Leaf Bar. We were both going through hard times. I had lost a job and had been unable to find another. A very kind and sympathetic sculptor-painter friend had allowed us to live rent-free in her unrented next-door apartment. To us it was a gift from heaven.

Every morning we would go off to Woolworth's on Oak Street for coffee. Usually we traded stories and dirty jokes. Rette knew gobs of both. Shyness was a part of his character, something which not everyone would perceive. It surfaced in his subtle moments. I can remember him debating himself whether or not he should ask for another sugar for his coffee. He simply had to get up the nerve to do so. I sometimes am reminded how, filled with the emotional turmoil that haunted his tender and sensitive spirit, he could get up so early every morning and take long walks. He felt a part of life and wasn't about to sleep the day away. About noon I would begin my futile search for a job. Rette would begin his serenade with Bacchus.

The last time I saw him was August 1988. I was in New Orleans from Austin to give a poetry reading at the Maple Leaf. Relaxing at one of his favorite pubs on Oak Street, he read me a brand new "dog poem" on one of his famous napkins. I laughed out loud. "I have a new love," he told me in my ear. "Really, a new girlfriend!" I shouted out loud. "Shh-hhh, not so loud," he whispered. "She's right behind me." He winced. He was embarrassed, like the little boy who loves his schoolteacher but is too afraid to tell her.

Thinking about Rette, I sometimes wonder how he would've looked without a beard, as I never saw him that way. I imagine now in the Heaven of Bearded Poets, telling jokes. He would be knocking them dead, if they weren't already.

New Orleans, November 1990

Nancy Harris

Introduction to the 15th Anniversary Edition of the *Maple Leaf Rag*

I couldn't help thinking of the contrast to fifteen years ago, this past Sunday, February 13, 1994, when we held our 15th Annual Mardi Gras Extravaganza Open Mike Poetry Reading at the Maple Leaf Bar—8316 Oak Street in the Carrollton section of uptown New Orleans. Thirteen readers signed up; no one was in costume, no one was tripping, no one threw beer and wine glasses at the readers, no one punched out the teeth of a heckler. No need to enforce Everette Maddox's original rules for the event: "No holds barred, no fisticuffs, intolerance will not be tolerated." But it was a very successful reading; everyone who performed read quality work, including a leading Honduran poet in town for the past month who vowed to take back memories and experiences of the Maple Leaf readings to share with his fellow poets in Honduras.

I was first introduced to the readings at the Leaf in 1979. Writer John Stoss, whom I had met at a poetry writing workshop at the University of Arkansas, stopped by my house during the summer to visit and share poetry and told me that poets Everette Maddox and Robert Stock and painter Franz Heldner had started Sunday afternoon poetry readings. I stopped by the very next Sunday and have attended just about every poetry reading since then—it became my church and my salvation on Sunday afternoons. Soon, along with the live music, the readings caught on, mainly due to the outrageous personalities of Maddox and Stock. Bob Stock's death, in 1981, at the age of 58, was a shock to us all. He had been writing incredible new poetry at that point, and, ironically, had given up drinking and smoking, had been given the gift of new dentures, and was trying to get his life back together. The last words he ever said to me, at a reading at the Leaf, were: "I'd give anything for a scotch and a cigarette." And he did smoke a cigarette the day he stopped breathing, but his emphysema-stricken lungs could no longer do the job.

To his great credit, Everette Maddox carried on, commandeering the readings solo with his humor and charisma and his pithy, short poems. Likewise, Everette's introductions of readers sometimes were more entertaining than what followed. One that we all remember is his reflective introduction of poet Helen Toye "whose voice has launched a thousand sips."

What has remained constant over the years—before and since Everette's death in 1989—has been the diversity of the writers who have presented their work. There have been academic writers to be sure, but, more often, poets outside the universities who work at varying jobs (doctors, lawyers, plumbers, electricians, tree surgeons, welders, housewives, offshore workers, musicians, painters, college students, high school teachers, carpenters, dancers, waiters and waitresses, librarians, you name it). Some quite accomplished and published, others just starting out and gathering inspiration and direction from attending. During the Jazz & Heritage Fair of 1991, the poet William Matthews, author of *Blues If You Want*, was invited to read and a capacity crowd greeted him. This diversity, along with a fairly loose structure, has allowed the readings to be spontaneous and full of surprises. Often, since New Orleans is a tourist city, out-of-town poets, who see the reading listed in *The Times-Picayune*, will drop by, and we always try to make a place for them to read after the regularly scheduled readers.

Readings are not solely confined to poetry. There have been performances of short plays, fiction, nonfiction, multimedia events, and musician/songwriters, too. Usually the readings are scheduled a month ahead of time with one to multiple reader/ performer(s) on the docket.

Strangely (or not) the sequence of the fifteen-year life of the Maple Leaf readings can be broken down into five-year periods. The first five years were the weirdest—from the legacy of the 60s and 70s—up until 1984. These were the years of the now legendary and near apocryphal stories: such as the Mardi Gras open mike reading when a particularly obnoxious heckler was punched out by a (now well-established with tenure) poet who had prior professional boxing experience. The blow, only meant to deter, unfortunately removed a few front teeth from the drunk. Pianist James Booker also played at the Leaf during this time. Between '84 and '89, the last five years of Everette's life, the readings continued to grow in popularity. There were also other readings in the city. Poet Lee M. Grue, who established the New Orleans Poetry Forum, had monthly readings at her Backyard Poetry Theatre in the Bywater section of New Orleans, and Borsodi's Coffeehouse had monthly readings on Freret Street, but the Maple Leaf was the only regular weekly reading series open to the public.

In addition, mention should be made of the publications and presses spawned by the advent and subsequent history of the series. Poet and publisher Maxine Cassin, who had already established the New Orleans Poetry Journal Press by the time the readings started, offered to publish the first *Maple Leaf Rag* anthology. It contained poets who had read at the Leaf during the first two years. It was edited by Maxine, Everette, and Yorke Corbin. Now, fourteen years later, under circumstances no one could have foreseen, we present the 15th Anniversary edition.

Rereading Yorke Corbin's introduction to the first *Rag*, certain ironies jump out (with a fourteen-year periscope of hindsight). I quote:

> Whether Maple Leaf Rag becomes a tradition remains to be seen . . . But the notion that there should be further anthologies of work by New Orleans poets is an important one . . . This book is a first step toward establishing a literary community in New Orleans, and one measure of its success will be in whether further steps ensue.

Well, we did endure! and this fourteen-year hiatus is not only proof that a literary community did indeed arise but that it expanded beyond the confines of New Orleans. Writers from many states and countries have been lured to the exotic notoriety of the Maple Leaf readings in recent years.

In 1982, Cassin's press followed the *Rag* with a collection of Everette Maddox's poetry, *The Everette Maddox Song Book*. The

Song Book, which I was privileged to help edit in a small way, was carved out of a large manuscript. A second collection, *Bar Scotch*, was published by Pirogue Publishing in 1988. Pirogue, a press started by Bill Roberts and Hank Staples (now a part owner of the Leaf), also published poems by Julie Kane, *Body and Soul*. My book, *The Ape Woman Story*, was published by Pirogue in 1989, nine months after Everette died. My sorrow that he never saw the book greatly diminished my joy and dream of its publication.

Since Everette's death in February 1989 to the present, the last five-year segment of the readings, I have been experiencing what it is like to actually administer a reading series with a national reputation. During the first year after his death, poets Julie Kane, Helen Toye, and myself, ran the series together. For various reasons, Julie and Helen dropped out after the first year, and I guess I am the only poetry junkie addicted enough to commit myself to being there every Sunday afternoon of the year.

I have learned a lot about myself and others over the past fifteen years. I know I have grown more compassionate and tolerant about the readers and their work. In the early days (being in my arrogant twenties) I have recollections of giggling insanely (along with willing cohorts) at poets whose work I thought belonged on Hallmark greeting cards. But now, going on two decades, I must say I have realized remarkable discoveries and turnarounds by poets who initially read and then continued struggling and improving their art. Beginners as well as established writers are welcome here. We all learn from each other. So my laughter has diminished and my respect has grown for anyone who has the guts to stand up to the microphone and address the audience in a meaningful way.

When people now ask what the criteria are for reading, I just say, "Let me get my book and see what is the next available date." I think every sincere writer deserves to be heard with respect and admiration, and if anyone disagrees or is offended, they have the right to get up and leave. Sure, there have been gigantic egos (needing to be surgically removed) ranting and raving and absolutely certain of their genius, but it's all part of the whole experience. Actually, to me, the unsung heroes and heroines of the reading series are those regular "audients" who are not writers, but those who come just to appreciate or be stimulated by the poetry and fiction read.

One of the many rewarding experiences of undiscovered talent occurred just a few months ago. A hesitant newcomer, a man in his mid-thirties, signed up to read. He'd never read in front of a public audience before. Right before the reading started, he said to me, "I'm so nervous. I'm just an electrician; I only have a high school education." Well, he got up there and read some genuine poetry with the stage presence of one who had done it many times. Everyone was blown away by his work and his presentation. His name is Kerry Poree and one of his poems is in this 15th Anniversary Anthology.

When Everette died he left a manuscript of poems written on napkins and bar coasters during the final months of his life. These scraps of paper were gathered in a paper grocery store bag and saved from destruction by Hank Staples. Hank was going to publish these poems, but after four years of other financial obligations a group of us decided to take matters into our own hands. On a historic night full of strange confluences, synchronicities, and bizarre encounters, at the wedding party for poets Ralph Adamo and Sue Barker, we met up with fiction writer/teacher J. Travis who wanted to follow in his father's footsteps and start a small press.

Hence, Travis, Adamo, Bill Maddox (Everette's brother), Ken Fontenot, and myself (with editorial assistance from Helen Toye and Fred Kasten) worked together and released Everette's posthumous collection, *American Waste*, on Valentine's Day 1993. Since then Travis and Portals Press of New Orleans have published a science fiction novel (*The Camel's Back*) by Tom Whalen and Michael Presti and agreed to publish this 15th Anniversary edition of the *Maple Leaf Rag*.

Finally, thanks have to go to the owners of the Maple Leaf Bar who have supported these readings since 1979. Thank you Carl Brown, John Parsons, Bill Odom, Jim Stratton, and Hank Staples. It's been a long, strange journey and we hope it continues!

We tried to calculate the number of writers who have read/performed here over the fifteen-year span. We think at least a thousand people have. We tried to reach as many ex-readers as possible by sending out flyers, placing an ad in *Poets & Writers*, and through local publicity. Not all were reached and space limitations eliminated some good writers. However, this edition presents over a hundred people who have read at the Leaf. Hopefully there will be a future anthology. Fifteen years ago, few thought this reading series would be going on this long. I certainly had no inkling that I would take on the responsibility of running the readings. But every Sunday I feel Everette's presence and call on his spirit to help me carry on—Umpteen!

We hope this anthology will be a fitting memorial not only to Everette, but to everyone who has read at the Maple Leaf during the past fifteen years, whether or not they submitted work or were included herein.

See you at the "Leaf"!

Mardi Gras Day, 1994

Rodney Jones

Some Notes on Everette Maddox

When the poet Everette Maddox died in New Orleans, in February of 1989, more than four hundred persons showed up for his funeral march. It began on Oak Street, at the Maple Leaf Bar, and followed a Dixieland Band to Carrollton Station, where it paused at the Maple Leaf. Fred Kasten, the local radio eminence, walked at the front of the procession, carrying Maddox's ashes, and, in the crowd, one could see not only the legions of local friends, but a good number from Alabama, and also many others, friends of a lifetime, who had come from even farther, from North Carolina, Illinois, New York, and Connecticut, to pay their respects. I understand that, at this last service, Bob Woolf and Fred Kasten, who had twenty years earlier collaborated with Maddox to write and publish poems under the pseudonym of Buck Potatox, spoke eloquently and with great sincerity, but I could not hear, for I was unable to shoulder my way through the crowd. What did impress me and what impresses me still is that this man, who had been out of work for most of the past decade and, during the last five years of his life, without a home, was able to command the sort of respect that more typically graces the send-off of a governor or an archbishop.

And I believe that it was either Robin Gaston or Fred Kasten who reported to me that Rush Limbaugh, later that week, took the occasion of one of his incomparable radio broadcasts to lampoon the magnitude of this funeral service, which celebrated the life of a man well-known for unemployment and drinking, as more evidence of liberal decadence. I do not know if this story is true, but if it is, Rush sure got it right that time.

He would still be known as Rette for many years when I first met him. This would have been early 1968, in Tuscaloosa, Alabama, and I like to think it would have been him and Bob Woolf coming back from a night of drinking to the room next to mine, which Rette had just rented, and that this song, which Rette often sang to the tune of "I'm Looking Over a Four-leaf Clover," would have arrived before the faces:

I'm looking over my cousin Grover
who married a Belgian whore—

The voices, raspy from smoke, loudening over the protests from downstairs:

The night was foggy
and Grover was drunk
His dick was soggy
and her pussy stunk—

The protests, more obstreperous now, a broom bumping against the ceiling underneath me, the song unraveling now:

No need explaining
He's still complaining
His gonads are in a cast
I'm looking over my cousin Grover
His first piece may be his last—

And finally, the door springing open, and rolling into the wrong room, both of them shit-faced, Woolf, tall and dressed like an engineering student, and Maddox, the skinniest man I had ever seen, but natty and tweedy, with a face that bore a disarming resemblance to both Stonewall Jackson and D. H. Lawrence.

And it would have been Maddox who hopped spryly to his feet and approached me, at first with the look of picaresque and entertaining bemusement that I would come to recognize as the trademark and logos of his most casual inebriation, but then a transformation would have taken place, and almost imperceptibly, precipitately, the face would have shifted gears; the picaresque smile straightened and sobered to the serious business of greeting. He presented a hand, thin and blue-veined and gnarled as the hand of a hump-backed grandmother propped up in a wheelchair for Sunday visitors, and a look of bashfulness that had been summoned reluctantly but inexorably to sociability. It was a gaze that bestowed in all its dutiful and remarkable shyness a feeling of gravity and importance, and the voice joined to that gaze, hoarse and countrified, so one got that a sense of a weld scabbed over but beaded solidly underneath.

"Howdy," he would have said, and he would have made a little of that polite conversation that they make down there, asking where I was from, and what my parents did for a living, and I might have talked a little. I might even have told him that I liked Faulkner, that I was trying to write fiction, and that I had just broken up with a beautiful girl, for I would have been certain by then that I was engaged in conversation with a suave and old-fashioned gentleman, who now would have begun to pace back and forth across the rug, puffing gleefully at his pipe.

But then something would have happened to make the face change gears again. It might have been a spark from the pipe burning a hole in his lapel, or it might have been something that Woolf or I said that set off one of his glamorous cussing sprees, which would possess a striking combination of elevated and scatological language. And I would have been both chagrined and amazed, having never heard something like this in my life. And he would have gone on. And it would have been then that I would have tried to say something that might be of comfort, to which he would have responded as he started.

I heard it. I am not saying I believed it, but belief is a door that hangs halfway open, is not only the thing itself, that large opening to susceptibility, but the smaller more helpless opening to the suggestion of what might but couldn't be true, what once was and should be again, and this was the rut that Maddox paced, scowling and muttering now and then, "Fucking greatness," and then he did something that I have never seen another man do. He doubled the four fingers of his right hand into a half-fist, raised it to his jutting chin, and moved it back and forth like a chimpanzee. "Nookie," he said, extruding the word and bending it like a softened tube. "Oh God," he groaned, "I love her ass, and I'm like pore old Gatsby. I don't stand a chance in hell. Oh God, she's so fucking beautiful." I do not mean to mislead you, gentle reader, for that is the way it would have happened, and then, suddenly, Maddox would have been talking about Maude Gonne and Fanny Brawne. He would be quoting Keats and Yeats and Dylan Thomas, and it would go on until he either passed out or the sun came up, and if you were like Bob Woolf, or Carl Peterson, or myself, it would have left you stunned and with the unquestioning impression that you had encountered genius.

He was, at that time, by consensus, the most talented graduate student that anyone in the English Department at the University of Alabama had ever seen. To hang out with him in those days was to feel the world suddenly magicked into fiction, was to move in a landscape where the images and characters of poems and stories seemed as real as shrubs and parking meters. And also, there was his own mythology, which he could weave in an instant, heroic carica-tures of people he had known in Prattville, his hometown, legends of numerous local characters, comparisons of local beauties to the classic heroines of literature. He never fell in love with a girl, but with a tradition of women, so he would refer to one as the tall, proud Yeatsian girl and another as the buxom country wench. He would speak for a moment of some woman's unattainability. The next moment he would be talking about the figures on Keats' Grecian urn, and then suddenly he would be speaking of this history of philosophy, of linguistics, of Hank Williams, or the particular charms of some musical instrument, or Eugene O'Neill.

He held court those days at the Chukker, a bar in downtown Tuscaloosa, where by midnight, you would not infrequently discover him regaling a table with stories, playing a little wooden flute, or climbing onto a table to do the inimitable Maddox shuffle, a sort of Alabama version of a vaudevillian tap dance, which climaxed with his unzipping his pants and dangling his index finger from his fly. "Nookie," he would holler at the top of his voice and raise his face to the ceiling, baring his teeth and scratching his chin like a chimpanzee, all of this much to the delight and amazement of all of us who sat in his audience. There was rarely a night when he did not pass out at least once, and rarely a night when he did not wake up and walk the streets. And if you walked with him in the early spring, you might hear him extolling the virtues of the various sweet and heartbreaking essences, wisteria and morning glories, or this and that girl he had his eye on, and followed around but didn't stand a chance with, and later, he might stand on the stairway of one of the campus buildings and quote the whole of "Ode on a Grecian Urn" or "Somewhere I Have Never Traveled," and you would have been convinced, again and again, that you were in the presence of literary genius, and you might have been willing to stay up later and try to convince him not to kill himself, for he had reasons, aside from his romances, to be depressed. His father had only recently died, and his mother was then on her deathbed.

But at the time, all of this seemed less a life of self-destruction than a life of affirmation. His presence was a gift, as though one had stumbled inside a very well-written book, and anyone seeking to understand the man behind the poems should know that, from a very early point in his life, books were his religion and poets and writers his gods. He and his brother Bill had grown up in the red clay hills outside of Prattville, Alabama, and somehow their ideal grownups had not been soldiers or football players, but Hemingway and Faulkner and Fitzgerald and Thomas Wolfe. So this identity was of such long standing when I met him that it had become the very fabric of the man. And he did not identify just with authors, but with the great cities that he read about in books, and with composers and artists, with George Gershwin and Mahler and Picasso. He wanted to live a life that, like Eudora Welty's description of Faulkner's fiction, was twice as true as life.

Poetry, he believed then, was language with voltage. It was the most conscious of linguistic constructs and should be beautifully wrought, but meant nothing if it did not convey passion. It should speak intelligently in the voice of its time and, as well, it should sing. He had taken some of these notions from a poetry writing seminar that he took with August Mason, a brilliant but eccentric teacher, who, according to local legend, had been asked to retire after throwing a dog out of the third story window of Morgan Hall. Maddox was not the only talented poet in this seminar, whose other members included John Martin Finlay, Minnie Bruce Pratt, and Marvin Weaver. In fact, when I first met him, he professed envy for the work of these other poets and, on occasions, despair that his own work somehow did not match theirs, but I am not confident that I drew the right conclusions, as Rette Maddox indulged his Olympian talent for cussing and complaining to such an extent that it is nearly impossible to winnow the chaff from the seed. At any rate, when I first met him, he had been working for more than a year on a thirty-six-line poem in rhyming quatrains called "To a Young Girl Playing an Oboe," and it seemed to give him great sorrow. He was fond of repeating the maxim that "no poem is ever finished, only abandoned," and it seemed clear to me that he did not have any high opinion for his prospects of ever finishing "To a Young Girl Playing an Oboe." When the poem was selected as one of the winners in the 1968 Hallmark Honor Prize of the Kansas City State poetry contest, it did not much change his mind, but at least he did go on to other poems, and took some confidence from the victory.

One of these poems that he worked on in the spring of 1968 was "Notes for a Poem about the Past," and I would like to quote it here if only to show Rette's typical attention to craft and form at that time:

> Here, when you stand and smoke in sweet clover
> By tall cathedral clocks pigeons cajole,
> On a flagstone square where shabby pushcarts roll
> At morning down streets narrow enough to spit over—
>
> You are pilgrim. You, and the rest, are going,
> Always, to the site of battle, of king's decree—
> To where shells pile up, and an antique sea
> That Homer knew, Odysseus sailed, is blowing.
>
> I saw you listen when a streetcar lurched
> Past pirates' gathering-places, saw you stare
> At gargoyles, surly opponents to the dare
> Made by clouds passing back of where they've perched.
>
> Had not time been (ignore the paradox),
> You'd sup with Shakespeare, swill a pint with Browne,
> Angle with Walton, clap for Liszt, and frown
> With Marlowe at fierce stars above the rocks. . .

You talk about the future, but you want
The past with a yearning more than sensual—
Rows of grey armor, lions couchant in a hall
Mighty with echoes. Places like these flaunt

Their pastness at us. A well-made stick in hand,
We'd amble, time permitting, in otrocentro
Gardens at dawn, precisely cut—memento,
Though, of bewigged heads in which they were planned.

Past must be past, and we can never unravel
Its skein, that's disappearing momently—
Things of our own from which we're never free
Bear down on us, remind us we can travel

Forever without finding what we seek:
What was before. At night venetian blinds
Rattle in air-conditioned rooms . . . The mind's
A hurricane of drums. The dead years shriek.

All of the elements of his apprentice work suggest a thorough familiarity with the work of poets that he revered at the time, first among them, Yeats, but also Snodgrass, Nemerov, Dickey, Shapiro, Merrill, Cummings, Allen Tate, Eliot, Wilbur, Williams, Stevens, Justice, and Larkin.

Neither did he limit poetry to genre, for at times, I would come into his room late at night and he would read me long stretches of James Joyce's *Ulysses.* He delighted in the Rabelaisian passages, the vulgarities of Buck Mulligan and Molly Bloom. He would read these passages with something like the fervor of an evangelist, his cheeks swelling and reddening, his voice rising and cracking, his pipe smoking like a revolver, and after an hour or so, he would switch to Hemingway and read from *The Sun Also Rises,* the part where Bill and Jake are riding the bus into the mountains to go trout fishing. Sometimes he would stop for a good long stretch and cuss at his pipe, and then he would talk for a while about Emmaline Granger or Gatsby, for fictional characters seemed as real to him as novelists or poets, and also, at times, he would read from one or another of the new critics, Warren or Tate or Eliot, and there would be snippets from Pound and stories of Rimbaud. He would read Jarrell's essay on Whitman. There would be tears in his eyes when he quoted Keats, and that would be an exit, for then he would start talking about Fanny Brawne, and Maude Gonne, the women who had forsaken writers, and finally his own lost loves, and I would listen a good long time before admitting that my own heart was broken, and by then it would be morning.

I was, like Bob Woolf and a few other devout Maddox followers, a bad conventional student for having stayed up so many nights with Rette, and I do not know that it occurred to any of us that he was our teacher, for, though his learning far exceeded ours, we thought of him as a friend and equal, as though we had absorbed the bounty of his erudition like dew and Robert Penn Warren and T.S. Eliot were longstanding family friends. And it was not just the sharing of books, for he took us on pilgrimages to the cities that he loved, to Chicago, St. Louis, New Orleans, and New York, and one journey with him was worth a seminar, for he talked every mile of the way, not just of poetry, but of architecture, music, and painting, of railroads and history, and of interesting people he had known. One freezing winter night, he rode north with me through the Mississippi hill country in a car with no heater to piss on William Faulkner's grave, and on another occasion, he and Bob Woolf drove to Asheville, North Carolina, to visit Thomas Wolfe's family home. I do not know how he stood us, but he did, and I believe that one of his greatest pleasures was to see us opening before these miracles, these great cities and books that he loved.

He also read our fledging efforts at writing, and he was generous enough to laugh at us, and yet to leave some sense that we might, by dint of work and further reading, miraculously rise above our limitations. He was, more than most poets, truthful. In fact, he told one student in his poetry writing class at the University of Alabama that he would give him the grade of A if he promised never to write another poem. The man told me about it years later at Rette's funeral and expressed no small gratitude, but with me, at least, Rette Maddox was gentler. He would allow sometimes that I had written one good line, and he would urge me to build on that good line, his general notion being that a good task for a beginner was to write one good line after another. The end result might not be good poetry, but it would certainly be good training. The other part of the training was to read, and not just the great poets, but the great fiction writers and critics. Beyond this, thinking and suffering were the keys. This is what he told me, and I have no reason to think he told himself anything different, for he was no respecter of persons. To the end, his eye was downward, and his friends were always, in addition to young poets, people who held nine to five jobs, people who worked on boats and swept the floors of the bars he frequented.

During the years at Tuscaloosa, he read several poets who had a profound influence on his notion of poetry and of the role of the poet. He was tremendously impressed with the work of Alan Dugan and by the *Dream Songs* of John Berryman, and, later, by the work of James Tate, Michael Benedikt, Mark Strand, and Charles Simic. This was the time when the poet James Seay came to teach at the university, and Rette immediately took to Seay and Seay to Rette, though their spheres of influence differed, Seay working days in the lecture halls, Rette working nights at the Chukker and at various parties that gathered after closing time. Seay's first book, *Let Not Your Hart*, appeared, and not long afterwards, Howard Moss, the poetry editor of *The New Yorker*, accepted Rette's poem "Shades Mountain," an accomplished but atypical poem that he chose never to collect. These accomplishments made us all feel a sense of importance, almost of mission. This did not cease as marijuana and LSD rushed through our community, and, for most of us in the fledgling writers group, these drugs were not just social aids, but lenses through which we began to view literature differently, which is to say that reading was part and parcel of our hallucinations and that we sought the work that complemented our ongoing visions.

With Maddox, this was no simple matter. For most of us, the natural choice might be one of the ambassadors of whatever brand of surrealism was hottest that month, but Rette, as he tripped, was just as likely to read aloud poems by James Merrill or Karl Shapiro or Ezra Pound, giggling with Byzantine delight at passages that no doubt sent others into long jags of cognitive dissonance, for I do seem to remember those who left his presence at those times, and if the poetry did not do the trick, he might just launch into a five-minute cussing spell, a wonderful and mostly original convulsion of language, though it always seemed to include the adjectives "unconscionable," "egregious," and "ball-biting."

On one of these nights, we came up with an idea for a school of poetry: the Bowel Movement. We planned readings and publications, and Maddox delighted in all of this, suggesting P. T. Barnum's theme as our verbal logos: *This way to the egress.* This was Maddox in his Baudelaire period. Baudelaire walked a lobster on a leash to the opera. Maddox, on the other hand, began to keep possums in his house.

They were filthy, mean-spirited, testicular, so primal that their principal behavior was to hid under the furniture, to bare their teeth, scowl, and hiss at the slightest approach, but Rette loved them, for these were literary possums. He had managed somehow to obtain them after writing "Thirteen Ways of Being Looked at by A Possum," a parody of Wallace Stevens' "Thirteen Ways of Looking at A Blackbird," and a poem that is in many ways superior to Steven's poem. He was twenty-five years old when Michael Benedikt accepted the poem for *The Paris Review*, and it thrilled him more than his earlier acceptance by *The New Yorker*. He talked much, during these days, of promoting his own poems through possum T-shirts and possum festivals, even of a magazine to be called *Possum*—Was it ever published? So much of the record of Rette's early life has vanished, and much of it, like those undomesticatable possums, of a singularly entertaining nature. In addition to the Bowel Movement and the possums, he, together with his good friends Fred Kasten and Bob Woolf, invented a poet with the unlikely name Buck Potatox and, using that name, began publishing a number of highly inventive poems. A great deal of tongue-in-cheek play characterizes all of this, but also, it was during this time that he began writing the cartooning and self-caricaturing poems that marked the end of his apprenticeship and the beginning of his commitment to an aesthetic that, combined with his fondness to drink, probably sealed his academic fate.

The first evidence of this turn was probably his decision not to finish his dissertation, and I would like to emphasize that it was a decision, not just a result of his many late night conferences with Bacchus or his general disposition, for nothing proved easier for Rette Maddox than the writing of scholarly papers. To watch him work was to witness mastery. To begin with, there would be the pacing, back and forth across the room, each circuit gathering centrifugal force and momentum, like the winding of a crank, back and forth like that, sometimes for five minutes until something caught. The eyes would spark. The pipe clamped between the teeth would puff more fiercely, and then he would hunch over the typewriter like a stockcar driver, and the two fingers flying across the keyboard would set off a fusillade, beautiful, clean, and violent, until the platen had devoured a page, another, another, and then he would stop, go over to the bookcase, open a book to a seemingly random passage, from which he would extricate an phrase or paraphrase, go back to the typewriter, interlard it in his text, and, proceeding forward with the same unwavering velocity, complete three more pages before breaking to pace again. Again that winding of the crank, and then the fierce puffing of the pipe, and then the clean white sheets of bonded paper rolling through the platen, the pause to extricate and interlard, and again the driven speed, which seemed to occur of a natural force, with no more energy expended than a cow might use browsing through a morning of clover. Again and again and again, until the thesis, which seemed to have been snatched from a moving train, had marched its subordinate ideas and arbitrarily inducted resources to such victories as all theses aspire to: a grade, a measurement of respectability.

I am not saying it was I. A. Richards, but it was something. The authorities that he had gathered helter-skelter—Jung, Freud, Warren, Levin, whoever—would be woven around the central idea so resourcefully and with such effortlessness that it seemed less a paper than a conversation of intelligent men moderated by a narrator who seemed bent on turning the symposium into a farce. Neither were there typos or spelling errors. The margins were all correct, and the footnotes hung like plumb-bobs at the bottom of each page. The prose was seeded with *bons mots*. There were snippets of Latin and French, subtle allusions, puns, and references to various critical schools of thought, and twenty pages of such fare would take him perhaps two hours.

But he despised this ability within himself, loathed, reviled, and desecrated it. He liked to explain it humbly. There were different kinds of luck, he would say: luck with bitches, luck with money, luck with music, luck with poetry. The gift that allowed him to create the lucid and erudite discourse of papers for college literature courses in a very short period and with whatever resources he had at hand was what he called academic luck, and he talked about it as though it were more of a curse than a gift. Of course, such talk was partly posturing, Rette's typical gambit of elevating the listener's ego by caricaturing himself, but there was also clearly substance to these anti-academic thoughts. In short, he saw the Puritan dross of genteel respectability tainting every lecture hall. He saw the pretense of the diction and the manner, and it was not a model of behavior that he felt comfortable emulating. On the other hand, he was even less comfortable with the clubbiness and careerism of the poet-teachers rolling off the assembly lines in the burgeoning MFA programs in creative writing. Though he would continue to work in colleges and universities for several more years, first at the University of Alabama, then at Xavier and the University of New Orleans, his most valuable teaching always took place outside the classroom, in his own apartments, on the road, and in bars, and the only writing that would prove valuable to him was poetry.

His high esteem for the art was never more obvious than when one watched him composing a poem. As when he composed academic prose, he worked by fits and starts, pacing at times, puffing fiercely at the pipe, attacking the keyboard as though manning a machine gun being charged by a brigade of Puritans, but unlike prose-composition, one could sense the pressure here. There was a look of private and utter desperation on his face and no easy negotiations with silence, but rather a pushing against an immense weight, for he never believed that a poem could be willed into being, but that it was of a sudden fluency, a gift, as magical and unlikely as any of the rest of creation, and still that one had to work hard at that birthing, for poems were miracles to Rette Maddox. If he had trouble believing in those miracles or in his own worthiness to be the stage on which they occurred, one should never doubt his intention to rise to that level, for the torture and beauty of his life were shaped and confirmed in that pressure, and his mature poems, in very telling ways, document his escape from those pressures.

The best poems in his four published books strike me as some of the most companionable and beautifully wrought poems of our time. We may tend to underestimate the strengths of these poems because of a single flaw in a few poems that he chose unwisely—I believe—to place near the beginning of his first full volume, *The Everette Maddox Song Book.* These poems are not just evidence of—but monuments to—self-pity: We see it in whole poems like "Anonymous" and "Gift" and in lines like "Nothing/ is relevant since/ losing you is what/ my life is about." I do not see any reason to put a good face on these poems or the tendency in his character, for the truth is that Rette Maddox published a few poems that are not just bad—they are heroically and aggressively bad, and they draw so much attention to themselves that they may, for many readers, dull the attention that his strong poems deserve. At the same time, even in that first volume, he sometimes managed to turn the man-done-wrong theme to good ends, as in the "The Miracle":

> "Things are tight," the man
> said, tightening
> his quasi-friendly grin.
> "We can't give you
> any money, and
> we don't want these here
> poems either." He
> tightened his tie. "Fact
> is, the old cosmic
> gravy train's ground to
> a halt. It's the end
> of the line. From now
> on, there's going
> to be no more nothing."
> He went on, lighting

a cigar: "We don't
wish we could help, but
even if we did,
we couldn't. It's not
our fault, by God, it's
just tight all over."
He brought his fist down
on the burnished desk
and lo! from that tight
place there jetted forth
rivers of living water.

The most salient feature of Maddox's strong poems is consciousness, which is to say that no poet announced himself and his themes more lucidly and directly, or had a more well-defined notion of how to go about the business of entertaining and enlightening his audience, which was also very consciously defined by the framing of his poems. Friends are almost always included in his poems, so it is not only Maddox's consciousness, but the consciousness of others that is honed in on and held against the backdrop of his subject. He writes in "What I Do":

Somebody makes a crack like
"I'd rather have a bottle in front of me
than a frontal lobotomy,"
and I seize that fleeting crack
and bang and hammer it, in a fury
of incompetent affection, until
it's fixed: an imperishable plank
in the platform of good feeling.
Oh there's nothing to it, but
I do it well. So now
that I know what it is I do,
what my calling is, I hang out
my shingle. It reads: CRACKS FIXED,
and in more modest scrawl: Lines
End-Stopped while you wait.

The same sort of motion occurs in an earlier poem, "Maintenance," in which he likens himself to a janitor who comes, sweeping up snippets of insights that his friends have thrown away. He begins that poem, "It's a thankless task/ sweeping up the halls of consciousness./ My friends are all such fools/ I can't help liking them./ They want to create or destroy,/ and somebody has to just keep order." For Maddox, the duty of the poet was less to create consciousness than to recognize, transmit, and order consciousness, for poetry was not just the "little/ black ants of print," but evidence and provocation of a special awareness, a primal condition of creation that existed in the world beyond the page. The made thing of poetry should never disguise that fleeting glimpse under eternity's skirt, but find and report that consciousness, which might as likely emanate from overheard conversations and encounters with children as from listening to Mahler or meditating on history. In essence, most of Maddox's poems are about poetry, but only if we define poetry as not just the linguistic phenomenon but as our most valuable awareness of the experience of our time on earth.

He worked mostly in a syllabic line that he adapted from Alan Dugan's line and made it his own, and he did it for the reasons that should be clear to anyone: because it allowed him to render the virtues of plain American speech with formal grace, and because it proved less wieldy than the metered lines of his apprenticeship. He also worked in free verse, but he did not quite approve of it or trust it, for he was, by temperament, a formal man, who even near the end of his life, when he was sleeping in the bed of a dump truck, continued to sport a tie and tweed jacket. As well, his poems are marked by the constant resistance of subject to treatment: the more serious the subject, the lighter the treatment, and vice-versa. In all of these elements, he was both tactician and craftsman, and his mastery of the art continued to grow throughout his life, although the time he had to practice his art fell off at approximately the same rate, so at the end, in those last few months when he was again inspired to write, he never wasted time cutting to the chase, so you know instantly whether it is there or not, and when it is there, you had better be damn well prepared, for as Ralph Adamo has pointed out, it works like a haiku, bam, and is gone.

As I have mentioned, there are weak poems in *The Everette Maddox Song Book*, but the poet of *Bar Scotch*, his second full-length book, is rarely off target. I do not mean to suggest a mystical step to another plane, for many of the poems in *Bar Scotch* pre-date selections in *The Song Book*, only that the selections for the second volume suggest Maddox's maturing knowledge of what he was up to: the rage against the Puritan ethic, the Dionysian celebration of sociability, the faith in the imagination, the relentless investigations of moments.

Neither does he waste much time with sentimentality, but instead squares off with the reader in the first poem, "Nothing Personal":

> This poem was written out of
> a deep dark stomachache.
> It had to fight its way up
> through a rotten mood
> and a foul mouth to issue
> in snarls, curses, tongueouts,
> obscene fingers and broken
> beer bottles to be hurled
> at you, busybody reader:
> Beat it! Go away! I'm not
> writing today. But it's
> nothing personal: Come back
> tonight, when the full moon
> falls in my Scotch and all's
> well on the patio with
> my lots of friends, and I'll
> kiss your ass and make it well.

Like most poets of true decadence, Maddox rails at a host of the conventions of ordinary society, at the prescriptive platitudes of the workaday world, and the straitlaced behavioral mores of the middle class, but he differs from typical American decadents in that his poems do not bear witness to a superior and mystical solitude, for, mainly, his poems are addressed to and contain friends. They take place, not in fields or on cliffs, but in bars and on city streets. He is not, like James Wright, alone, surveying a ruined landscape, but drinking with pals, and, if the foundation of the drinking is common misery, the goal is transcendence, communion.

I do not see any reason to assume that the character of the poet differs in any significant way from the character of the man, for there was about him a distinctive fear of loneliness that differed from his ongoing estrangement from the women he idolized, and the fear was based in nightmare, in the early deaths of his parents, and in his own sense of powerlessness. In public, he could often transform this depression by engaging in literary conversations, or by his wonderful, unique habit of turning his friends into myths, or more dangerously, through self-caricature, but to see him alone was to see him either occupied with a task or flung down into such an abyss of self-loathing and suicidal brooding that no words of encouragement could reach him. So it was the darkness on one hand and the whiskey on the other, and only a rare, ever-narrowing moment where poetry was possible, but in such moments, he wrote with more conviction and mastery than ever before. "Cleaning the Cruiser," a poem that he wrested from the menial work of a job he held briefly at the Louisiana Maritime Museum, deserves quoting whole:

> The model of the cruiser *New Orleans*
> is smaller than life
> but larger than me. The glass case
> with table stands six feet
> seven inches high (I'm 5'8"
> sober) and about fifteen
> feet long. How I clean it,
> once a month, on a small aluminum
> stepladder, is, first, to brasso
> the dim brass frame all over
> with a rag—a pain in the aft,
> as well as futile. Next, as to

the glass: one squirt of windex
under a paper towel becomes
a sort of filthy halo, a swirl
of drunkard's breath, which I rub
and rub, until at some point suddenly
everything disappears except
what appears to be nothing
but the reality of the fake
ship itself, its gray guns and planes
as plain as rain beneath my raised
hand . . . Dangerous point!
at which I imagine that I may fall,
or crash, through that drab
clarity, and hit the deck,
bound for the Philippines. Mean draft
indeed! into World War II,
which I only remember in sepia . . .
On the other hand,
talk about your escapes!
When the present storm is on, isn't
the violent past the safest place to be?
Oh I would do it—run away
and fight my father's war
all over again, to wear
the black gold-buttoned coat
that hung in some dream-closet
of my childhood, and find, at armistice,
you. Kiss me once,
I'd say, and kiss me twice,
and kiss me once again,
it's been a long, long time.

    It does not seem pertinent to even ask what he might have done
if he had been able to find a woman who would have endured his
complaints or if he had been given a stipend by some altruistic institution, for, clearly, he would have not kept either. Neither do I have
the impression that his last decline was altogether sad, for his oldest

and most loyal friends, the surviving duo of the Buck Potatox Trio, have told me that, in many ways, the last days of his life were his happiest, for he was mostly free of the job responsibilities that clearly bored him, and neither do I imagine that he would have felt guilty for having bummed a meal off a buddy, or for having slept on someone's couch. And when he was finally at rock-bottom, wandering the streets, and sleeping in the bed of a dump-truck, I do not imagine that even that would have killed his spirit, for he often professed, "Health ain't good for you," and his life suggests that it was a true sentiment. His life was not so much a sinking into despair, as a conscious dive that featured much acrobatic twisting and somersaulting. There was muscle in it, and unbendable will, and grace, and style, and even dignity, but perhaps, most poignantly and perversely, there was the release from the muse, which he would have felt keenly and with perhaps equal proportions of celebration and self-torture. So I believe that it was not only his unrequited love for Suzy but an unquestioning faith in his own approaching death that set him to writing the poems of *American Waste*.

That last book marks the victory of hopelessness. It is written utterly without illusion or literary pretensions, and it captures so palpably the nuances of Maddox's speaking voice that to read it is to almost touch the man: the savage world-cartooning wit, the sense of beauty and civilization, the carnal-cry, the fascination with history, the resigned and stoically self-caricaturing romantic. It is, as Bob Woolf pointed out to me in a late night phone conversation, jazz, and in particular, New Orleans jazz, but it also seems the work of the oldest young man in the world, one who is holding up all the props of misbegotten adolescence and childhood, and glorying in the rot and sad foolishness of it all, as here in "What I Said To The Sky":

> I reeled out of a 6-martini
> candlelit dinner
> & stood in the usual gutter
> clutching what was left
> of the 20th century
> & looked up into a sky

the color of a bruise
It looked like Mr. Hyde
in Classics Illustrated
& I shook my fist
at the God that had vacated years ago
overdue on the moral rent
& said "I came up a romantic idealist
& life has made me a mean
cynical pessimistic piss-ant
fuck you & the clouds you rolled in on"
& some wise-ass passer-by said
"But what about Suzy"
& I said "Suzy
blew the last blast
on my toy trumpet
that's all"

And everywhere else in the book, that melody of completion and exhausted potential resonates perversely, joyously, as it ranges freely in a vernacular that feels essentially plush and emotionally luxurious.

The book required much in the way of editing, for the original manuscript ran close to a hundred pages, and Maddox had not established a clear order for the poems. He had written the poems out in block print, all caps, on whatever paper was handy, and the feel of improvisation was not lessened by the fact that many of the poems were written on bar napkins or that they were couched in an unrelenting vernacular, but, clearly, most of these poems were not first drafts, but pieces that were very consciously crafted to strike with a sudden and woefully playful force. What Ralph Adamo and others did in editing the book was mainly to cut the poems that seemed less than finished or fragmentary and to establish an order that respected thematic unities. I would make no claims that *American Waste* is Rette Maddox's best book, but it is the volume that best represents the behavior and spirit of the man, and I have increasingly come to see that such representation is the thing that matters most. The truth of poetry is the truth of a life or the poetry is nothing, and the truth of Rette Maddox's life was more often than not bleak and sad, but gilded with the kind of wit that allows him to dress up "like Albert the Alligator," as he courts his Suzy, and to announce to a doubting Turtle that he will win her by playing on a banjo, an instrument he's never played in his life, "the complete works of Rimsky-Korsakov."

It is mainly the equality and fierceness of the wit that characterizes these poems. It is a courtly wit that is drunk on jazz, and it finds its bearings in extraordinary imaginings that rise from ordinary situations: the sweet "gusts from girls" that the poet smells as he goes to take a leak, the performance of a bad band, the restoration of the Sistine Chapel, a visit to Houston, sightings of tits and memories of old songs, the theft of either a poem or "7 dollars & 31 cents" as the poet visits the men's room, the repair of a cooler. And there are two splendid heartbreaking poems: "Heaven," and "Home in Their Biblical Beds," which goes like this:

> The very spiritual
> bodies of women
> flow away
> in white dresses
> in Poe & Rosetti
> The most famous
> flow-away being
> Millet's "Ophelia"
> in the basement
> of the Tate Gallery
> How come people
> don't really flow away
> but grind & grown
> & crackle & waste into a naturalistic stick
> like my mother did
> at St. Jude's
> in Montgomery
> 20 years ago

Now, five years after his death, I wonder what will become of these poems, if some young people, in love with the romance of death, will discover them and make of him, as they have made of

Frank Stanford, some sort of national legend. For my part, I care nothing for the romance of death, but the best poems of Everette Maddox possess a singular emotional wit and even genius. I would hope that many will find them, and that some publisher with real clout will someday see fit to do a meaningful *Greatest Hits of Everette Maddox* from the three published volumes. In the meantime, I hope that some serious and hard-minded scholar will be able to track down the dozens of early poems that got written but never published, for some of them belong with the very best work of one of our finest neglected poets.

Julie Kane

Valley of the Kings: Last Days of Everette Maddox

Late in the last October of poet Everette Maddox's life, I emerged from a tomb in Egypt's Valley of the Kings and grasped something about Everette's poetry for the first time. I had been gazing at three-thousand-year-old tomb paintings of jackal-like dogs, ibis-like birds, and stylized papyrus reeds. Now, blinking under the rays of a gold sun disk crowning a brilliant blue sky, I could see the same dogs nosing around the tomb entrance in hopes of handouts, the same birds wheeling in the direction of the river, the same river dotted with the sails of *felucca* boats, their design unchanged for three millennia. All of a sudden I understood why Everette chose to write obsessively about a two-block by two-block square of the Carrollton neighborhood of New Orleans and the characters who populated it, rather than continuing to chase after the Big Subjects and heavy symbolism of his early poems. Make art out of what's around you, those tomb paintings seemed to be saying, and the ordinary elements of your surroundings can sometimes take on the power and force of myth.

I was in love with Bill Petre, a part-time bartender at the Maple Leaf Club in New Orleans, at the time of that two-week trip to Egypt in the fall of 1988. After a tour with the Navy in Vietnam, Bill had gone to art school on the GI Bill, managed an art gallery in the French Quarter, and had a couple of one-man shows of his oils and pastels. He had started bartending at night so that he'd have "light to paint during the days"—except that he often drank so hard that he'd still be sleeping off a hangover as Ra's chariot sank over the west bank of the Mississippi River. By the time I met him, he had been fired from all of the best music clubs in New Orleans— Tipitina's, the Dream Palace, the Bon Temps—and now he was on probation at the Leaf, the last stop on the trolley line. He was six feet tall, with graying gold hair tied back in a ponytail and a gap in his smile where he'd knocked out two teeth crashing a new but uninsured Volkswagen Jetta into a concrete overpass on Interstate-

10. On the June night that I had fallen in love with him, dancing to Snooks Eaglin live at a party on the *batture*—that narrow strip of land between the levee and the river where squatters lived in illegal driftwood houses—he kept murmuring, "You don't want to get involved with me, I'm a drunk." He was correct, of course, but I didn't listen, carried away by the colored lights strung in the trees, the river muck sucking at my sandals with each dance step, the river lap-lap-lapping just a few feet behind us, and the flamenco rhythms of Snooks's guitar. The party was being thrown by the wealthy boyfriend of Suzy Malone, Everette's latest poetic muse. Formerly a lead singer in The Pfister Sisters, a forties-style girl group, and recently divorced from Tommy Malone of The Radiators, a legendary New Orleans rock band, the beautiful Suzy was now bartending part time at Muddy Waters' nightclub, across the street from the Maple Leaf. She had long, auburn hair to her waist and a sprinkling of cinnamon freckles on her nose, and she always had a smile for Everette; she made it clear that she felt honored and touched to be the inspiration for his latest poems.

The Maple Leaf was the last stop on the line for Everette as well as Bill. Since his arrival in New Orleans in 1975, Everette had lost three teaching jobs, a wife, a stepdaughter, a sports car, and a succession of apartments to excessive drinking. Now he was officially homeless, his address in the prestigious *Directory of American Poets and Fiction Writers* listed as "8316 Oak Street"—the address of the Maple Leaf, where he washed bar towels and emceed the weekly Sunday afternoon poetry readings. He would usually be there when the bar opened up around noon, and be there when it closed around four or five in the morning. On the coldest nights of the year, Bill and the other bartenders would often take pity on Everette and deadbolt him inside the club when they locked it up at closing time, although it was most decidedly against fire code regulations.

Bill, Everette, and James Booker—the gifted R&B pianist who used to play regular Monday night gigs at the Maple Leaf, when he wasn't too messed up on alcohol or heroin, and who'd died young just a couple of years before—began to populate the poems about the Maple Leaf that I started writing after I got back from Egypt. In a sense, all three men were the same person—the self-destructing artist, the "genius of the place"—and my unconscious mind knew it long before my rational mind did. Knew, as well, that they formed a three-way mirror to reflect back my own wasted potential and continuing downward spiral.

One Sunday evening in late November, after the poetry reading, I invited Everette and some other good friends back to my apartment to eat homemade chili and view the slides that I had shot in Egypt. But Everette got sick on the chili and left early, complaining that his stomach and throat had been bothering him lately. Later in the week, having dinner with my friend Mary Darken Murray (now "Herrington")—a pediatrician who wrote poetry and sometimes came to the Sunday readings—I mentioned that Everette hadn't been feeling well, and she said that she might drop by the Leaf with her black bag to check up on him. She did, and she diagnosed him with acid reflux and pneumonia and prescribed some liquid medication for him. Bill and the other bartenders stashed it in the Maple Leaf cooler and served it up to Everette in a shot glass every four or six hours or however often he was supposed to take it—they took good care of him.

But even though Everette was taking his medicine, washed down with plenty of bar scotch, he didn't seem to be getting any better. Bill Roberts, who had founded Pirogue Publishing the year before to bring out my *Body and Soul,* Everette's *Bar Scotch,* and his own *Stories on the Drift,* had scheduled several readings to promote all three books around that time. Bill, AKA "The Long Island Cajun," had grown up around New York City and earned an MFA in fiction writing from SUNY-Stony Brook, but he was working for a diving gas company out in the boonies of Louisiana, affecting a Cajun accent, and spending an awful lot of time angling for catfish in a wooden pirogue. He was a character straight out of the movie *Five Easy Pieces,* where Jack Nicholson is hiding out from his well-to-do family and artsy side amidst a bunch of Gulf Coast oilpatch workers. The weekend before we were to read at Ruby's Roadhouse in Mandeville, across Lake Pontchartrain from New Orleans, Bill somehow got his hands on an alligator and marinated it in rum for twenty-four hours and then stewed it in a crockpot and brought it with him to the reading. But Everette still wasn't eating, not even his literary patron's booze-soaked alligator, and his mood was sullen.

The following month, Bill Roberts drove us to another three-some reading at the East Baton Rouge Parish Library. Afterwards, we went out to eat with Richard "Buzz" Kilbourne, a poet and attorney from a small town north of Baton Rouge. When Everette got up to go to the men's room, Buzz leaned over the table and whispered, "His color is terrible, Julie. He looks jaundiced." It had been months since Buzz had seen Everette, so the change in Everette's appearance was obvious to him, although those of us who were around him all the time couldn't really see it. When Everette got back to the table, I peered hard at him—eyes as blue as bottle gentians, the only flower that blooms in Louisiana in late fall; coal-black hair swept back from a pale, domed forehead; skeletal frame animating a tweed jacket and tie—but couldn't see what Buzz was talking about. Everette looked like nothing so much as "a defeated Confederate general, leading his tattered troops," as Buzz had once put it.

Of course, it was winter, and Everette hated the cold, which could be partly to blame for his unhealthy pallor and bad mood. Even indoors, wrapped in a navy blue wool pea coat with the collar turned up, he shivered and cursed the weather. He had outworn his welcome on too many friends' sofas by peeing all over their bath-room floors, setting fire to their carpets with his live pipe embers, or leaving their front doors standing open when he woke up around noon and wandered off in search of a steadying drink. Everette could not be bothered with the conventions of domesticity, such as aiming for the john or employing a house key. Once, when I had tried to take him to apply for food stamps, he had recoiled in disgust and protested, "Now, what good would it do me to be walking down Oak Street with a pack of weenies under my arm?" But his unhousebroken status left him sleeping most nights in the broken-down truck belonging to Terri, the daytime bartender at the Leaf—out of the wind, but not the cold.

The weekend of January 27 to 29, at least, Everette was going to be warm. Bill Roberts was driving us to Alabama and Florida in his pickup truck, which had a loaded gun in the glove compartment and a fishing tackle box in the bed to support his assumed Cajun persona. It would have had a hunting dog in the back, too, except that Bill had put "Old Pink" to sleep after the dog developed a rash on his penis; the vet had told Bill he needed to apply ointment to the affected area a couple of times a day, and Bill just couldn't handle it. ("PINKIE MUST DIE!" Bill's business partner, Hank Staples, used to hiss when Bill walked in the Leaf.) That Friday, Bill Roberts picked me up at my apartment on the corner of Dublin and Birch streets in Carrollton. Everette had persuaded me to move from the west bank of New Orleans to Carrollton two years earlier by proclaiming, "It's the Montmartre of New Orleans!" (And so it was, when Everette was alive.) My place was only five blocks from the Maple Leaf, so that was our next stop, to collect Everette. I don't remember Everette as carrying any luggage with him, other than the usual plastic go-cup of scotch that he took with him whenever he left the bar. Bill said that he wanted to get some coffee before we got on the highway, and Everette said that we should go to a certain burger place near the Huey P. Long Bridge in Jefferson Parish, because he hadn't eaten in days but their burgers were small enough for him to swallow. Bill wanted to know why Everette couldn't just go to the nearest McDonald's or Burger King and cut a regular-sized burger into smaller pieces, but Everette refused to even entertain such a ridiculous idea, so Bill gave in and detoured to Jefferson Parish.

"I can only swallow things that are very, very small," Everette explained as he nibbled at the edge of a burger the size and shape of a matchbox. Then he began to choke and turn purple, scaring me and Bill into jumping to our feet in the restaurant booth, ready to pound him on the back or attempt the Heimlich Maneuver. When the tiny plug of burger finally shot out of Everette's mouth and into the napkin, Bill and I lost our appetites for our own burgers. Everette, too, abandoned the idea of eating and went back to nursing his scotch.

We piled back into Bill's pickup truck, all three of us wedged into the front. Ten or fifteen miles out of town, Everette let out a low moan. "Oh, Gaw-w-w-w-w-w-d!"

91

"What? What is it?" Bill snapped.

"My pipe. I left it back there on the table."

"Well, don't worry about it. I'll buy you another pipe the next time we stop."

"No-o-o-o-o-o-o!" Everette moaned. "It's not just *any* pipe. You don't understand. It can't possibly be replaced."

"Jesus H. Christ!" Bill shrieked, but he turned the truck around, sped back to the mini-square-burger place, screeched to a halt in the parking lot, and dashed inside while Everette and I tried hard not to look at each other, like little kids afraid of Dad's wrath. Bill emerged clutching the pipe. "Here's your fucking pipe. All right? Are you happy?" Everette was. After a long and satisfying smoke, he climbed into the covered bed section, stretched out between the fishing tackle box and the overnight bags, and went to sleep, leaving me to make conversation with Bill, which was a little awkward.

Bill and I had been lovers for a few months back in 1985, disastrously so—we could never seem to get together without drinking too much and picking a fight. A couple of times we had taken Everette out to dinner with us as a human shield. Given that the relationship had been so combative, you can just imagine the tenor of the post-relationship. Bill had barely spoken to me in the two and a half years since the breakup—except once, when he came to me with the idea of starting up Pirogue and publishing *Body and Soul* as its first book. The funny thing was, Bill still liked my poetry, even though he couldn't stand me as a person. Just recently, for example, he had written me a formal business letter on Pirogue Publishing stationery vetoing my choice of an author's publicity photo for *Body and Soul.* He'd be damned if he was going to pay for a photo of me "fawning over a cat," was the highlight of that missive. Ironically, the *Times Picayune* had declined to review *Body and Soul* when it came out, having been tipped off that I was Bill's "girlfriend" several years after the fact and assuming that Pirogue was some kind of vanity press.

The other half of Pirogue, Hank Staples, was also not your typical publishing executive. With his burly build and wavy, center-parted brown hair, Hank in his bar apron could have passed for a nineteenth-century barber or shopkeeper. Indeed, he even lived above the "shop," on the second floor of the Maple Leaf, where he bartended a couple of nights a week. Everette and his brother William used to crash there on occasion, until Everette wore out his welcome and William smashed several dozen bottles of Maple Leaf booze on the barroom floor one night and got permanently eighty-sixed from the premises. James Booker used to get carried up there, too, from time to time in years gone by: Hank referred to the screened porch room with a mattress on the floor as the "Booker Memorial Vomitorium." Around the bar, Hank was known for howling at the moon whenever Walter "Wolfman" Washington played, which was fairly often. Unbeknownst to most of us, Hank was toting a roman numeral like a concealed weapon: he was Henry Lee Staples IV of Virginia, and when a relative died and he inherited a wad of cash, the first thing he did was invest in Pirogue with Bill Roberts—all because he believed in Everette's poetry and wanted to help bring out Everette's second book. The second thing Hank did with his inheritance was to buy a share of the Maple Leaf, becoming a business partner rather than a mere employee. Despite his elevation to the ranks of management, Hank continued to bay at the moon whenever Wolfman played.

But, back to the Pirogue Reading Tour of January 1989. We made it to Montgomery without further mishap, crashed for the night with some old friends of Everette, and gave a well-received reading at Christopher's Restaurant at two in the afternoon the following day. The folks at Christopher's had strung up bunches of purple, green, and gold balloons in our honor, because we were from New Orleans and Mardi Gras was only about ten days off. After the reading, Everette and I were having a good time talking to people and signing our books, but Bill wanted to hit the road and get to Florida before too late, so he whisked us into the pickup truck and handed us a pint of Southern Comfort to keep us occupied.

Somewhere on a rural Florida highway a few hours later, the pickup truck ran out of gas. "Jesus H. Christ!" shouted Bill, pounding his fists on the steering wheel. Everette was asleep in the back—or so it seemed. "I'm going to have to hitchhike into the next town for gas," Bill said. "Where are we? Have you seen any road signs?"

"No," I said—but I was so far gone on Southern Comfort, I wouldn't have noticed the giant floodlit HOLLYWOOD sign, at that point. Bill cursed again, got out of the truck, slammed the door, walked about twenty yards down the road, and stuck out his thumb. A blast of cold air had entered the truck when he got out, and the warmth from the heater was already beginning to fade, and not a single car had passed in either direction in the ten minutes or so since we had coasted off onto the shoulder. And it was even colder in the truck an hour later, when a yellow Baptist church bus finally stopped and allowed Bill to climb on board. Shivering uncontrollably by then, I glanced back to Everette and saw that his eyes were cracked open. "You're awake!" I accused.

"I've *been* awake," he said. "I just thought it was best to keep a low profile in this situation. I'm a coward at heart, you know."

I laughed and passed Everette the last of the Southern Comfort, and we talked about love and poetry until the yellow church bus reappeared an hour or so later on the other side of the highway, whereupon Everette dropped back down to a horizontal position and resumed feigning sleep.

I should have tried feigning sleep, myself, because after Bill had poured enough gas in the tank to get us going again, he decided to pull off at the next exit to fill 'er up and get a cup of coffee, and when I got out at the restaurant and called my home phone to check for messages, I discovered that Bill Petre—who had broken up with me a couple of weeks earlier—had left a drunken and apologetic and romantic message on my answering machine. I called him back, and just as the two of us were cooing at one another and making plans to see each other as soon as I got back to town, a recaffeinated Bill Roberts came striding past me, barking, "Get off the phone, we're leaving now."

"Okay, just a sec," I called after him. But, by the time I hung up and went back out to the parking lot, the truck was gone. Bill had taken off without me. "Everette won't let Bill leave me here, when he wakes up and discovers what's happened," I told myself. Or would he, the little opportunist? Even in my drunken state, it occurred to me that a poet on tour for Norton or Graywolf probably wouldn't be likely to find herself in such a situation. Too smashed to do anything about it, however, I went back inside, dropped another quarter down the pay phone slot, and dialed Bill Petre back. About twenty minutes into our middle-school conversation, I saw and heard the truck screech back into the parking lot. I hung up and ran outside before Bill Roberts could come in and get me.

It turned out that we were only about ten minutes from Fort Walton Beach—Bill had already dropped Everette off. We rode in silence before pulling up outside a handsome, two-story wooden house that backed right up on the water of Choctawhatchee Bay. The friendly young couple who owned the place welcomed us, putting me in my own guest room and Bill and Everette in a shared room for the night. I woke up early the next morning and slipped out back to admire the bay view. Who should be out there but Everette?—huddled in damp sand with his knees drawn up to his chest, shivering. "I was coughing so hard that Bill kicked me out of the room," he explained.

"Oh, shit," I said, and sat with him out there for awhile, trying to cheer him up. Images from the past summer kept running through my mind, images of Everette happy and seemingly healthy, in contrast with the wraith who was sitting beside me now. Everette sitting at a table on the back patio of the Maple Leaf reading a review of *Bar Scotch* in the early edition of the Sunday *Times Picayune* and crowing, "I feel like I'm sitting in Sardi's, waiting for my Broadway reviews to roll off the presses." Everette reveling in attention from dozens of his friends and fans at the autograph party for the book the next day. Everette in love with love at the July wedding of Brent and Terri, the two main bartenders at the Leaf. Everette jokingly commanding the Tony Bazley Quintet to "Hit it, boys!" at our jazz poetry reading at Muddy Water's nightclub in late August. . .

Toward noon, Everette's friends served up a pot of chicken gumbo, but Everette wouldn't touch it, claiming that the chicken pieces were too big. "Just drink the broth. I'll fish the chicken out," I said, but he refused and said he'd just stick to his scotch.

That afternoon at the Fort Walton Beach Art Museum, before

an audience of about twenty or thirty people, Everette gave one of the best performances I'd ever seen him deliver. His comic timing was perfect, particularly while reading the racy parts of "Of Rust": "Somebody said the best / words, in any order, / were *Alone in bed. E.g. / In bed alone. In alone / bed. Bed alone in.* But / I think the best words / are *In bed with you,* and / the best order is / *In you with bed. . . . "* By the time he got to the last lines of "Even Odd," I was pinching my arm to keep from crying over the crazy vocation that was keeping us both stringing words together and ricocheting around the South drunk in a pickup truck instead of marrying and having children and holding down normal jobs and lives: "The language wants / to love you: let it."

I don't remember much about the ride home to New Orleans, but a day or so after, I phoned Doctor Mary and told her about the choking episode and Everette's alarming inability to swallow anything but scotch. She called a medical colleague to see if he'd be willing to run some upper GI tests on Everette as a favor to her, and the guy said yes. So she stopped by the Leaf and convinced Everette that he should go have the tests. He was feeling so bad by then that he went along with the plan—you couldn't have dragged him to a doctor if he was feeling like himself. The night before the barium swallow, I gave him an envelope with enough cash for round-trip cab fare and drinking money afterward, since I couldn't get off from work to take him.

"It's esophageal cancer. His throat is almost totally closed over," Mary told me on the phone a week later, after the tests had been run and the X rays developed.

"Well, geez. Can't they operate and remove the tumor?"

"Sometimes they operate as a palliative measure—to make the patient more comfortable. But Everette's not strong enough for that," she said. Then she started talking about getting Everette into Charity Hospital, where they could get some IV fluids into him and keep him warm.

"But he hates hospitals," I said. "Why not just let him stay at the Leaf? I mean, he's happy there."

"Because his throat is going to close over completely, and he's not going to be able to swallow scotch or even water any more, and then he's going to die of dehydration right there at the bar, and it's going to be a slow, horrible, agonizing death," she told me. "I wouldn't wish it on anyone."

"Oh, God," was all I could say. "Oh, God."

Mary got Everette admitted to Charity Hospital that same week. She made sure to tell the on-duty residents that a celebrity poet was coming their way, and she told me that the staff gave him the royal treatment when he arrived. But when I dropped by the old Art Deco hospital on Tulane Avenue to visit him on Friday afternoon, just before Bill Petre and I were going to leave for a weekend at the Mississippi Gulf Coast, I could hear him shouting and moaning from the moment I stepped off the sixth-floor elevator. I followed the commotion down the hall and into a long, narrow ward room with half a dozen hospital beds on each side, all but one occupied by an African-American male staring murderously in Everette's direction. Everette himself was in the bed all the way to the end, by the window. He was half-sitting, half-lying, inclined at a strange angle, and as I got closer I could see that his arms were straightjacketed. "Pick me up!" he commanded. "Help me!" I wrapped my arms around his shoulders and scooted his rear end closer to the end of the bed so that he could sit up straight. That seemed to calm him down a bit, and he stopped thrashing and shouting, but he didn't seem to recognize me. I said something about the bad cold spell outside and asked him if he were warm enough and he said yes, it was the first time in weeks he'd been warm enough. That made me feel a little bit better about his being in there.

I was still wondering why the hell Everette was straightjacketed, given that they were supposed to be giving him the "celebrity treatment"—apparently the celebrity they had in mind was Ezra Pound—but I had to leave the ward and wander up and down the hall for awhile before I could find anybody who worked there. I stopped a doctor, but he didn't speak English. Then I found a nurse, who explained that Everette was in arm restraints because he'd been hallucinating. I asked her if she could give him something to sedate him, but she just turned her back on me, and when I went back into Everette's ward room, his eyes were closed and his roommates were staring murderously at me instead of him, so I decided it was probably time to leave. I called Mary before leaving town and she said that she'd been begging the staff at Charity to give Everette an alcohol drip, but that they would only give him Valium, and she said she'd try to see if she could get the dosage increased.

That day, February tenth, was Day 3 of sobriety for me and Bill Petre—we had given up drinking together for Lent. We drove to Bay St. Louis that evening and had a sober weekend together, just like normal people: staying in a little seaside motel, eating raw oysters and fried softshell crabs, watching the bottle-nosed dolphins perform at the Marine Life Oceanarium, breathing in the restorative salt air, and remembering it all the next day, which was kind of unusual for us. On a deserted beach of the Gulf Islands National Seashore, Bill pointed to Horn Island, a crescent of sand and scrub trees lying a couple of miles off the coast. He explained that that was where his favorite artist, Walter Anderson, used to live alone for months at a time, sleeping under his overturned rowboat, painting the things he saw around him, and lashing himself to a tree during hurricanes. Back on shore, Anderson had covered the walls and ceiling of his bedroom with stylized images of blue crabs and brown pelicans and stars and ocean waves, multiplied in rows by his paintbrush. A couple of years after our Gulf Coast trip, that little tomblike bedroom chamber would be loaded on a flatbed truck and moved, intact, to the newly opened Walter Anderson Museum of Art in Ocean Springs.

On Day 6 of our newfound sobriety, Bill Petre and I drove back to New Orleans in time for him to work his customary Monday night shift at the Leaf, and I headed off to my History of the Vietnam War class at the University of New Orleans. Some time after the class ended at 8:45 and I arrived home to my shotgun half-double in the "Montmartre of New Orleans," Bill phoned me from the Leaf.

"It's Everette," he said. "He's dead."

And even though Everette's entire life, like that of a young pharaoh, had been one long preparation for the passage from brief, flickering existence into eternity, into the world of his poems, furnished with all of the images from his daily life, but burnished, stylized, so that the mythic could be seen to shine through every instance of the singular and the personal—even so, I could not believe that his spark had been extinguished so soon.

David Kunian

From *He Was a Mess:*
The Short Life of Poet Everette Maddox
(Radio Documentary)

Narrator: He was a poet, a teacher, an inspiration, a barfly: Everette Hawthorne Maddox fulfilled many roles during his short time on this earth. His talents took him from his hometown of Prattville, Alabama, to college and graduate work in Tuscaloosa to his eventual home in New Orleans. Whether instructing in school, sitting at the Maple Leaf Bar, or conducting poetry readings in the Maple Leaf back patio, Everette took on the life of a poet. His published writings were few, but he influenced everyone with whom he came in contact, whether at the bars he frequented, the readings he organized, or the classes he taught. In the coming minutes, you will hear many of his friends recall his intelligence and his foibles, his kindnesses and his darkness, his life and his death. It was a short life, but one that was lived on his terms and his terms alone. He would admit shortly before his death to his long-time friend Fred Kasten that "He was a mess." So listen now as he is remembered by those who knew him in *"He Was a Mess": The Short Life of New Orleans Poet Everette Maddox.*

. . .

Narrator: Everette Hawthorne Maddox was born in 1944 outside of Prattville, Alabama, a small town about fifteen miles from Montgomery. His father held many professions, while his mother taught school part time. He had a younger brother, Bill, who later joined him in New Orleans. Everette's former wife Celia recalls what she knows about his parents.

Celia Maddox (CM): I think the parents might have met when they both worked on a newspaper when they were young. So there was sort of a faint aroma of glamour about them. They were extremely important to him. They remained enigmatic to me. I couldn't put a complete picture together of whether they were these brilliant but unfortunate people or slovenly types. Their fortunes never rose very high. Their father did lots of jobs from being some kind of itinerant preacher to working in the cotton gin mill.

Narrator: New Orleans writer and producer Fred Kasten knew Everette well, both in Alabama and later in New Orleans.

FK: His immediate family . . . it's not too strong a word to say that they were cursed. No one lived past fifty. All died of cancer or alcoholism in one case. His father was a jack of all trades. At one point he was a sign painter, a preacher, a salesman. His mother—I don't believe she had been to college. I don't think she had formal education to speak of, but she was widely read. He and his younger brother Bill's love of literature come from her.

Narrator: College and adult friend Bob Woolf remembers Everette at the University of Alabama.

Bob Woolf (BW): He was an excellent scholar. He was probably the best-read person I've ever known. He had no problem in graduate school or anything like that. Except for poetry, he would have gone on to finish his Ph.D.

FK: Visually he was a very dapper guy. Seersucker in the summer, tweed in the fall. He drove a sports car. He had a beard before it had been fashionable for many people to have beards. He was well-trimmed and well-turned-out. He was in graduate school for a good bit of that time and then I think he gave up the idea of ever completing the Ph.D., but he did start teaching poetry writing. One of his gifts was teaching. He was a really wonderful teacher in an informal context, but also in the classroom.

CM: We were married in Tuscaloosa at the University Club. That was '75 or '76, and I think it wasn't too long after that that we moved to New Orleans. He got a job at Xavier University there. We moved into a great apartment, 2900 Prytania. There's a poem about that, too. It was Scott Fitzgerald's old apartment briefly when he was courting Zelda and he had to sort of make it or break it in order to get the girl, and so that was of course just perfect.

Narrator: Tom Bonner was Everette's supervisor at Xavier University in New Orleans.

Tom Bonner (TB): Everette came down for an interview and he was perfectly charming and open, interesting, and we decided to hire him. He made a good appearance. In fact, he reminded me very much of Edgar Allan Poe in terms of features. Slender, slightly dark, dark hair. Gentle. He had an ironic sense of humor, and he seemed to be caring about the people he was conversing and ultimately would be working with. But one of the things that I did discover as we were going through was that his first published poem was in *The New Yorker*. That's a rare thing for any poet. Most poets start off in the smaller literary magazines and work their way up. He had begun there.

He had worked for us for about two years when his drinking problem became more evident on campus. There was a pattern of behavior where he was having a hard time, ah, maintaining a certain decorum. For example, he would sometimes walk across campus with a glass of scotch and on a largely undergraduate campus, Roman Catholic campus, that was a bit uncomfortable. And that, I think, well, he was never confronted directly about that, but it was an accumulation of moments like that that indicated he had done a really good job for us and it was perhaps a good time for him to go someplace else where the pressures were less. And there were pressures. He was teaching a full course load of four courses a semester, and he was trying to write in the middle of that as well, and he was having some family difficulties.

Narrator: Here Celia Maddox remembers Everette during this time and his effect on their lives.

CM: I think he was resolutely on this steady downward spiral when I met him, and it took me a couple of years to realize that that was a conscious choice. It wasn't just a matter of circumstance. It just got to be too much for me. I couldn't do this. I had a child, and I don't know what I was doing with her, but I just wanted to have a real life. I saw that it wasn't going to ever be any different, so with some great regret, I had to kind of move on. This is not the right life, yeah.

Narrator: Poet Bill Lavender was a friend of both Everette and Celia.

Bill Lavender (BL): Oh, yeah, he was really depressed, especially around the time of the divorce. It was kind of a vicious cycle. He was depressed in the first place about not being able to hold a job, and then the more he got depressed the more he drank, so that made it absolutely impossible for him to hold a job, and that made him more depressed, and the more depressed he got, the more he was a drain on Celia, and the more she had to pull away to save her own skin, and the more he got depressed then, so right about the divorce was a real low point, as far as I know.

Narrator: At this point, several artists got the inspiration to do something with the wealth of poetry being created in New Orleans in the early 1980s. Sculptor Franz Heldner recalls the discussion of these plans with both Maddox and poet Bob Stock, plans which were hatched, of course, at the Maple Leaf Bar in New Orleans.

FH: And we're all sitting in the Maple Leaf and it's the middle of the oil bust, and these two guys were being really down. I said, "Hey, kids, let's put on a show." You know? "Let's have a reading. Let's do readings." "Where?" "Here." Well, they went "argh argh argh." You know. Well, I knew one of the owners very well and I talked to him, and indeed we started it. What does it take to get a bunch of writers to read their own work? Not much. So it had a life of its own. When I left, Everette took it over and made it into the grand flower, the real crown of local readings that it has become. And that was Everette's doing.

Narrator: People who gathered when Everette read have all agreed that Everette was a gracious host and an utterly spellbinding reader.

FH: If you try to figure out how long Beethoven's 9th Symphony is, you never—I've looked at the CDs and I can figure the time. But if the 9th Symphony transports you and takes you beyond time, you don't give a rat's ass about how long it's taking. And that indeed is how Everette spoke. You didn't think about it at the time, the consideration, the heat, the fact that your beer on the table was getting flat, any of it. He could indeed transport. He was an excellent reader, of anybody—Mark Twain, himself. You name it.

Narrator: The readings were held every Sunday at the Maple Leaf, and Everette was paid twenty dollars each week to be the master of ceremonies for them. He taught at a couple of places, but these jobs soon ended, and Everette couldn't or wouldn't find work. He was a full-time poet, but other aspects of his life suffered. Fred Kasten describes Everette's life at this time.

FK: It wasn't too much longer after that that he basically became homeless. He moved from friend to friend for a while. There were a couple of places where he shared apartments with people, but for most of the latter half of '87 and all of '88, he was sometimes locked in the bar at night. He slept in the back of a dump truck that was parked on Dante Street. Sometimes he was known to sleep on the bench behind what was then the Winn Dixie in the Riverbend. There's a little park there. In fact, one of the great stories is that one morning he woke up using the previous day's *Times Picayune* as cover and his name was on the society pages of the Picayune for being at a party for the first Tennessee Williams Festival where he was a panelist.

Narrator: Professor and poet Julie Kane met Maddox at his haunts around Oak Street and the Maple Leaf.

JK: He was funny. He had so many contradictions. He was a man who late in his life was sleeping in the Maple Leaf and in the Steak and Egg and on the steps of the Catholic church near the Maple Leaf, but if people tried to give him clothes, he would not accept them unless they were Brooks Brothers or designers that were kind of cutting edge fashion.
That was the wonderful thing. You could stop in the Maple Leaf at any hour of the day or night and have a brilliant conversation. He was always a larger-than-life, vivid personality. The bar people there

were all proud of him. They all knew they had something special in Everette there.

Narrator: Hank Staples is one of the current owners of the Maple Leaf. He was a bartender there in Everette's time and also published his second book, *Bar Scotch*. In his many hours at the bar he witnessed Maddox's great memory of literature.

Hank Staples (HS): He could quote pages and pages of so many authors just off the top of his head. He really liked Thomas Wolfe, and he could talk about *Look Homeward, Angel*. You might mention some part of the book you liked, and he might quote from that part of the book. He could do that over and over with different authors and different poems.

Narrator: College classmate Bob Woolf was a great friend, fan, and appreciator of Maddox's work.

BW: There were a lot of laughs. Some of the poems were funny and not meant to be funny, but there was enough irony in them. I guess irony was the predominant thing, and the language was just so good. It was an enjoyable thing to listen to. It seemed particularly American and, of course, he liked to read. He liked to read in bars. That's where he really preferred to read. Easier to get a drink there, I guess.

. . .

Narrator: Everette Maddox first met Ralph Adamo at a poetry reading soon after Maddox moved from Alabama. They became friends and Adamo later was one of the editors of Everette's posthumous book *American Waste*. Here he describes Everette's poetry.

Ralph Adamo (RA): Everette embraced the role of public poet. It fit the poems which have all sorts of levels, but on one level they're accessible. They tend to have some humor in them. They're friendly. Plus he had a great delivery. He was a robust and terrific reader. And he was a terrific M.C. He was what an M.C. should have been. He was entertaining, encouraging, kind.

The first published book was Everette and some friends including me tearing apart his first three or four manuscripts that hadn't been published and selecting the best of them. And the second book was the best of what didn't go into the first book that he already had by 1980 or '81. Then he didn't write for a long time. His life was in trouble. His wife had left him. He was having an increasingly [difficult time] not making a living and not having a place to live.

John Travis published the last book, *American Waste*, and those poems are [a] more plain spoken, desperate voice in the last work, sometimes exhilarated, sometimes incredibly sad, frequently very funny. But he wrote all those poems in the last six months of his life. It was really something he wrote right up until the day he went into the hospital.

Narrator: By 1988, Everette started writing again. Fred Kasten speaks about his new bursts of creativity.

FK: By the last few months of his life when he started writing again for the first time in a long time, really he hadn't written significantly in a decade. There are poems in the batch of work, the best of which are collected in the volume *American Waste*, which are his best.

Narrator: Many poems in *American Waste* describe scenes on Oak Street where the bars the Maple Leaf and Muddy Waters beckon to thirsty people of all persuasions. Muddy Waters is gone now, but as Hank Staples was collecting the poetry that makes up *American Waste*, he was observing Everette and his various infatuations.

HS: His current platonic love interest was Suzy Malone, who was working at Muddy Waters. And he would come over and say, "I made up a poem about Suzy!" and he would recite. I kept saying, "Write it down, Everette, write it down." And finally I said, "Write it down, Everette, and I'll hold the poems for you. You write them and I'll hold them and I'll save them. I'll publish another book." That's what I told him because I had published *Bar Scotch*. And he started doing it. At first he was reluctant to do it. He wouldn't do it and all this and that. We had this old K&B bag, the kind with a handle on it. It was paper. If it had been plastic, Everette wouldn't have permitted it. I kept it in that. It started out he was reluctant, but then he was coming up and saying, "Archives." And sometimes in a day he'd hand me three or four poems. They just stayed at my place for a few years. Anyway, they were on Abita Beer coasters, bar napkins. Some are on flyers from Muddy Waters. Several Muddy Waters' menus have an Everette Maddox poem on the back, and I can tell you the poetry was a lot better than the food.

Narrator: It became evident to Maddox's friends by 1988 and 1989 that Everette's life had assumed a certain trajectory. It was a difficult dilemma, as Fred Kasten explains.

FK: And I think it was clear to people without him even expressing it openly that he was on the path he had chosen and there was nothing by the way of an intervention in his drinking or anything along those lines that ever got seriously considered. I think it was because it was widely understood that after that session he would go back to living the way he had determined that he was going to live out his days. Short of that, I don't think there was much changing him. And I think even though it was discussed on occasion, "Should we do something? Try get him in detox?" or any of these things, pretty much everybody said that much as we hate it, there isn't much that we can do. Maybe that was a mistake on his friends' part. I don't know. I don't think so, and when you look at his family history, there's a lot to be said about [heredity] having a heavy hand in his fate, because essentially everyone in his family met the same fate. He himself faced life the same way, with a good bit of wisdom and a strong sense of irony and a deep wit and a lot of dignity.
. . .
FK: There's a Henry Miller line that says there is no power on Earth that can loosen the grip of a man who has his hands on his own throat. In many respects, that's what Everette certainly proved.

CM: I had a couple of experiences toward the end. He died in February, right? In December I was back in New Orleans. I had long since moved to Connecticut, and I was back in town and decided to jump in a cab and go up to the Maple Leaf and see if I could dig him up. Of course, I saw him there sitting at the third stool, and instead of saying, "Hi, Rette, hi! It's me," I just kind of sidled up next to him. We began to talk. And we talked for fifteen or twenty minutes until something I said made him turn his head and look at me. And I realized that was the first second he realized who he was talking to. And that was really scary. I was just so taken aback by that, by how his senses had narrowed, that I just flat had to leave the place. It was too scary.

Narrator: At the beginning of 1989, poet Julie Kane realized how ill Everette had become.

JK: The last few days of January Bill Roberts took me and Everette on a reading tour to Alabama and Florida. He put out our two books on Pirogue. I didn't realize—up until that point Mary Murray, who is now Mary Herrington, who is a physician who used to come to Maple Leaf readings—she'd make house calls to the Maple Leaf to check up on Everette because I believe she diagnosed him with pneumonia or bronchitis or one of those respiratory things, and she had prescribed medicine to him. Well, he was not feeling good and losing weight and complaining about not feeling well. I remember when we started on this trip, we stopped to get something to eat, and Everette wouldn't swallow. He could only eat things that were very, very tiny. And that seemed ominous. When we got back I told Mary that "I think it's more than pneumonia. I think something may be wrong with his throat."

Narrator: Poet and doctor Mary Darken Herrington.

Mary Harrington Darkin (MHD): It turned out he had cancer of the esophagus and it was just closing his throat up and he couldn't swallow. You looked and his whole throat was full of tumor. It was obviously hopeless. And he said very cheerfully, "Should I tell my friends that I'm dying?" (Laughs.) I said, "Well, you know, we should get you into Charity Hospital and see if there's anything they can do where you can at least get some fluid in you," because he was getting dehydrated.

Narrator: Dusty Phillips is a welder and self-proclaimed river rat. He and Everette were friends and drinking partners. Dusty saw Everette the day Maddox went into Charity Hospital.

Dusty Phillips (DP): This time he was going to go in the hospital. And he was sitting on the bench outside waiting for his ride to go to Charity Hospital. And ah, I'd walked out of the bar and was going across the street to the other bar. I stopped to speak to him and say hello. He told me, "I'm going to the hospital, and I ain't coming back." Yeah. He said it to two or three people.

RA: I wasn't here for it. I wasn't here for his last night in the Maple Leaf. I heard the next day he was at the hospital. Supposedly when he was finally talked into being taken off to Charity, the last thing he said to some people was, "If anybody tries to bury me in Ala-goddamn-bama, there's going to be some serious haunting going on."

When I visited him, he was conscious and really pissed off, in just terrible humor. The second or third time he wasn't really conscious. I read the beginning of *Ulysses* to him because that's his favorite book. I read it for an hour or so, and then I left. I got a call a few hours later that he had died.

DP: We went in, and he was lying there. I tucked in the sheet and tucked in the blanket all around him. I talked to him. I'm not really a Buddhist, but if I had a particularly organized belief system, it would be Buddhism. I was standing over Everette and I chanted the *Om Mani Padme Huum* and I would say it as deeply as I could and make my voice resonate as much as I could. I put my hand on his chest and his head. And his eyes popped open and his head came up off the pillow and he looked and said, "Oh, you came to see me." Then his head fell back down on the pillow and he didn't speak again.

Narrator: Nancy Harris, current mistress of ceremonies and organizer of the Everette Maddox Memorial Reading Series, remembers hearing of Everette's demise.

Nancy Harris (NH): And it was just a shock. I was at work and my friend Julie called me and told me that he had died. I was stunned. Everybody knew he was going in the hospital, but everybody had this silly faith that he would be OK. It was right after Mardi Gras.

It was February. He died February 13th, the day before Valentine's Day, 1989.

Narrator: Fred Kasten recalls that people came from everywhere for Everette's farewell.

FK: We had a wake at my house on Saturday night. It was just a thousand-square-foot shotgun and it was packed. I remember being in my kitchen, which was in the middle of the house by the refrigerator, just unable to move. And at some point poet Rodney Jones wanted to get a look at the ashes. He pried the lid off the urn and spilled a few onto the fireplace. And we always joke that Maddox is the only guy we know who actually gained weight after he was dead, because when we swept up the ashes a little bit extra got in there, too.

Narrator: The next day Everette Maddox's funeral paraded through his neighborhood. It stopped at each of the bars he called home before ending at the Maple Leaf. Dusty Phillips.

DP: I really loved, well, the dementedness of this place. Here's a guy who died of the effects of alcohol, basically, and his funeral is being celebrated by the biggest gang of drunks you can find in a bar with a really heavy style. Everybody dressed up. They had a fantastic band. We processed around the neighborhood through the streets from bar to bar and back down Oak Street. As we came down Oak Street, here's five hundred people marching, and everybody fell silent pretty much, and I remember Deborah Gunther was out front with the band, and we marched a good ways in silence, everybody anticipating the next song, and I remember Scott Ray yelled out, "Cut him loose!" And then Deborah called out, "Don't you have one more song for my boy?" Right then the clouds opened up and the sun, the sun came through. It was uncanny. Right in the first notes of the tuba, first notes of "[Oh, When] the Saints . . ." and everybody's step lightened up and we second-lined dancing back to the bar.

HS: It was just packed. In six days a homeless poet from Prattville, Alabama, had brought people from all over the South to attend the funeral.

FK: . . . He had always expressed a desire to be buried on the Maple Leaf patio, which is in fact where most of him is, most of the ashes, that is. It's right under a stone, a slightly used gravestone—well, it's a mistake on the carving is what we were told, not a used gravestone, though there is another name on the other side, and a very nice plaque now marks the site of his burial. Some of his ashes, a ceremony was held and some of his ashes were placed in the Mississippi. So he's around the world and in the Maple Leaf.

Narrator: Dusty Philips knew of Everette's love of the Mississippi River, and he took his ashes there.

DP: So, they gave me the box with the remains, and I let it be known to anyone who might be interested that this isn't a funeral, this is just—we're going to dispose of the remains. So . . . when we went down to the river, it was a little bit high and a lot of flotsam along the shoreline, so it would be hard to make a good cast, you know, out into the open water. So I took my knife out of my pocket and popped the top off and I walked on a log out as far as I could. A tugboat came by and a bunch of little waves upset my balance. The seven beers I had beforehand didn't have anything to do with that. It didn't, not at that point. I was beyond seven beers. (Laughs.) I went in the river. I got baptized up just past my knees. I took the container and swung it in a wide arc like that and all the black ashes went flying in the air and fell in a thousand little splashes in the river and that was that. He was in the bosom of the river.

BW: His significance is a lasting significance, and it's in his work to the extent that his work remains extant, remains read. That stands by itself. In his personal life, if you can separate the two, he touched a lot of people in a lot of different ways. He gave some of them direction because of his own interests and passions. He really did have a lot of influence in a lot of different people. I may be really badly wrong about this, but I think his work will find a growing audience. It may be a slow growing thing, but I don't think he's going to disappear. I really don't. His work is going to last. It's too good.

FK: Oh, I wish he was still around. We all miss him still.

NH: I try to keep the readings going the way he had, in his spirit. When I open up any of his books and read his poems, I can hear his voice. And that's why I like readings, because even if the poet is dead, and you've heard him read a lot, you can hear his voice. He had a very distinctive voice. His poems are very short and very compact. When he read them, it's almost like they became bigger.

Everette Maddox (EM): Everybody should have an epitaph ready, just in case, and this is mine. It's called "Hypothetical Self-Epitaph."

> What if I just caved in,
> gave out, pulled over
> to the side of
> the road of life,
> & expired like an old
> driver's license?
> You might say He didn't
> get far in 31 years.
> But I'd say That's
> all right, it was
> the world's longest trip
> on an empty tank.

FK: He started talking to me in November and brought it up several times that year: what he wanted was an epitaph, which he eventually got on the marker and stone on the patio of the Maple Leaf. HE WAS A MESS. And he was.

William Lavender

"Living Water": Notes for an Essay on Everette Maddox

Books, print, texts. Manuscripts left behind, here in the world, along with everything else, after the writer has been removed from it. It is left to us survivors to perform the necessary ministrations upon these texts, just as it is left to us to minister to the dead body. The former, we reassemble (or build entirely anew, as the case may be); the latter, we reduce to ashes. In 1989, I lifted up the plastic container about the size of a cigar box that held Everette Maddox's ashes, to feel the heft, and can report that his ashes seemed quite weighty for their small volume, about the density of clay. And I want to report, now, that the four small volumes of his work that I have in hand have an equal amount of a different kind of density, that "richness," that "depth" that critics always look for, and always find.

I knew Everette better in his early days in New Orleans, the late seventies. He and I and his wife, Celia, and my wife, Debbie, were quite close for a while. After he and Celia divorced, the balance of this relationship was lost, and we gradually lost touch with both of them. "The Miracle" was first published in the 1976 chapbook, *The Thirteen*

> ### The Miracle
>
> "Things are tight," the man
> said, tightening his
> quasi-friendly grin.
> "We can't give you a
> job, we can't give you
> any money, and
> we don't want these here
> poems either." He
> tightened his tie. "Fact
> is, the old cosmic
> gravy train's ground to
> a halt. It's the end
> of the line. From now
> on there's going to
> be no more nothing."
> He went on, lighting
> a cigar: "We don't
> wish we could help, but
> even if we did,
> we couldn't. It's not
> our fault, by God, it's
> just tight all over."
> He brought his fist down
> on the burnished desk
> and lo! from that tight
> place there jetted forth
> rivers of living water.
>
> (Everette Maddox, c. 1974)[1]

113

Original Poems. My copy of the chapbook is inscribed: "For Bill & Debbie—in hopes it will someday be worth its price—nothing. Luck and love, Rette." I have always found "The Miracle" to be a strangely compelling poem, strange because I didn't understand it, or didn't have a way to understand it. In *Bar Scotch* there is a poem called "The Jerk" that has a similar theme (portrait of a bourgeois bureaucrat) and is similarly organized around a pun, but "The Jerk" has none of the eerie resonance of "The Miracle." The jerk in the later poem is merely that, a silly, suburban academic. But the bureaucrat of "The Miracle" is a patriarch. His voice is the voice of real power, of authority, of decision over life and death, and yet, in good bureaucratic fashion, within quotation marks, qualified, hedged, hiding behind a kind of royal "we." This Father has not the ability to dole, to spend, to grant life, but merely to announce his austerity with a sadistic relish, to disclaim responsibility, to refer the subject to some impossibly higher, "cosmic," authority. God at the end of an interminable succession of desks, forever the next floor up, the next office down the hall. But the poem is not a monologue; neither is it descriptive. It is a window upon an exchange, or an attempted exchange, a barter. It is an ironic and foiled exchange, as is, indeed, the exchange attempted by Jesus and the Samaritan woman. Both the poem and the passage from the Bible indicate negotiations of gifts; grants and poems in the one, waters normal and living in the other, but the negotiation that is taking place in the poem is the same one that Everette referred to when he inscribed my copy of the chapbook. He is attempting to trade his poems for "nothing." "From now/ on there's going to/ be no more nothing," says the bureaucrat. The currency of the barter has changed, or rather has become real currency. From now on poems will only be traded for some-thing; they will be commodities. The no-thing that the poet desires will be withheld. The reification of poetry is a theme that we can follow throughout Everette's work, the paradox of the exchange, the necessity of the receipt when one had thought to make a gift.

When I first met Everette everyone called him Rette. It was a nickname he cultivated and relished, for he had a vision of the South that was as nostalgic and lurid as *Gone With The Wind.* When he and Celia moved to New Orleans from Tuscaloosa, the first house they rented was the house where F. Scott Fitzgerald had stayed when he was in New Orleans, and Everette took this as a sign. His heroes were, in fact, not poets but fiction writers, Fitzgerald, Joyce, Barth. He was fond of quoting Barth to the effect that novelists were not frustrated poets but vice versa. He had a fantasy of himself as a kind of Southern Fitzgerald, a dandy. He almost always, even when his poverty was extreme, wore a tie, and he once told me that one of his main ambitions was to be able to afford a Brooks Brothers suit. One morning in the late eighties I ran into him in the French Quarter on my way to work. I hadn't seen him in years, and I was struck by his decline. Always thin, he looked now to be literally starving. His hand was cool and weightless in mine. He was filthy and he stank and had obviously been sleeping outside. On his feet, though, were a ragged pair of wing-tips, and his filthy blue oxford shirt was buttoned to the top, and he was wearing a dirty red tie.

What is an image? What, more concretely, does an image do? What is its function, its necessity, its meaning? When I was in undergraduate school, I had a professor of creative writing who often quoted Lorca's saying that the poet is "professor of the five senses." As if painters and sculptors and musicians, not to mention fiction writers, were not also instructors of perception. I wonder, even, if those who produce nothing in the way of art, those who live and speak and struggle and die and whose bodies are reduced to ashes and leave behind them no texts or artifacts to which their names can be proprietarily attached, I wonder if even these have not earned some tenure of sight and sound. But maybe an image doesn't have as much to do with the senses as Lorca and we have thought; maybe it's only a convention of language, a genre. Pound defined the term as "that which presents an intellectual and emotional complex in an instant of time."[2] This doesn't seem to pertain as much to the senses as to psychology. We could almost read a clinical meaning in that term "complex." The point is that our model of the image is generically Freudian; images mean in the same way that dream symbols mean. What Everette Maddox and myself and most poets I know were taught in the university work-shops in the seventies was a kind of hegemony of the Freudian image. Thus we were taught that displacement and sublimation, i.e. metaphor and metonymy, are the grist of poetry. What was ignored in these workshops was in fact what should have been most obvious about the scene, that poetry, with all its images and rhetoric, is primarily a discursive activity. That images are as conventional as rhyme schemes. That they exist for the purpose of poets talking to each other.

I've never written formal criticism of a poet I knew personally. My critical work tends, I think, toward the analytic, which can be appropriate when dealing with "literature," but is more problematic when dealing with a friend. One genre that has always frustrated me is the review, or the "appreciation"; I've never been able to capture that tone of quick yet authoritative yet tasteful praise: ". . . though the work is sometimes _____, on the whole the book is _____ and _____, represents the poet's _____est work to date, and some of the most _____ and _____ work to come out of _____." How I envy those writers (and their jobs!) who can fill in these blanks with such inspired responses that the template seems to disappear. If I had that "gift," it would be so easy, it seems, to write this essay on a "departed poet and friend." But then, as I think about it, I realize it would still have its difficulties; it would be as touchy as, for example, selecting the right card from a display at K&B. The card that would be appropriate for the occasion, the one that would elicit just the right balance of laughter and tears, the one that would "feel" right with "Everette" at the top and "Bill" at the bottom. It's the repeatability of statements that gives them value. For language to be worth something, it should be as well-designed and indistinguishable in its individual occurrences as dollar bills. Then the economy of supply and demand will determine the price tag. What currencies, what "things," can these poems in *American Waste* be traded for?

But this "living water." Where did it come from? What does it mean? How did it find its paratactic way into this poem? I doubt that Everette knew the passage from the Book of John in any conscious way, or that he meant to refer to it specifically. He seems, even, to have conflated in memory the story of the Samaritan woman at the well with the Old Testament story of Moses striking the rock and the water welling out. Most of us who grew up in the South in the fifties and sixties were force-fed enough of the Bible at church or school or home that such stories and phrases have a vaguely familiar ring. Certain phrases, even, haunt with the force of

> 7 There cometh a woman of Samaria to draw water: Jesus saith unto her, Give me to drink.
> 8 (For his disciples were gone away unto the city to buy meat.)
> 9 Then saith the woman of Samaria unto him, How is it that thou, being a Jew, askest drink of me, which am a woman of Samaria? for the Jews have no dealings with the Samaritans.
> 10 Jesus answered and said unto her, If thou knewest the gift of God, and who it is that saith to thee, Give me to drink; thou wouldest have asked of him, and he would have given thee living water.[3]

compulsion, erupt at the most inappropriate times, immersing themselves in whatever genre happens to be flowing by. Do we, therefore, read the allusion or the image? Do we read the text or the "intention?" Or do we, somehow, just read the sound, living water, like a senseless murmur, not even a voice, out of some dim recess of the past, out of a primordial soup of exchangeable meanings, a soup of desire and family romance, of sperm and the Father's name, of nameless Woman, amniotic fluid, birth-blood, baptism, expulsion, exile. I don't know, here, if I'm reading Everette or myself reflected or some almost forgotten professor or a kind of pervasive social text. I can dip my hand into the language but, by its ebb and flow, it is never the same language twice.

Why do people write poetry? Rather, why do some people live and write the way that Everette lived and wrote, with that relentless urge toward self-destruction? There are numerous examples; Frank Stanford and Jack Spicer come immediately to mind. I suppose it could be argued that there are lots of self-destructive people around these days and that some of them just happen to be poets, but it seems to me that poets destroy themselves with a particular flair. When Jack Spicer was on his deathbed, he pulled his friend Robin Blaser close to him and said, "My vocabulary did this to me."[4] What Spicer was actually dying of was alcoholism, so he was in effect assigning the blame for his drinking to poetry, or perhaps exchanging the two terms, implying a kind of equivalence. For a more canonical citation we can also refer to Baudelaire's dictum, from "Get Drunk": ". . . be perpetually drunk! With wine, with poetry, or with virtue, as you please."[5] For Baudelaire drunkenness is ". . . the great thing: the only question. Not to feel the horrible burden of Time. . .".[6] The various intoxications are bolsters against time and death, but, in the case of poetry, not in the way we are used to thinking, not in the survival of the name with text as a surrogate body. Rather it is a self-righteousness and euphoria of the moment, the moment of composition, perhaps, or shortly after, the moment of *being in* the poem. One awakes, we imagine, from a poem as from any other drug, with a hangover, a hangover that only another poem can cure, a despair that must be stifled or released or distanced again and again, time after time, day after day. As with liquor one can gauge the quality of the goods by the intensity of the hangover, mild for the aged single-malts, ferocious with *Bar Scotch.*

It is 1975 or '76. Celia and Everette and Debbie and I driving home from the French Quarter in their VW at 7 a.m., the end of our evening out. We stop for breakfast at some restaurant, now demolished, whose name I can't remember, and stare into our coffee, nodding, in silence. Then Everette says, "The problem is, one thing. You can only do one thing. All those things out there to do, and you can only do one."

Many of the people I have talked to about Everette's poetry express, candidly, their disappointment that the posthumous book, *American Waste,* was not his best work. I disagree. What they miss in *Waste,* I think, is the more "chiseled," literary quality of the earlier poems. The poems in *The Everette Maddox Song Book* are crisper; they have definite and dramatic resolutions; the language is spare and stripped of inessentials and dialect; the images are crystalline; etc.

> Along with the small press magazines and books, poetry reading series are the most vital site of poetic activity in North America. Despite the striking vitality of poetry readings, readings are never reviewed in any of the nation's daily or weekly newspapers, even though these papers routinely review theater and dance and art events whose scale is comparable. I suspect the reason is that cultural editors, like most literary critics and scholars, wrongly assume that the book is the only significant site of a poet's work. Contemporary North American poetry is realized as significantly in its performances in live readings as it is in printed forms. Critical response to contemporary poems that fail to account for its performance are, for the most part, inadequate.
>
> (Charles Bernstein)[7]

The poems in *Waste* need to be cleaned up; some of them lack any resolution whatsoever; they're full of non sequiturs and dialect for its own sake; the images are "sloppy;" the logic is skewed. The poems in *Waste* need, in short, to be workshopped. They need to be edited, revised. If only he were not reduced to ashes we could sit down with him, all of us, and hammer out version s that would be entirely intelligible and offend no one. We could make them into the kind of poems that have currency, imbue them with a generality, a breadth of connotation that we are certain is secretly lurking below the surface of their specificity. For these are the qualities, generality, intelligibility, currency, that determine poetry's value, the markers that tell us one book is "better" than another, which one is worth more. The purpose of the creative writing programs has been to standardize this currency, to codify intelligibility for the general audience of their own creation. *American Waste* is utterly worthless; it has nothing to say about the plight of "man" or of the homeless or the downtrodden or the South or alcoholics or any other victims. Everette had to stop writing for seven years, he had to forget everything he had learned, before he could accomplish this poetry that is worth nothing.

Everette's great work was not any of the books but rather the Maple Leaf Bar's reading series. It was this work, and all the social connections and interactions necessitated by it, that brought, for example, the huge crowds to his funeral and to the series' fifteenth anniversary party, commemorated by the publication of a new issue of *The Maple Leaf Rag*. Everette was not alone in this work, of course. Such projects are always a group endeavor. They do not have authors; numerous people should be credited. Nancy Harris, who has continued the series since Everette's death, is most worthy of mention, but there are many others. My point is, however, not to compile a list of acknowledgments, but rather to get at the value of *American Waste*, a value which cannot be separated from Everette's work for the reading series. If we separate the book from the work, it is because we imagine that there are objective criteria to which the book must be submitted. We might look for the book's "music" (it sounds like a shot glass banging on a bar), its "honesty" (it's a series of poses and prevarications), and find it wanting. We might look for (as I glance through some of the things people have written about Everette's poetry) jauntiness, confluence, desperation, openness, spareness, grandeur, big-heartedness, attention to detail, for beautiful, sensual, free-flowing images. But none of these are in the book. Rather, they are there only if we bring them, only if they are already on the table before we ever open the book. All our criteria for evaluation are in fact creations of "extra-literary" works such as Everette's, social, political, psychological interactions, discourses that create the context in which it is possible for literature to emerge. The criteria that we have, or imagine that we have, all those phrases that haunt the genres of criticism and most poetry, are but the academic petrifications of works of the past. Worse, they are inventions with their own agendas, programs for the systematic erasure of the work and aggrandizement of the text, but thus also a certain breed of deconstruction, and even some of the critical movements that have sprung up in opposition to it. However we evaluate a text, whether we find it in remarkable rigors of craft or the trace of contradiction and repressed desire or the workings of capitalism or the pen of God, if we evaluate text and only text in our effort is in the service not of poetry but the academy. It is to this self-justifying academic endeavor that we owe, even, that greatest of the poetic smokescreens, the "test of time." We think that what matters for our poetry is what happens to it after we die, after the work is over and all that remains of us is a fading memory, a box full of ashes, and a text. We think, in a turn of mind that was made antique by the invention of the printing press, that our immortality is tied to the survival of a text with our name on it, as if heaven were this flat, insensate shuffling of pages through the halls of universities, or monasteries, or whatever institutions of the future may take over the care of the archives. But if we peel away the academic skin, the layers of critical truisms and the infantile lie of immortality in the text; if we look at our critical terms for what they are, genres in their own right, institutional habits, polemical models that any poem can be made to fit, then we are left with the poetry itself. Poetry is an activity, a work, something that people do rather than bequeath. Poetry as a work of which the text is only the spoor. No matter how "clear" the text, it is obfuscation if it does not trail back into the work.

I came to Everette and Celia's house one morning, it must have been around 1976. It was the second house, on Constance. He had been up all night, working on a new poem, which I believe was "Crunch" (in the *Song Book*, p. 35). He was sitting at the kitchen table, in front of his typewriter and about fifty neatly stacked sheets of typing paper. He handed me the top one, and I read the poem. He was still deeply involved in it and asked me if I was catching some of its more intricate workings, which of course I was not. He handed me the second sheet on the pile and asked me if I liked that version better. I could see, however, no difference between the two versions until he pointed it out to me, a deleted word. I asked him why he hadn't simply crossed the word out, and he told me that he had to see each revised version of the poem in a perfect copy, without extraneous marks. He leafed through the stack as he spoke, and I saw that each sheet was an almost identical version of the poem, but each, he assured me, with some slight variation. There was not a pencil mark in the whole pile. Not even a typo. He told me that when he made typing mistakes he immediately threw that copy away. I am thinking about this and the poems of *American Waste*, composed much later, when he had no typewriter nor even paper, written on napkins or the backs of band flyers or bar coasters. I am thinking that at a certain point the fact of the poems finally overwhelmed the thrall of print, and he was able to *see* them without having to imagine them as pages in a book. The poems reflect this change. In their specificity of setting, context, and address, they are poetry stripped of exchange value, products of a different work than the manufacture of pages. They are, simply, what they are, individual, discursive events.

Let us compare the waters of "The Miracle" and "How I Got In," two poems from the extremes of Everette's career and mature life. In each of them water exerts an elemental force, but in very different ways. In the earlier poem its force is eruptive, artesian, orgasmic. It controls the poem through a single unexpected burst of dramatic resolution, informing and overwhelming all that came before. The eruption of the living water retroactively imbues the bureaucrat's speech and the poet's silent response with an under-current of meaning, thus defining itself as a sublimated energy finally making its appearance, a consummation. And yet it too is

> How I Got In
> For *Wade*
>
> Well
> I was hanging
> up to my belt buckle in grief
> outside the Muddy Waters
> I had my dirty hands all over a
>   lamp post
> It looked so flooded with
> friends in there
> that I didn't see how
> I was going to gain access-
> Then somebody said
> "Know anybody?"
> I thought & said
> "I know Wade"
> & they said
> "Well Wade on in"
> & so I lit my torch
> & shook a leg
> & waded on in
> & had a hell of a time
>   (Everette Maddox, ca. 1988)[8]

only another symbol, only another dream awaiting interpretation. All the structures of this poem present themselves *en abime*, endless chains of substitutions, long corridors of psychological possibility. If there is an end to the chain, a figure so far in the distance that we cannot see beyond it, it is the scene of the family romance. The position of the poet in relation to the bureaucrat is that of the son to the father at the moment of expulsion from the marital chamber. He stands in wonder, awed to silence, as the father commands the feminine water from the mundane furniture of power.

In "How I Got In," water seems to have quite a different meaning. Rather, it seems to have no meaning at all, but only to pervade the poem as a sort of motif. Water is present not in the sense of words, but in their non-sense, in the accidental arrangements of the letters, in the long dead sources of the metaphors and names. This water does not erupt but seeps; it erodes meaning from under the words and images. The ground shifts beneath the simple expletive "well" and a friend's name and the name of a favorite bar, and the words are set afloat in a vertiginous freedom from reference. There is no Freudian reading of this poem because *the meaning is not the thing.* Not that the poem has no meaning, but that its meaning is entirely local or ungeneralized. Here we are given not a chain of substitutions but a specific event that is oddly saturated; "oddly" because the water of this poem does not have any causal, historical, or psycho- or otherwise logical relation to what it describes. The water is of the words, not the scene; it is what the scene is dissolved in. The scene itself, its image, remains murky, for the point is not to clarify but indeed to muddy; we are not meant to *see* something, but to remember we are swimming.

The language of the image: a language whose songs all decode to a single, universal referent, the primal scene. The "introspective" genres. A poetics that is produced, like any other, in a discursive work (what else is a workshop?), but it is a work to which the text cannot refer. The rules are the same as for the game of charades. The poet, then, is tied to a past by the umbilical chain of substitutions. A paradoxical past, universal yet private, common yet unmentionable in writing. A poet is a person who ~~drinks~~ writes alone in ~~his~~ her room.

What a strain it is to write this. I've been working on it, off and on, for over a month. Sometimes I think it's horrible, full of repressed (or indeed open) hostility, arch, an utter waste. Sometimes I think it's great and sing it to myself while falling asleep. Sometimes it is sheer drudgery, an assignment, and I have to have a glass of wine, or two, to get me started. Sometimes I can't wait to get started and have a glass of wine, or two, to celebrate.

There are other points of comparison between "The Miracle" and "How I Got In." The first poem, for example, is ironic, while the second is not. The one has a theme of exclusion, the other of inclusion; the one of expulsion, the other of entry and acceptance. "The Miracle," is, as it were, the starting point of "How I Got In," for it is a poem of grief, of being "up to my belt buckle in grief," a state of being that "How I Got In" leaves behind. The earlier poem presents a psychological scene, whereas the later one renders a social setting, a setting of which the poem itself, by way of its dedication, is a part. The two poems, also, are each constructed around an exchange, by which I mean both a discursive exchange, or dialogue, and a monetary exchange. In neither setting, of course, does money change hands, but in each case money haunts the dialogue. This is less obvious in "How I Got In" than in "The Miracle," where the genre of the one-sided conversation is obviously that of the rejection of an application for employment or some sort of stipend. In "How I Got In" the transaction is somewhat veiled, but the conversation that occurs at the center of the poem is certainly modeled upon an exchange between the poet and "somebody" collecting cover charges at the door of the bar, a situation in which if one knows anybody on the inside, in, for example, the band or its entourage, one can "gain access" even if destitute. In both poems money is the unavailable key to inclusion, to the esoteric realms of the family or the circle of friends, but in the second poem the lock is picked, so to speak, with a name and a pun, or rather an *enallage*, a name used as a verb. This wispy, almost meaningless trick of language circumvents the mercantile genre and the door that the bureaucrat of "The Miracle" had shut swings open. It is an exchange for nothing for nothing, but what changes in this moment?

As the sign of things in general, money is the ultimate generalization, the ultimate noun. Its definition is so broad, you could write a book, or several books, and exchange them for just this one word. By tradition, since time immemorial, money is decorated with the face of the patriarch that utters it.

Everette knew he was writing his best work in his last years, and he knew what it would get him. "[I]f I could have/ wrote like this/ when I was 20," he says, he could have gone to New York "& starved in/ grandeur."[9] Gone, obviously, is the Fitzgeraldian idea that one will be remunerated for writing well. Still, writing has its appeal, its "grandeur"; it still "beats hell/ out of baseball."[10] What is that appeal? What is it that one has when one is writing and doesn't have when not writing? Or, to continue a theme, do we *have* anything; does writing bestow upon us anything that can be signified as a noun? Richard Katrovas, working a bit hard, perhaps, to find a substantive, calls it "specialness,"[11] but I wonder if it isn't writing's verb, its activity, that is the basis of its value. Could this be so? Could these hopeless submissions to the magazines and small publishers on the perpetual verge of bankruptcy, these readings with twenty or ten or four people in the audience, and all of them other poets, or in Everette's case, the composing at the bar, giving a copy, perhaps, to Suzy or Wade, and hand writing another for the archive on a friend's dresser . . . could this be it? Is this the grandeur? If so, is it really better than baseball? But if it seems ludicrous that poetry might be only what it is, think how grand it would be to have your work anthologized by Norton, or forced upon university students after you're dead, or praised by critics to fatten their vitas. Poetry no more bestows immortality upon us than speaking does; its grandeur lies elsewhere.

Declension of the verb *to rette*: I rette; you rette; she rettes. To engage in a fatal nostalgia. To write in the thrall of the past, haunted by the past, stuck in the past. To find in the present the signature of the past. To see in present events primarily a mourning for what has passed. Rare: to overcome this; to write the present out of the past; to find the present through the murk of the past. (Past tense: *wrote*.)

One night, '76 or '77, Celia called, and Debbie answered the phone. Celia wanted us to come over to their apartment because there was nothing to do and they wanted company. Debbie told her it was too late, that we were already in our bathrobes, which we were. She presented the invitation to me and I grimaced, not wanting to get dressed again, or even get up from the couch. Celia persisted, but we would not be budged. A few minutes later after they hung up there was a knock on our door, and I opened it to find Rette and Celia in bathrobes. We played Scrabble, as I recall. Of the four of us, Everette was the worst player. He could always make a word, but didn't have the hang of playing for points. He could never seem to land his x on a triple letter score, or stretch his word to cover a premium square, or block his opponents from getting them. Not a night I thought, at the time, I would remember, but I do remember it now, so many years later, though I don't remember who won.

---

[1] Everette Maddox. *The Thirteen Original Poems.* New Orleans: Xavier UP, 1976. p. 6. The poem is also collected in *The Everette Maddox Song Book.* New Orleans: The New Orleans Poetry Journal P, 1982. p. 38. Maddox's only other books published to date are *Bar Scotch.* New Orleans: Pirogue Publishing, 1988; and *American Waste.* New Orleans: Portals P, 1993 (posthumous). For a brief textual and biographical outline, see Ralph Adamo's introduction to *American Waste.*

[2] In "A Retrospect." *Literary Essays of Ezra Pound.* Ed. T. S. Eliot. New York: New Directions, 1968. p. 4.

[3] King James Bible, *Book of St. John*, Chapter 4.

[4] cf. Robin Blaser's "The Practice of Outside," in *The Collected Books of Jack Spicer.* Los Angeles: Black Sparrow, 1975. p. 325.

[5] From *Paris Spleen*, trans. Louise Varèse. New York: New Directions, 1947 (1970).

[6] Varèse.

[7] Charles Bernstein. "Provisional Institutions: Alternative Presses and Poetic Innovation." Buffalo: Electronic Poetry Center, 1994. [Internet computer file available via gopher at wings.buffalo.edu (select Library, then Electronic Journals, then E-Journals Produced at UB.)]

[8] *American Waste.* p. 38.

[9] "Oh Man." *American Waste.* p. 80.

[10] "Writing Again." *American Waste.* p. 61.

[11] In "Artists and Bureaucracies: What Jimmy Carter and Vaclav Havel Can Teach Writers in the Academy." *New Orleans Review* 20.1-2 (Spring/ Summer 1994): 46.

Doug MacCash

On the Manuscript of *American Waste*

Writing Again

Writing again
after 7 yrs
isn't as good as
youth
whose last flush you
were to me
sweetheart
but it beats hell
out of baseball

Poet Everette Maddox died in 1989 of the combined effects of tobacco, excessive alcohol, and deficient nutrition. He was forty-four years old and had spent better than a decade without a regular home. He lived instead in the marginal shelter of the saloons, stoops, and doorways of a few square blocks of the Carrollton area of Uptown New Orleans. In the last months of his life, in obviously declining health, Maddox surprised those who knew him by returning to his writing. In that final creative outpouring, Maddox produced upwards of one hundred poems and poem fragments. These he wrote and rewrote in a quaking hand, on any available scrap of paper. He entrusted this accumulation of work to his friend and publisher Hank Staples, who stored the writing in a paper bag atop his bedroom bureau. Soon after Maddox's death this gathering of bits of paper was sorted and carefully edited by a committee of Maddox's friends. The edited collection was titled *American Waste*, introduced with an illuminating, sympathetic foreword by poet Ralph Adamo, and published by Portals Press in 1993.

Later that year, the poet's brother, William Maddox, and the other custodians of the disheveled manuscript donated the bundle of rough pages to the Historic New Orleans Collection (HNOC). The poems are irresistibly engaging. Maddox's themes vary. He writes with a humorous resignation about alcoholism and bar life, his persona pitiable, but never submerged in self-pity. He acknowledges in himself an unquenchable, almost adolescent lust which remains forever unrequited. He occasionally embraces the romance of Southern culture, but he just as frequently lampoons it. Maddox—the former English instructor—also perpetually toys with the language itself, finding the ironic possibilities in broken phrases and unlikely recombinations in practically every poem.

But in addition to the text, the physical manuscript is a poignant and resonant artifact. Cocooned within a worn Roubion Tile and Marble Co. paper sack are writings on the backs of Abita beer coasters, fluorescent pink cash register receipts, Xeroxed flyers announcing musical groups such as the Fuzzy Slippers from Hell or Shot Down in Ecuador, Jr. appearing in Muddy Waters or Carrollton Station or the Maple Leaf, a portion of a corrugated cardboard box, plain white paper napkins (perhaps from the Steak and Egg?), pages from a prescription pad advertising something called NOROXIN, and lined five-by-eight cards. This collection of soiled and tattered hand-written drafts embodies a rare unity of content, form, material, and even geographical reference. The hand-penned document contains much of the same spirit as the poetry itself.

In addition to Maddox's writings, the HNOC received the poet's collection of original and Xeroxed hand-bills announcing the many readings in the Maple Leaf poetry series over the years. This regularly scheduled reading, which has been presented on Sunday afternoons in the bar's patio since 1979, is said to be the longest-running poetry series in the South. Maddox was the host of the series from its inception until his death. This collection of brightly colored flyers features readings by local literary figures such as Andrei Codrescu, Robert Olen Butler, and Julie Kane, as well as practically every accomplished and aspiring writer in the region. There are also announcements of annual open-mike readings: the Boring reading, the Mardi Gras Extravaganza reading, the April Fools Who Can Read, Can Read reading, and others. Like the poetry manuscript, the sometimes energetic, sometimes lackadaisical appearance of the announcements themselves echoes the uneven quality of the poetry series. Again, the document is somehow perfectly mated with the message it bears.

Everette Maddox's last collection of poetry is rich with humor, but it is more burdened with pathos. The odd, unkempt manuscript is even further redolent of regret. The phrase *American Waste*— which was emblazoned on the side of a trash container on Oak Street—was chosen by Maddox before his death as a possible title for his next book. He probably suspected that it would become a *de facto* epitaph as well.

William Matthews

Dignity from Head to Toe

Everette Maddox's poems offer themselves to a reader, any reader, with a desperate friendliness so American it seems they must have been in sales only yesterday. Today they're between jobs. The source of their manic charm is revealed in "The Poem" (from *The Everette Maddox Song Book*, 1982, hereafter referred to as *TEMSB*).

> It's a rug: jump
> on a bump and
> another humps
>
> up. It won't stay
> smooth. It's nice skin
> that keeps breaking
>
> out in boils. It's
> a cathedral, with
> every word
>
> a little gar-
> goyle. A big grin
> with all the teeth
>
> snaggled. Because
> somewhere, down deep
> inside, every-
>
> thing is not all
> right.

Only someone who loves poetry idolatrously will make fun of it the way Maddox did. The "rug/ jump/ bump/ humps" cluster in his first stanza avidly violates good poetic taste. And why a rug? Maddox routinely proved Charles Simic's theorem that "Every cliché dreams of belonging to a great poem." This rug, too, will be pulled out from under our feet. Poetry can point to what's not at all right, but cannot change it.

In his *Rhyme's Reason: A Guide to English Verse*, John Hollander imitates Pope's "Essay on Criticism" by giving self-defining examples of each prosodic term he glosses, e.g., for dimeter:

> If she could write
> some verse tonight
> this dimeter
> would limit her.

Maddox wrote "The Poem" in dimeter, a line-length widely neglected, for reasons Hollander suggests, since Skelton. On the one hand, then Maddox's dimeter lines not only honor his debt to the tradition of English-language poetry but also assert his credentials—he can do the difficult and make it sound colloquial. On the other hand, Maddox often wrote in strict forms, I believe, in order to remind himself that the forms are only tools for writing poems; he didn't think of himself as making order out of chaos, but as making poems.

Here are the first few lines of "The Substance of a Late Night Phone Call" (*TEMSB*):

> I have stagnated
> for 13 years
> in Tuscaloosa,
> Alabama, and want
> badly to get out.
> However, my friend
> Bob Woolf in Mobile
> tells me he has
> left a trail
> of stagnation

all over the Southeast,
like a slug. . . .

The first eight lines of the poem are in syllabics, five syllables to
a line. Then Maddox lets the pattern go. Another poem in *TEMSB*,
"Breakfast," is a kind of syllabics sonnet: four tercets with three
syllables per line, and then a final couplet with two syllables per line.
Why would he be so strict in "The Poem," and start strictly in "The
Substance of a Late Night Phone Call" only to let his pattern tatter?
When then turn that tattered pattern back into something formal in
"Breakfast"? Because Maddox wrote out of a deep ambivalence
about the power and value of poetry, and such inconsistencies in his
formal practice embodied that ambivalence.

> life death eternal significance
> bullshit
> from now on I'm just
> going to make little whimsical gifts

So begins "Gift" (*TEMSB*). I don't think Maddox felt that
poetry was insignificant; he gave his life to it, or at least the part of
his life on which alcohol didn't hold a prior lien. And what, after all,
was Maddox's most characteristic rhetorical situation? Hopelessly
unrequited love, pursued with a mock-courtly but crazed persis-
tence. Especially in *American Waste* (hereafter referred to as *AW*)
the role of the unobtainable was played by Suzy, who served
Maddox as Laura served Petrarch.

But what else was unobtainable? Any guarantee that poetry
means more than whistling past the graveyard.

I have arrived, I see, at a familiar debate topic, often proposed
in Auden's famous formulation: "Poetry makes nothing happen."
Yes or no?

Poetry has little or no power over the world outside the poet as
reader. A beautiful little poem about the destruction of trees, such
as W. S. Merwin's "The Last One," doesn't still the snarl of chain
saws. Or, let's say it does, by seeping into the innermost conscious
of one reader after another. Still, this process is far slower than the

rate at which trees topple, and so it makes its readers sharply aware of the speed of loss far more efficiently than it saves trees. The world blunts poetry, the way paper blunts scissors.

But poetry's interior powers are great. Poets become, I believe, their bodies of work. People like to say that, for example, Philip Levine wrote such and such a poem because he is working class and Jewish and angry. But from his recent autobiographical essays, *The Bread of Time*, we learn, if we'd missed it in his poems, that his working class sympathies are, in sociological terms, an act of downward mobility. Poets call this faculty the imagination. Levine has chosen to treat his anger, Jewishness, and sense of sympathy with hard laborers as important, just as Elizabeth Bishop chose to treat her reticence as important, or as Robert Frost chose to treat his slyness and ferocity as important. The skeptical might say these poets chose parts of their temperaments they couldn't have got rid of for love or money, but such choices are in fact the hardest of them all. The poets chose them over and over at the desk, where poetry reigns, and where the poets made not only their bodies of work but also, and just as crucially, themselves.

Maddox chose his fate carefully, I think. Here's "Oh Man" (*AW*).

> Oh man
> I was standing
> on the corner
> rooting in my pocket
> for carfare
> & pulled out a
> rumpled poem
> & thought
> to nobody in
> particular
> if I could have
> wrote like this
> when I was 20
> I'd 've hung out my
> cardboard sign
> on what was then

             a U.S. highway
             & hitchhiked to
             New York
             & starved in
             grandeur

 This poem is as carefully rumpled and informal as his earlier
"The Poem" was carefully regular and formal.
 In each case the care has been disguised a little. Maddox died in
a unique situation—both homeless and widely beloved. There were
not the only opposites he loved to blur: formal and informal, destitute and dignified, courtly lover and drunk with a sodden dick in
trembling hand in the men's room of The Maple Leaf Bar, street
poet and prosodist, Rhett Butler and Rette Maddox, et al. It's a
life's work to make ambivalence a religious condition, and what will
be your reward, should you do it well or ill?

             Out of print
             at God's
             Bookshop

These lines comprise one of the epigrams gathered together as "Bar
Coasters" (*AW*).
 Let's take a look at "Oh Man."

             Oh man
             I was standing
             on the corner

If "The Poem" refers by metrics to Skelton and English prosody,
these lines refer to the blues ("I was standin' on the corner/ of
Twelfth Street & Vine"), and/ or to rhythm & blues. One tradition
is aggressively Anglophile and white; the other is American, black,
and aggressively informal.

             rooting in my
             pocket
             for carfare

"Rooting" is a pig's verb, although it has here an important secondary meaning: "cheering" or "hoping for." The euphemistic "carfare," which is what down-at-the-heels-gentility calls "busfare," is brilliant.

> & I pulled out a
> rumpled poem
> & I thought
> to nobody in
> particular

We'd expect "crumpled" for that balled poem in his pocket, but here the "rumpled" part, the poem, serves for the whole, the man. Or is it the other way around? There's a subliminal rhyme between "& I pulled out a/ [rumpled] poem" and "and I pulled out a plum." What a good boy am I? the poem wants both to ask and not to ask. Having it both ways ("nobody in/ particular") was one of Maddox's specialties.

> if I could have
> wrote like this
> when I was 20

The answer, of course, is yes and no. At 20 he'd have not made such a blaring error for effect as "wrote." He'd have been a good boy, and he'd have wound up being rather like the aging, muddled good boy who wrote this poem.

> I'd 've hung out my

("shingle," as idiom would lead us to expect, as if the good boy were setting out to practice medicine or law)

> cardboard sign
> on what was then
> a U.S. highway

(as opposed to the more recently built limited access interstates, often with laws against hitchhiking)

> & hitchhiked to
> New York
> & starved in
> grandeur

The implication is that by staying south, Maddox starved in, if not squalor, something less than grandeur. But his grandeur is internal and portable, and in this love of ambivalence he insisted that his grandeur be also seedy. The tone should be like the effect of the cover of *American Waste*, a title one of whose intentions is to refer to the author himself. But the cover photograph shows Maddox reading at The Maple Leaf, dressed splendidly in a three piece suit.
In "Sunrise in Montgomery" (*AW*) we learn the provenance of that suit. The title continues into the poem, the beginning of its first sentence.

> Sucks
> my heart up
> through the vest
> of my hand-me-up
> little brother's 3-piece suit
> I wore to the poultry reading—
> Walt rolls goggle-eyed
> with the post-excitements
> Bill & Momo get it on
> Ella on the tape sings
> "The very thought of you"
> Barb says "I wish I was on Baronne Street"
> But I think she says
> "I wish I owned Baronne Street"
> & I think "Me too Hon'
> we'd all be at the Fairmont

chawing diamond corn flakes"

The Scott Fitzgerald tone (a corn flake as big as The Ritz?) here and at the end of "Oh Man" is also ambivalent. Maddox is making fun of the disease of the provinces—the sure conviction that if it happens here it can't amount to much. Grandeur, he knew, is eternal. But while he's mocking in that tone, he also participates in its elegies: he knew that by devoting himself to poetry, which makes so little happen except within, he had missed much. That he missed it by choice and with chivalrous mockery doesn't lessen the occasional melancholy. Here's "Cameo of Suzy" (*AW*).

> This is not a funny
> poem
> about the life of
> glamour & beauty
> I wanted when I was
> young
> You weren't too late,
> I was.
> You were the lovely
> face
> I glimpsed in the
> lobby
> leaving the B movie
> of my life

And yet Maddox arranged to leave all choice behind him, to be as quixotically and irreversibly committed as the man in any courtly love pairing. To be past the point of no return made the venture real and meant that the game was being played with real money on the table.

The editors of *American Waste* (for Maddox did not arrange the manuscript) made an intuitively fine decision to end the book with "Flowing on the Bench."

> As I was going to sleep
> on the iron bench

in the back of the bar
I felt all right
I felt I was joining something
Not the Kiwanis Club
No
I felt like one river joining another
I felt like the Mississippi
flowing into the Ohio
Right where Jim & I
passed Cairo in the fog
Right where the book got good

Sharon Olinka

Leaving the Past

In September 1979 I moved to New Orleans. I never knew I'd be affected by the psychic residue of other people's stories. Someone named Robert Stock, who had died. And a woman poet uptown who wrote well about loss. It all seemed like a Clarence John Laughlin photo, full of light and shadow, foreboding. Pieces of an arm, a leg, or a veiled face. The veil charcoal colored, like ashes.

In the 1980s, New Orleans had a lively poetry scene that centered around the Maple Leaf Bar, the New Orleans Poetry Forum, UNO, Tulane, and a few coffee houses. I was a housewife with low self-esteem, and I had begun to take writing workshops. Martha McFerren and Lee Meitzen Grue were the arbiters of taste at the time. Martha disliked poetry that was "sensitive" or "political." Lee Meitzen Grue conducted workshops at her house and organized readings. And then there was Everette.

I was charmed by Everette Maddox's old-fashioned courtesy, his wit, and yes, his sensitivity. A true Libra, if I remember correctly. His critiques regarding my early poems were never calculated to hurt.

I remember spending a few hours one summer afternoon just talking with him, at the Maple Leaf. He spoke of that woman he sent a rose to every year, with utter reverence. I thought, *wow, how romantic.* But also, *that isn't real.* He wasn't there, in that moment, in that drink we shared. He was in a dream of the past: a rose and a girl's face.

After a while, I began to notice that Everette was sexy, in a strange way. I knew I was attracted. He was too, because he got more awkward around me, with a catch in his voice, and significant looks. It got harder to talk to him and be around him. Something was just wrong. There were things around us, darkness and the past all pushing against our words. Little chips of stone from other people's houses. And I wasn't free to be with him.

I stopped going to workshops. I began to think that New

Orleans wasn't the right place for me in terms of job opportunities, or where to go with my writing. I thought I might do better elsewhere. My husband got a job in Los Angeles. We made plans to leave.

My farewell reading was at the Maple Leaf. I read with Richard Katrovas. It was like a party. People even brought presents, which touched me. After the reading, the crowd gradually left the bar. I was alone, except for Everette.

He reached out for me and kissed me. It was a hungry, possessive kiss—I was surprised by how strong he was. It couldn't go any further. I was leaving in two days. All I thought was, *I have to leave. Go to! He'll keep me here! No!* Sadly, he let go of me. He wished me luck.

Three years later, in Los Angeles, I dreamed a black bird swooped down on me and started beating its wings, brushing its head against my face. I later realized that was the same week Everette died. I put the image of the bird in my poem "Bird of Death."

Dear Everette, you're still with me. The shy housewife took risks later on . . . oh, if you only knew. I've had a hell of a time. I won't even list all of it, what's the point, just that I grabbed for the big brass ring of the whole world, held on, and won't let go. You'll always be a part of me that belongs in dreams. In the beautiful houses of New Orleans, their light and shade. Their figures in black veils. But no matter how well F. Scott Fitzgerald wrote it, things just don't drift back to the past. They move on.

Randall Schroth

Everette Maddox

What impressed me most was his timing. Reading at the Cafe Brasil in New Orleans in December, he fell down going up on the steps without spilling his scotch. It looked like he landed hard on his hip, but he fluttered back up with some help.

I figured it was part of Everette's act, to get immediate support from the audience. Then he stood there swaying, leaning against an invisible wall, trying to focus on his notes. Could he do it? Already he had the full attention of over a hundred people, jammed into a big bar on Chartres Street so tight that other folks were leaning in three big doors from the sidewalk to see what was going on. They seemed to hold him up in spite of himself.

With the first poem, he listed far to the left to balance his drink, but Basil Rathbone in his prime couldn't have said it better. Everette knew it so well he didn't need his eyes to focus. By the last line, you knew there were times when the man could focus better than anyone.

He held up his new book, *Bar Scotch*, in one hand, a real scotch in the other, and grinned. That was Everette's balancing act, paradox and vision. But the timing! His pauses were measured out in milliseconds on a scale of perfect pitch that's available to only a handful of musicians and a few of God's chosen poets and comedians. If the heartbeat is our standard or most available rhythm, I figure Everette must have had some extra valves. He'd twist a note to that exact point where you'd have to laugh or gasp and let go.

He finished up on his feet. We'd seen a man juggle the hermeneutic discrepancies of body, mind, spirit, and soul like so many cue balls; a major drunk and soulful pinball wizard and poet at full tilt. We'd got more than our money's worth.

But after all it had more to do with "grace." When Everette put together those readings at the Maple Leaf Bar every Sunday, he'd show up sober, in a clean suit, and do the introductions in the old southern manner, with humor and grace that you see imitated in the movies but seldom in real life.

The man was one of New Orleans' better citizens, slept on its bars and its sidewalks, died in February (1989) at forty-four.

Gail White

Poets in New Orleans: A Reminiscence

New Orleans in the 1970s: Nixon was president, the Vietnam war was on, the sixties counter-culture was still with us, and the poets met for monthly readings in the summerhouse in Lee Grue's back yard on Lesseps Street.

Lee, every inch a poet in layers of flowing white drapery, backed us all with moral support and a place to read. For the readings we sat on folding chairs, and for a small donation you could dedicate a chair to a poet of your choice, and his/ her name would be painted on the back of the chair.

The Big Easy is a hard-drinking city, and the poets lead all the rest. Among my memories I find the following:

Robert Stock, who had once known Allen Ginsberg and now looked like Buffalo Bill, would drink from a hip flask between poems as he gave a reading. At the time I thought this rather pretentious of him, but looking back I have no doubt it was a necessity.

I remember Everette Maddox saying he had the world's largest collection of hand-written rejection slips from the poetry editor of *The New Yorker.* He had been published there a couple of times, but his style had moved on, and he failed to convince the editor that the change was for the better.

It may be rumor, not memory, that tells me Everette was once found drunk at sunrise on the steps of the Mater Dolorosa church, but the rumor was entirely credible in those days.

On one occasion I entertained the local poets at my shotgun house on Bartholomew Street. I put out all the liquor I thought the occasion required, and hid my personal supply under the sink. The poets unearthed and drank it all, including a friend's private stash of bourbon which he kept in a bottle labeled "CLOROX." It was in memory of this occasion that I wrote the poem "Partying with the Intelligentsia."

It was 1986 when I left New Orleans and moved to Lafayette. The first people I met were recovering alcoholics. I didn't even know there was such a thing. I had come to regard mild intoxication as the proper state of man. But my all-night singing and drinking days were over, and I started to forget my once impressive supply of bawdy limericks. Jack Parker's Viking Party has given place to Anne Rice's Hallow'een bash, and I can only dream of the House of the Rising Sun.

POETRY & SONG LYRICS

Ralph Adamo

Notes Toward an Elegy

The nurse says
He's the one at the end
making all the noise

Our stupid questions put him to sleep at last

      * * *

Trying now to die
his cold chest bare
A broke stick on the swollen river of public death

A convict is wheeled to the bed on his left
Space, lovely and musical, to his right

And the bad-tooth smell of death
the good thief turned his tv down
and (said he) said a prayer

      * * *

They sent the death cart for him
a few breaths too soon
Then the snoring began
It was not a
by hell damn your eyes roar
but a husk
of the poet's breath
that lingered
He's back the doctor said
He won't be long

Ralph Adamo

Poem Ending Everette

Well, pal, it's yer birthday
and you're dead.
What do you make of that?

An airy celebration
of thin air? Emaciated
air, spruced up and comma'd,
volatile, flammable even, bright
as a shade of sunlight slicing
the possum-scented river,
oh them possums you brung
to market in New Orleans, pocketfuls
of possums, a possum under every hat, young ladies
in thrall to your multi-possumed gamble, your
dollar down, way down, your drinking hand
steady as a young gunfighter's,
and your pupils
lined up on every side. You said
"I'm Everette Maddox, surgeon
to the enchanted forests of whiskey and song,
and I have left my Ala Goddamned Bama birth dust and
bullhockey for the icy winds
of Carrollton where I don't reckon
I'll ever get warm or be bored,
or kiss another pissfaced poor stranger of a butt
for a drink of this goody-forsaken fate to bust a gut
kicked in by America, and by American Poetry,
that slime they track to tenure
up at the University. Well,
NOT ON MY BIRTHDAY THEY DON'T.
On my birthday they shout UMPTEEN,
they sing oh-my-darling, they deal
POETRY, man, down and dirty."

147

I wrestle the word *friend* from the freezing bench
and hustle that sleepless grin
into the piano man's limo,
his bony butt and Booker's
barely dinting the plush, their quarrelsome spirits
primed for a wide ride down Carrollton Ave, oh my,
oh my.
It's as though the bar had lost its marrow,
its grimace, its one redemptively cynical thought.
Everette.

Grace Bauer

Three: for James Booker on St. Patrick's Eve (From "Blues Elegies")

Even the Krishnas cruising Bourbon Street
had their shamrock scam today, sticking us
with a little *Erin Go Braugh* in the name
of their un-Irish gods. And then
in walks this Brit with a knack
for the inimitable and he starts
coaxing the ivories into blues so deep
you'd swear he'd just done hard time
in Angola. He warms us up
with some Fess, a little Fats, then breaks
into *Junco Partner*, and we're out there
on the dance floor swirling like ice in scotch,
like we've gone back two years to Booker's last night
at the Leaf, that crazy Halloween the moon
made him play his heart out—like we had
never hear him play before—and we had heard
him play plenty. And so three days later
we were hardly surprised when he collapsed
like a tired dancer and they rushed him
to Charity for too little too late.
Tonight it's like he's fingering the keys
again and we're right there with him
as he wails *Please Send Me Someone To Love*
in another man's voice.

Grace Bauer

On Finding a Note to Everette Maddox in My Library Book, New Orleans, 1979

This town isn't big enough
for poets to hide in.
We bump into each other
as surely as cabs
in New York.

The note is from some poet, who says
"I'm beginning to start to wonder
about becoming mildly curious
about the fate of the poems."
I couldn't resist
reading something like that.
Rhett, I think your friend
is pissed.

I have spent this winter
hiding, hibernating
in a bare, cold house.
My desk is cluttered.
My typewriter ribbon is worn.
Words fall as heavy
as the rain outside.
I have so much to say
to no one.

I found the note
in a book by Berryman
on page one hundred sixty two,
a poem called CANTATRICE.
"Misunderstanding, Misunderstanding,

Misunderstanding"
reads the first line.
Who knows how long
your name has marked those words.

Grace Bauer

Second Lining at My Own Jazz Funeral

For Rette & Nancy

There ain't a saint among us
but we go marching in
to July's white heat, armed
with black umbrellas
and bottles of Dixie beer.

The drummer's on a roll
and tries to woo me
with Amazing Grace, but I'm
distracted by the sax man
who's wailing for Eliza Jane.

When our entourage turns off Oak
to strut toward the batture,
I hesitate, then head back
to the bar, not ready
to say goodbye to the river

that has run through ten years
of my life like a Huck Finn fantod,
or the friends I'm afraid
may forget my face too quickly,
or the lover whose bed
another presence will grace

before I'm even out
of this town—where even the dead
have their parade and their party
and get buried above ground
so the water
won't get in their bones.

Stan Bemis

The Goddamned Absence

From one man who loved him to another:
I envied Dusty the particles of dust
the ritual at the River
a separation from the substantial
Walking in the Orleans streets
to the bleat of Dixie couldn't give the sense
though all those tears were shed:
Our brother's gone.
The guy who lived for poetry and intoxication
and, though shabby, had
refinements beyond the Garden District's.
I know that life just couldn't
be boiled down
into a pile of ashes.
Not that sparkle and sneer and holy laughter,
his odd timidity
his exquisite delicacy with a flow of words
cannot be just more sludge
on the breeze-swept Mississippi's
polluted waters
But to have held his remains in my hand
would have empowered me
with a sense of tangibility.
I've not made peace
with the Goddamned absence.
I saw him maybe a week
before he made his exit and
for a man who'd said continuously,
I'm dying—he looked all right,
the bastard.
He can't be dead but I guess
he is.

I mean, I haven't seen him for
a long time.
But I can't help believing
he's re-lighting his pipe somewhere.
In my mind I envision him saying
to Jesus, Moses, Mohammed, Mary Glover Patterson Eddy,
and all the others
"Poetry in the rear"—
I'd wish I'd said goodbye and touched him
One last time.

Steve Brooks

Dead Poets Society (Song Lyrics)

Tyger, tyger, burning bright,
Through the forests of the night.
Everette's was the hand and eye
Could frame thy fearful symmetry.
Everette
Could cage it in a

Line of thought, a line of verse.
Everette knew what words were worth.
And Everette's words were diamond words.
Whenever you heard them, something stirred
Inside of you.
'Cause that's what poets do.

Oh, Everette, he never et
A square meal in thirty years.
But men don't live by bread alone,
And you could find him any time,
Slouched up on his high chair,
Drinking scotch,
And staring at his crotch.

He slept on sofas, slept on floors.
Some nights he slept out of doors.
Napkin backs and envelopes
Were the places Everette wrote
His masterworks,
And all of us young Turks

Gathered up the scraps
That Everette tossed into our laps.

And that's how Everette won his fame:
We'd print them under Everette's name,
Every year or two,
'Cause that's what poets do.

Who was the man behind the mask?
None of us ever dared to ask.
Poetry was Everette's shield and sword.
Despair could be its own reward,
When despair was polished hard,
Until it shone, like a precious stone,
When all of the pain could sparkle through.
'Cause that's what poets do.

And all of us at the Maple Leaf
Knew that he would come to grief.
Some folks live so close to death,
That you can swear you smell it on their breath.

Yes, poets dream, and poets drink,
And poets live life on the brink.
Poets smoke, and poets die,
And if you ever ask them why,
They'll tell you, they don't have a clue.
They'll tell you,
It's just what poets do.

So, Everette's body turned to ash,
And we all had a mighty bash.
People came from near and far,
To toast the bard at the bard's bar.
We knew he would have done the same for us.

And Everette, wherever you are,
Leaning on some heavenly bar,
Sloshed upon some sacred stool,
Where God serves His holy fools—

Even while you damn Him to His face—
Everette, I know you've got His grace.

And as I listened at your wake,
I saw how only you could make
A triumph out of tragedy,
Tragedy into a divine comedy.
Your words, your words will outlive you.
'Cause, Everette,
That's what poets do.

George Burton III

Sonnet for Everette Maddox

(The good ol' possum-bard!)

The gnome feels a shuffle coming on,
that Shakespearian rag, so elegant.
Early in the morning, crowd about gone,
bar scotch clouding your intelligence.
Some Chaplinesque humor on cloven feet.
Forty-four years past our folks danced lightly,
not rhythm and blues or a reggae beat;
now we know Artie Shaw only slightly.
I wanted to see you a few more times.
At Mardi Gras you were the King of *Wrecks*.
I regaled you with my triumphs and crimes,
and all you wanted was some red-hot sex!
   Apparently art is the child of pain;
    your despair and death in the New Orleans rain.

Maxine Cassin

Happy Hour

At Qué Sera you said,
"The street lights are coming on,"
as a streetcar full of celebrants sped by.
"This moment will never come again . . ."
though the trolley once traveled round the
bend
when we could ride the belt for seven cents.

Since then I have passed a host of friends
who disappeared along the tracks.
Though your song is playing somewhere
without end,
the dark conductor clangs and clangs
and clangs.

Maxine Cassin

The Old Odor

Dead fish assault my senses in this steaming patio
as I listen to this reader who has come a long way
not to be heard. Please don't mention it
to the impervious crowd inside
as they cheer the home-team on toward the End Zone
of the brand new 25 inch TV screen.
Let no one turn around to watch that spectacular interception
of a fumbled word mid-air.
Ignore this faithful tribe as they swat flies
in blistering sunlight—trochees, spondees—
and even comply with management's request
to return all empties to the bar.
All for you, dear Poet,
Your pittance of a wage,
your Sundays of free Scotch—
your haven and your hell
to which you are consigned
until the final Go-Cup
when the goalposts are pulled down.

Maxine Cassin

The Medium

When the rates are low
on Saturdays and on Sunday afternoons—
invariably they call.
Having heard the news,
they need to know
every detail of those final hours.
Then, growing bolder,
might I just recall
a time you spoke of them—
that is—if you spoke of them at all?

I draw my breath
and listen for the taps—
one: *to go away*
two: *to join the ranks*
three: *believe, perhaps.*
four: *come back? No thanks.*

I couch my answers in the soothing phrase
aspirated through my mouthpiece, "natural death."
They sigh relief it was not suicide,
that is, no sudden wound,
no draught delectable as cyanide
or act of will the timid seem to dread.

Taut as any wire,
I let their voices speak
through me to you
in variations of the conference call—
as dreamers link together
underground and overhead.

Eventually outrageous bills come due.
Until that day I summon you to hear.
Hear it, Everette—
you who *heard it all.*

Christopher Chambers

Dear Maddox

And surely he knows about Ransom and Tate.
Your own reflections doing very well, I believe,
though less impressive in the complimentary sense.
The writer's facility of the use of poetical stuff

in your own reflections does very well, I believe,
perhaps beyond rightness: better than rightness.
The writer's facility of the use of poetical stuff,
a gift that he should learn to take right advantage of,

is perhaps beyond rightness: better than rightness.
A little of the poetical is tolerable in poems,
a gift that he should learn to take right advantage of.
I will write more later if I can see the way to go.

Yes, a little of the poetical is tolerable in poems,
if it is possible to find out who it is he represents.
I will write more later if I can see the way to go,
for surely he knows about Ransom and Tate.

Christopher Chambers

Dear Maddox

I cannot imagine what he has been reading
with benefit of mind and the rhythms of English speech.
He searches the full unblemished darkness
sometimes not helpfully, and sometimes hurtfully.

With benefit of mind and the rhythms of English speech
this is his solo, friends and relatives,
sometimes not helpfully, and sometimes hurtfully
the pale comes to marred, and the marred to imperfection.

This is his solo, friends and relatives,
to swell progress, he starts a scene or two,
the pale coming to marred, and the marred to imperfection.
There are a good many words that fill up verses,

swelling progress, starting a scene or two,
for black is black without the benefit of full.
There are a good many words that fill up verses,
and I cannot imagine what he has been reading.

Christopher Chambers

Dear Maddox

There is one which begins: observe how he negotiates his way,
not in scope and depth and comprehension of man on earth
as I intimated yesterday in a stroke of self-obliteration.
One in which blackness, lack of color, is both full and not paled.

Not in scope and depth and comprehension of man on earth
does a figure (the name of which I do not recollect, unless it be
oxymoron)
begin in blackness, lack of color, both full and not paled.
In the theatre, banister is a noun and I doubt it can be wrinkled,

a figure, the name of which I do not recollect, unless it be
oxymoron.
Of course Milton coined darkness visible which is special
in the theater where banister is a noun and it cannot be wrinkled.
I am fond of talking about my own image in the shop window glass,

and of course Milton coining darkness visible, how special.
As I intimated yesterday in a stroke of self-obliteration
I'm still fond of talking about my image in the shop window glass
an image which begins by observing how I negotiate my way.

Carlos Colon

One More Way of Looking at a Possum

```
        v e
        e   r
          e
          t
          t
        eee
      mmmmm
      aaaaaaa
      dddddd
      dddddd
        ooo
         x
```

Peter Cooley

Some Kind of Resurrection

Here in the street my friend and I could catch the elegy
within the bar where poets read each Sunday
until today, words raising the dead poets finally.

I caught small gulps: "genius," "prodigy,"
"major work not finished," and I played back his confession,
Scotch in hand, before I read a year ago

while we waited for the tanked-up crowd to settle down.
"My muse is gone, my woman and daughter,
all I've got is booze, want a drink?"

Next his introduction, grandiloquent if stumbling,
all the dates and names of books in place from memory.
But now, back in the streets of our gulf city,

a procession wove out of the bar, a woman poet friend
swathed in black as always, swayed at its head,
bearing a box labeled "Rhett's ashes,"

and a jazzband followed, all the members drunk.
Dumbly I followed, all the New Orleans poets followed
the piper who should have borne us into the Mississippi

to baptize ourselves and be cleansed of this addiction
to celebrate the death of the poet as our own
in the bar's neighborhood, those homes he frequented,

door after door, adopting him, throwing him out.
Shall I say for the sake of the poem: he rose again?
Not from this crowd proclaiming his name

since the bearer of the box and all who chose communion
were admitted, door opening on door
to receive a cup, another, then another

until the multitudes swelled, then, lunging, drunk, dispersed.
I turned to my friend, a poet,
neither of us drinking, though we used to together

constantly, and both of us confessed
to the other we hated our guts this minute
for refusing to drink when he'd want us to

so we wouldn't judge him on this, his final day.
And who were we to say he wouldn't have found
other ways to do himself in, considering

the ones we'd tried, separately, together?
And both of us agreed we were no friend
to him or to each other or anyone, ever.

Joel Dailey

Impossumibilities

Every telephone
in the world
rings in your ears, etc.

The bashful possum
who resides in your beard
is sick of crumbs, etc.

Like a revolving door
that won't quit;
like the sun,

God's apparent
luminous yo-yo
and its shenanigans;

like the days
shadowing
one another down Oak St.

and turning in at
The Leaf;
these Impossumibilities

are hard as edges
fixed to these
temporary coordinates

that rip the flesh,
spill blood,
guts, memories—

pure Impossumibilities—
the very contents
of our lives.

Ken Fontenot

Poem Ending with Resolutions, Half-Baked

I can tell you the man
who taught me how to laugh
like this and like this
and like this,
and I can tell you the girl
in Austin, Texas, in 1974
who said "that's *pun*ishment"
when I made a pun.
I can tell you how Billy Larmieu
never forgave me to this day
the day I made his eye
his blackened pride.
And because hands remember
the insult of hands I can tell you
how many pieces of one-inch tubes
will fit in a barrel
the size of my uncle's belly.

How many times I have said shit,
and walked out, my face
blazing like Wyatt Earp's!
And this year I'm saying
to hell with each thread
of my emotional wardrobe.
I'm saying what's good
for Ginsberg is good for me.
I'm going to steal everything I can
from my beloved Whitman, too,
believe you me. I'm going to steal
from Phil and Chuck, from Jerry and Marvin,
from John Keats, from Rhett Maddox,

and especially from poor Robert Bridges
whom nobody reads any more.
I'm going to hitch my bed
to a tree. I'm going to bake Kantian
bread. I'm going to find
all the lost bears, their paws
patting me on the back,
my only job ever well-done.

Ken Fontenot

Winter and the Moon Tugs at the Mind

1
The window shivers. It too.
Last night in this shanty, this leaky house,
I almost froze. The landlord
told me nothing about winter here.
I am fatter than a summer cow.
My shoes are older than a grandma's eyeglasses.
My brain is foggier than a used computer.
Now who could have said *that* in 1935?
The foggier the brain, the less money
you have to make it still foggier.
One sip. Just one sip, brother, and *oooh-ieee.*

2
He's left-handed. Lately he dreams
he kisses our mother, rubs her neck,
combs her hair, she who is no longer alive,
but quite young in this dream, a virgin.
He's my brother Hank, who wrote so awful
in second grade Miss Dickerson kept him back.
He still chicken-scratches, still waddles around,
still sleeps twelve hours a night and can't get up.
I'll take my sister's handwriting any day.
Why do girls especially write so pretty?
Ah, who writes with his left hand covers his words.
Show me a man with an illegible hand
and I'll show you a man
who always dreams he's being chased.

3
Friday night. I meet him at the bar.

He looks and walks like Hank. It's colder than Venus.
He is my other self,
myself made otherwise by all his talk, his glow.
I like my women fussy, he says. *And chatty.*
At night I like my women made up like whores.
I buy him one Scotch. Two. I lose count.
He knows people I knew.
He rakes my past over the coals of niceties.
When he brushes his hand in the air
the women with him leave.
When he clears his throat they return.
If he told me the moon were orange, I'd agree.
If he said he were broke, I'd lend him money.
Did you ever feel the world was a black tuxedo
and you were a pair of brown shoes?
He laughs at all his own jokes.
I forget his name. I think of him now.
He makes you laugh, wipe your eyes.
He shows me some poems. As Dante would.
He is my other self,
myself made otherwise by all his wisdom.

Louis Gallo

Yeah

He lifted his head
from the bar
to tell me
he'd recently met
a Rod McKuen clone.
Seems Rod's a corporation now,
he said, the Colonel Sanders
of fried poetry.
Such talk, of course,
brought John Keats to mind.
"What *doesn't* bring Keats
to mind?" he asked,
more serious than prayer,
more loquacious than blood.

Michael Greene

Captain Maddox

I had been falling down drunk
For 2 days, when she up and
Says,
"Look, O weird one, let's go to the
Maple Leaf in New Orleans."
So I went.
And if memory serves,
There stood a certain
Captain Maddox,
Toothpick held daintily
Between his teeth
As he whistled
"Buffalo Gals"
Softly
In counterpoint to the
Leadsman's cry of "MARK TWAIN."
Jesus, I thought, this beats
the peewaddin' out of
Fucking cows!
Captain Maddox
Spinning the wheel down hard,
Turned,
Clicked his heels,
And said,
"Welcome aboard, pilgrim!
There's whiskey and cigars
In the texas for them that
Wants 'em."
Then the drunk next to me exclaimed,
"By the Shadow of Death, but he's a lightning poet!"
What else could I do but agree?

William Harmon

Free Refills

Rette, dear ferrous templar of the tutti-
frutti crusade, when we first
met, in Tuscaloosa in '74 or so, you quoted
a line
of mine which I knew only a
true poet would recognize the worth of—I blush
to repeat
it
but must:
Vanilla villas upon the moron moon;
the last
time, '84, New
Orleans, you said you felt the
most beautiful
words in English
were *Free Refills*; again I
was moved to admiration. What
a superlative poet you were, the
greatest Montgomery romantic since Zelda, and
a gentleman
of courtly chivalry and enterprise to boot (the Maple Leaf
Bar
where you drank all but lived
maintained the longest-established
weekly poetry readings anywhere). You
had a poem in *The New Yorker* at twenty-five
but none ever again
thereafter, only
what you called
the Crescent City's largest collection
of Howard Moss autographs—well,
ill
will, they

say, blows no real good. But
let me
nevertheless help myself to just
a second's worth of hoping the late Mr.
Moss undergoes a
moment of remorse there in whatever outlying precinct of
the afterlife
he finds himself consigned to,
a minor editor's sublimbo,
while *you,*
friend, belly up all day every
day to heaven's central bar
with Aristophanes, Ben Jonson, Lord
Byron, Hart Crane, etc; under
the eternal neon FREE REFILLS
to down
round
after round of paradise's
special bar scotch, that marvelous
and matchless single-malt
distillation known everywhere in the universe as Glenjehovah.

Nancy Harris

Memento Mori: The Black Box

your jazz funeral
was Black Orpheus
only a different
continent
a different rio
but the same old
carnival

the invisible skeleton
with hollow grin
ran unexposed, parading
through the crowds
clacking & clanking
with arrhythmic jerks
smoldering behind
every mourner's eyeballs

we drank
it all in, the dirge
of sounds, blue notes
the high balls
marching with unregimented
asymmetry around the corner
to a different bar

returning to a wake of free booze
& freely flowing tears
in the red tin rooms
of the Maple Leaf Bar
your only home for years
the black box: a ridiculous reminder

ashes to ashes & so it goes
put that in your pipe & smoke it
the black box
the night before
posed self-consciously
on Fred & Jenny's mantel
the tape recorder with your voice
coming out of another black box
& one of your drunk Alabama friends
picks it up & shakes it:
"Yup, it's Rette alright."
black humour that breaks the ice
in our drinks, in our souls

I pour a symbolic scotch
choking on its acrid taste & toast
you in the black box
haunting the mantel

wraith-like even in life
you constantly reminded us of death,
Everette, & love

the day we took you in the black box
the sky was bluer than it ever had a right to be
the day we took the black box
the sun so sharp its edges cut through us
the day we took you in the black box

down to the river, the beautiful, beautiful
muddy-brown, garbage-strewn river
yes, let us gather at the river
the day we took you in the black box
a month after you turned invisible
(except to Rosemary, who, a week later
saw you wavering, dandy like in your best suit

pipe & bar scotch in hand
in the doorway of Muddy Waters;
except to me: one night while watching TV
I felt engulfed by a palpable stench
of scotch incensing my livingroom;
except to Julie, whose Tarot reader said:
your friend doesn't believe he's dead yet
& he's pissed off)
I don't believe you're dead yet
& I'm pissed off that you can't feel
how the air changes around your skin
when a hurricane looms, how the sky
shifts, turning ominous & exciting

the day we took you in the black box
zigzagging through Carrollton streets
to the levee by the river, Mark Twain's river
Huck Finn's dreams, paddling through dark
muddy waters, now polluted with shiny cans
& golden brown beer bottles, portending
your next book's title, *American Waste*

six of us gathered at the river
beautiful, beautiful muddy-brown, garbage-strewn river
whose sibilant name called you home: Miss-iss-ippi
where Dusty plunges into the muck, arm stuck up
like an Arthurian knight,
keeping the black box out of the mire
rotting brown logs bobbing up & down
releases your ashes
into the river's mouth & we hope
the gulf stream carries them
somewhere south to an exotic spot—
at least in the opposite direction
to Alabama
we join hands in a circle
gathering around the empty black box

& we begin to believe in your death, in ours
& in the miraculous blue sky

Nancy Harris

My Dog Comes to the Word "Death"

For Mandrake, 1976-1990

death. death. death.
death. death. death. death. death.
if you repeat a word often enough
it becomes meaningless
just the hollow sound of a foreign tongue
you can't follow:
thump-thump, thump-thump, thump-thump-thump.

that being the noise Mandrake
beat out on the hardwood floors
clicking the clichés
in the middle of the night when I couldn't sleep
& he had ticks & fleas to scratch
& I had sheep to count:
one, two, three, four, five
da-da, da-da, da-da, da-da
throbbing hearbeats alive
with the backbone of poetry:
iamb, therefore I shrink.

here, Mandrake, here, Death!
his ashes are hermetically sealed in
in a shockingly small
pale green celadon urn
draped with a garland of lotuses
faintly etched
his photographs propped around it
various crystals from the mineral kingdom
guarding the circle of fire.

when I hold its cold roundness in my palms
I cry, disbelieving the gleaming brown eyes
pouring unqualified, unconditional love
from the polaroid above
are dead

dead as my friend Everette, the poet.
a year for deadness. my job is dead. a love is dead.
once, many years ago, after a poetry reading
some writer friends came home with me
to eat red beans & rice & we typed out
tap-tap, tap-tap-tap
an exquisite corpse on my smith-corona.
Bob Stock was there & he's dead too.

that's when Everette grabbed Mandrake's box
of flavored dog biscuits & joyously
munching on a handful, washed it down
with swigs of scotch.

Mandrake set up a howling protest,
his eyes mournful,
so we gave him some biscuits, too
his favorite being the pale green ones.

now, many of my best friends are in heaven
& many of them are here.

which way do I turn for comfort?
tick-tock, tick-tock, tick-tock, tick-tock

Nancy Harris

Unemployed in Fall #2

For Everette Maddox, 1992

a decade later you're dead
& I'm unemployed again.
some things never change.
some things are
forever.

this time I can't visit you
at the Maple Leaf, or is it
house of the rising sun?

actually at this point in my day
the sun is setting over my house
& you I imagine flying above
my roof in your Sunday best
coattails flying in the wind
a glass of bar scotch held aloft
never spilling any of your spirits
across Carrollton, Oak Street
the Riverbend & in your bird's-eye-view
the sky a blue fall luminescent painting
perhaps by Chagall:
some crows, bees, dragonflies
adding natural interest

what's new? nothing much, here.
same old antique bottles, colored glass
& prisms still fill my windows with light
& fluctuating tones, patterns, shimmering spectrums.
& speaking of spectral matters, I miss you
& want to know what you do now to occupy

your unemployed days & nights beyond time?

this morning, once again, the jehovah's witnesses
came to my door, awakened by Guinevere's barking,
not the doorbell. & this decade Mandrake's dead
who was at my side, always loyal. this time
my joblessness is stranger, more surreal
& more real. will I ever work again?
can't even collect unemployment, just dust.

& speaking of dust, I've been dusting off old poems,
many written when you were still here, taking me back
to lost decades, not worth finding.

an old friend of yours, Sam, showed up at the Leaf on Sunday
just as drunkenly obnoxious as ever,
not hearing about your death
until recently:
coming back to haunt his past, let bygones be.

Well, a few years later, he'll be gone, too
bones drenched in alcohol, formaldehyde,
whatever

found dead in his bed
& I won't even feel guilty
that I didn't answer
his last incoherent letter
that I'll put aside, shaking my head
fluttering, my tongue forming
the word "weird"
a hummingbird blurs for a moment
fuchsia, across my field
of vision

Karen Head

Abortive Midnight Journal Entry

Here in Nebraska, I am buried
under snow and self-pity.
If only you weren't buried too,
we could consult your dictionary—
look for words that mean something—
toast my newest job rejection letter.
The reward for having advanced
education is not employment—
at least not the paying kind.
Days like this, I want to drift
down to the Maple Leaf Bar—
drink Louisiana humidity,
thickened gin cotton-coating
my throat, until the slow burn
erases all thoughts of poetry.

Harry de la Houssaye

Rette's Old Clothes

You worked as a writer in the schools
until teachers and students complained
you reeked of alcohol. So you lived
on the twenty dollars a week
you earned by running a reading series
at the Maple Leaf Bar. Your teeth blackened.
Your eyes became dim. Your glasses became useless.
You stopped writing. Homeless, sleeping
in church vestibules or on park benches
you waited for the bars to open at noon.

At the end you burst open with poetry,
scribbling it on napkins and paper bags.
When scotch and cancer closed your throat
you died the death you wanted.
Your obituary in the *Times-Picayune* noted
your homelessness, your early promise,
unfulfilled, the two books of poetry
you left behind, along with friends
to mourn your death at forty-four.

But it did not mention your Brooks Brothers clothes
or how they were soiled because
you slept in them. Rette, they were a sign
of your dignity as you devoured the food
I bought you, like the starving man
you were, or as you saved all year
to buy Holly flowers on her birthday.
When she married someone else
you fell in love with barmaids and waitresses.
The last of Everette Maddox,
brilliant graduate student, evaporated

and with your fine clothes in tatters
you belonged completely to the street.

I prefer to remember how your eyes
sparked as you talked about Mark Twain
and the river. That was your dream
when you moved to New Orleans from
the red clay hills of Alabama—
to write about the river and its towns.
Here you lived for poetic moments:
buying pipe tobacco at the drugstore,
drinking your morning coffee at Woolworth's,
having your first drink of the day
at the Maple Leaf, and because you refined
your life beyond redemption,
you had to die to become the conscience
of the city you loved.

Rodney Jones

Elegy for a Bad Example

If there is no heaven and you are in it,
What does that make me? An idiot?
Your paradise was never the afterlife,
Only the usual after-hours party,
The one with beer and marijuana,

Where the priest, after explaining the rigors
of extreme unction, happily relieves
Himself on the hostess's potted plant;
Where the engineering student roars
Off naked on the sociologist's Harley;

Where the farm boy turns Buddhist
And the new marriage makes a fist.
Oh but you are not there to quote Berryman,
To enjoin all stupid dreamers to wake up
By the profound example of passing out.

No, in the real heaven that doesn't exist,
You are only the aging of a premonition.
You have no business here. You only occur
To me on a day of many absences
When I give the lecture on attendance.

Rodney Jones

Born Again

How slowly I came away from that vision of death
As a stage and stood before the butcher case,
Confessional of the cynics, pickled pig's feet,
Shining chops, insensitive to transcendence.
I had not seen the eyes of the lamb when I took
The white gristle in one paw, and I had not
Heard the lowing of the calves when I let
The grease drift down my chin and my arms.
The colors must have moved me more than the taste.
The reds at the hams and the shoulders
Might have been bars lit for the night.
I took them in my mouth and I left them ash.
I loved the roasts and in particular I loved
The duck, the veal, and the filet mignon
Before the cardiologists left me weeds and fish.
Only then I gave in a little to guilt.
Only then I began to look east for wisdom,
But not until Everette Maddox died
Did I begin to believe in reincarnation.
The dance he had done on tables made
Me look for him in the cat, and the way
He had curled up drunk pointed to the dog.
His brain was his glory. I did not like it
How he set a feast in his liver and his heart.
Those last months he slept in a dump truck.
He scribbled constantly in the Maple Leaf
And at Carrollton Station. I hated it
How he suffered so proudly and inconsolably.
In the letters, especially, you can see the scope.
He carried the nineteenth century with him.
He moved like a bird between Twain and Keats.

But it was not the brain and it was not the meat.
Not until I got my knife under the seal
Of the plastic urn and ran my fingers
Through the grit and the splinters of bone
Did I begin to believe the soul meant other
Than ancient desperation and lonely desire,
And not until we marched through the streets
Did I begin to look into the eyes of men
With something other than courtesy and fear.
Bob Woolf glided in his dark suit. Sam
Maisel fidgeted. There were four hundred.
Fred Kasten had the ashes just behind the band.
I could see Boswell, Schilling, and Smith,
And the rest of life, dripping from hooks,
Jerusalem of lamb or Mecca of beef,
But just that once I saw the heavens open
And heard the soul shrieking as it entered the tree.
For just that minute I was out of my mind with grief.

Julie Kane

The Bartender's Hair

Those nights I smelled a barroom in your hair,
I dreamed I saw you standing like a god
at closing time with Maddox huddled there

in the navy peacoat he used to wear,
thin as an X ray, pouring over his Scotch
in a plastic cup, a barroom in his hair.

It was the change in the bedroom air
that woke me mornings at four o'clock
to find you lying beside me there,

rum fumes rising from your skin like a layer
of fog on the highway, and bar rags washed
in disinfectant in your barroom hair.

Where was Maddox? Sleeping on the stairs
of Mater Dolorosa, the Mother of Our Sorrows,
those nights I smelled a barroom in your hair,
the ghosts of cigars and perfume there.

Julie Kane

Everything but Blue

After Diane Ackerman

Although your eyes were everything but blue,
unable to digest the blue in light
(as most of us would turn away blue food,

not having eaten in a day or two);
although they were watery, rabbity, nearsighted,
farsighted, naked, and everything but blue,

it is by them that I remember you
the time of year blue china sells to brides
because there is no blue at all in food.

Ask any coroner: He'll swear it's true
our eyes turn greenish-brownish when we die,
just as a newborn baby's eyes are blue.

Your eyes were cinders when we carried you
to heave the ashes at the riverside
for greenish-brownish alligator food.

The river and the reeds were green-brown, too.
Above our heads, a February sky
absorbed white light but scattered back the blue
as you could keep down Scotch, but not our food.

Julie Kane

The Maple Leaf Bar

I wanted to understand the place:
the pressed tin ceiling and the out-of-tune
piano where the late James Booker played

in a rhinestone eyepatch and purple cape.
Bottles in sunlight like Arabian jewels:
I wanted to understand the place.

Maddox asleep like a cat onstage.
Kittens asleep in the storage room.
Red Sox, Celtics, and Bruins played

in bars that kept my uncles late
They came home singing until they puked.
I wanted to understand the Saints.

What did you think, with your boyish face,
a bar rag tucked in you blue-jeans loop,
giving me all your change to play

the jukebox with? Another crazy barfly making eyes at you?
I wanted to understand the place,
to play with words like Booker played.

Julie Kane

Mapleworld; or, Six Flags Over the Maple Leaf

So ye old Maple Leaf has gone the way of all of the Cool. It
has been co-opted. Nothing escapes, because if you've heard of it
and it's not your usual, and you go there and you think it's cool,
others will follow, scribes will wax, poets will villanelle in the
washroom behind the bar, journalists will broadcast first in cool
papers and then real papers, then comes the new paint, micro-
brews, shitters sans orange algae, and no eau de crotch sweat,
only stuff with the name on it like vacationers' slides, but then
when the poets' minds go, it really is gone, and some other shit
becomes cool, but cool has changed. Who in Annapolis wants to
hear about how Tip's and the Maple Leaf "used to be"? Do we
want to hear about some "cool" Frisco haunt? No.

—M., via e-mail

You'd hardly recognize the Maple Leaf:
the bathrooms with their dim red Christmas bulbs
mercifully obscuring a half-inch-deep

primordial ooze, now eat-on-clean
for the Hard-Rock-T-shirt-clad multitudes whose guidebooks canonize the Maple Leaf

the way it wasn't when we'd roll our jeans
to wade on in through the primeval flood
that covered up the heads a half-inch deep.

Dial soap dispensers and hot-air machines
are waging war on our *E. coli* bugs:
you'd hardly recognize the Maple Leaf.

Like shotgun shacks transformed to "galleries,"
our funky hovel has been gussied up
in Disneyesque façade a half-inch deep.

Who cares about the way things *used* to be,
except us creatures of the slime, who love
the darkness and the dead?—the Maple Leaf
with Booker playing, Maddox "just asleep."

Fred Kasten

The Wages of Poetry (Song Lyrics)

*For Everette Maddox on the occasion of his being alive
and celebrating the 6th anniversary of the Maple Leaf
Reading Series*

Universal blues
and little local truths
awkward and complex
tools you use
it takes a skilled hand
to make an image hold

The wages of poetry seem kind of low.

Through barely working eons
no time off allowed you know
from keeping one eye sober
every place you go
remembering what you see
if not what you say

The wages of poetry are due for a raise.

In lost generations
and generations without souls
poets patch the language
fixing up the holes
like singing the blues
it ain't all sad you know

But the wages of poetry seem kind of low.

Universal blues

and little local truths
awkward and complex
tools you use
it takes a skilled hand
to make an image hold

The wages of poetry are just too damn low.

William S. Maddox

Peace on Earth

In 1981, my brother Everette and I planned a good Christmas
for ourselves, the first one we had spent together in fifteen
years. We would go spend a couple of days at Bob Woolf's house
in Mobile, drive back Christmas morning, and have the big
traditional dinner with Bob Stock's widow, and then go to
the Prytania Theater that night and see "Gone With The Wind."
So we drove from New Orleans to Mobile in my big Chrysler
Cordoba which I later converted drunkenly to scrap metal
at the corner of Lowerline and Willow and spent two days at
Bob Woolf's. We ate and drank and talked like crazy, then
Christmas Eve I finally had to go to bed and leave the talking
to them. We drove back Christmas morning hungover and tired
but happy. We got to Mrs. Stock's about noon and found the
whole extended family there, cooking turkey and peeling potatoes
and washing vegetables. We nibbled on dip and chips for a
while, chatted with the folks, and felt great since we knew
we would have a good meal and then catch the movie at eight.
Three or four o'clock came and that chip and dip stuff was
getting pretty old. But they were still all merrily peeling
potatoes and cooking turkey and washing vegetables so we tried
to fit in even though there wasn't quite enough to drink for
us to feel as merry as them. They had a big family, after
all, and there was only the two of us. Then it got to be
six o'clock and we were getting a little edgy and more than
a bit hungry but they were still washing vegetables and peeling
potatoes and cooking turkey. If I'm not mistaken we began
to get a little short with the Stock clan but I'm not sure
they noticed because they were all very busy and full of good
cheer. At about seven, Rette and I had a secret confabulation
in the bathroom and set a private ultimatum: 7:30 it was
time to blow it. We nervously watched the clock as we sat

there in hungry straight chairs in the kitchen while they
cooked turkey and peeled potatoes and washed vegetables;
the dip was all gone. When we announced at 7:30 thanks for
the good time but we were going to the movie, they were stunned
but gracious. We stopped at the Time Saver on the way and
got a pint of vodka for me and pint of scotch for Rette
which we cheerfully sneaked into the theater under our heavy
coats. It was a hell of a movie as always, made better by
the Christmas dinner we had of vodka, scotch, and popcorn.
Afterward we went to the Maple Leaf Bar which was morosely
populated by all the people who didn't have wives and children
or husbands and children or otherwise big people in their
lives instead of the people who always seem sort of little
when you're not in love. We all sat there and drank and watched
the clock tick and when it got to be 12:01 and it wasn't
Christmas any more, a mighty cheer went up from the bar and
we went on—thank you, God, thank you, Jesus, thank you,
Jeffrey Hunter—we went on with our uncelebrated but mercifully
undistracted lives.

Martha McFerren

Southern Gothic

For Everette Maddox and Eugene Walter

Poet in New York, revised. "Where are you from?"
asks the woman in the Horn and Hardart
of the man with a tie wider than he is.
"Alabama," he answers. She's uncorked.

From her green beans she rises. "When,"
she yells in compassion, "will you SLIME
stop murdering Negroes?" and this frail man,
who only did damage to himself
with too much Scotch, hunkers down
in a city of razor wire, not thinking
to holler in return, "When will you YANKEES
stop mugging the Hasidim for their diamonds?"

You don't need this, Everette.
Come home, listen to your own folks
make idiots of themselves. And come back,
Eugene, from Rome, where the Communists
beat you up. Come home and let your own folks
work you over at Mardi Gras.

And go home, me,
where it's a mess, but a warmer, cheaper one.
Where nobody stares at my flat noises,
nobody stands on good geography
waiting, wide-white-eyed, for me to swig
a jar of moonshine and go South blind,
to kick a hound dog, whip out the whip.
They're sure I carry it, that lush disease
known as Gothic.

I should tell them,
That's man stuff, anyway. We womenfolk,
we only sat saying things. Like the woman
at the asylum, slamming down her hand
and shouting, "I will not play another card,
Ouida Keeton, until you tell me
what you did with the rest of your mother!"

Okay, so Miss Ouida, *she* took some action,
but usually we talk.

     "They sewed
that tube to her BLADDER, and all the curl
fell out of her hair. Never did come back
'cept for one little patch."
    "She had
a heart attack and laid there
three days next to the clothesline
with her face in the clematis
and the ANTS ate her."

Miss Mae Marie
asked the cop with the ice cream,
"You all find out 'bout them two men
that was hangin' in the TREE?"
Oh, not the Klan this time, just a suicide
with company.

The only person I know
who ever got whipped was my Uncle Jesse,
because, in 1910, he left off plowing
and slipped away to the schoolhouse.
His father tied him around a tree, beat him
ignorant with a buggy whip.
They do it to
kids up North, too. They just do it indoors.

Christopher Munford

The Day After Easter in New Orleans

There are days when the city
is sunken and sullen

when the sun rises without comment
as it rose this morning
and there is no one
to see it

when there is nothing on the lake
no boat
no flake of sail or
bobbing gull

when the general atop his column
in Lee Circle is gray
is gray
as streaks of rain darken and ruin
his granite greatcoat

when great squadrons
of cloud sweep in at night
from the gulf
gathering over the delta
the swamps

swinging low to attend the river
to drain the color from the sky
to rain onto the city
this fine pitying mist

when it is too wet for the

deserted maiden aunt
(her name is Patience)
to be in the dripping garden
behind the Spanish wall

when it is too late to dress
for the weather
because the weather is in us
and we are dank
we are dull
we are the suspended silt
in the river
the purling mud in the current

the soil
sweeping gently out to sea.

Kay Murphy

Oh, Everette, There Is No Reason Why

Why is it you, dead, not me, why
my best friend at the time lived,
two bullets in her skull, still serving
drinks, swapping pills for vodka
behind a ratty, enameled bar;
before that, my ex-husband; dehydration,
malnutrition, midwest hospital
I couldn't bring myself to visit,
but my son did, sad son who finds it
next to impossible to stay alive, like you.
Both of you, bar rags of bones, but
he won't make forty-five, or sonnets.

Let me tell you why every time
I cock back my hair in some bar,
feel a bar lip rub my belly, a rail
notch my arch, suck a long neck,
teach Fitzgerald, Christ! hear
a good damned poem even, taste
whiskey on some lover's breath, I
think of you Everette. That some
whiskey-breathed lover said, knowing
me, he'd read your poem "The Reason Why"
but I'd be in the audience and couldn't
take it, shows you had more faith than I.
My husband drank himself to death,
same age as you. You're like family;
genetics **is** the reason, with no God.

Old cliché of despair and drunks,
these words, the strongest bond

our kind can count on, save you
for me. You, driving on an empty tank,
me, with what most thought was nothing,
arrived, from Midwest, from Tuscaloosa
to New Orleans at the same conclusion:
How many people could I say this to?
Everette, I don't think, tonight,
three days after another hellish holiday,
there's any reason I should continue
to take this, still counting syllables
to drag myself to the next dull line.
I've always counted my drinks to not die
like you. But you wrote as freely as you drank:
your drinks, prayers for death swallowed
whole; your poems, drinks for the living
spat out in lines still killing.

Sharon Olinka

Bird of Death

In my dream dark wings
brushed the ceiling.
Black bones,
you hold me still.
Little secrets.
Ball of fluff
from hell.

When your drinking
increased, job gone,
you went where no one
else would go,
and the corrupt, shell-pink
flowers of Prytania Street
remained with you.

Your eyes
pools of light
in a skull.
Bone points,
you cut me raw,
pulled me
to the deeper shade.
And I thank you.

People say
to me, I can't place you.
I tell them we're all
from another place, really,
its faint flower odor
of pure release
on our skin.

And I speak in a language
without translation,
flawed, but filled
with the gold lights
of sickness
and illumination.

A forbidden door
will free me.

I give you
this touch. This flight.

Spike Perkins

Streets of New Orleans

La Bohème is playing
in the streets of New Orleans
arias echo from wrought iron balconies
from Italy to Africa

the company and the characters
confuse roles and reality,
dying poets toast the spectacle
of their own tragedy
become grand opera

heroes become street acrobats,
balancing on the edge
of a boiling cauldron,
crippled crabs rise
like whales in a sea of gumbo
the Japanese cinematographers
have invaded La Scala—
the monsters are real,
the spices are intoxicating,
the play addicting

the cooks have taken over the orchestra
commandeering kettledrums, the
rhythm simmers slowly
it's a funeral march and a mating dance
no one can stop moving to
the conductor is copulating with
the widow, the concertmaster
is playing violin with his teeth

a soft rain falls, but no
curtain, the opera is unending
the audience has joined the chorus,
musicians patrol the seething streets
and the tenor is running for mayor

Spike Perkins

Hurricane Season

They published the names today,
an echo of ancient demons
summoned just that way, like banns
of a wedding the guest will flee.
Alternating evocation of male
and female, equal opportunity ferocity.

I remember our lights went out
after a birthday dinner
of barbequed shrimp and bourbon,
Everette and I and Juan
howled "chinga tu madre" through the oaks
while we slept.

After midnight
Hank found Marty, a naked priestess
drunk as we, in the rain-drenched doorway,
and woke the groggy poet to drive
to Alabama through the waning winds,
his triumphant revenge on Montgomery
the last hurricane season of his life.

It beats me how they choose
them—is it a curse or a fearsome
compliment to bear the name
attached to such a storm?
Is there a meteorological protocol
about it—no evil bosses, mothers-in-law,
ex-lovers, bad sons or daughters?

In New Orleans we sit
below sea level, a city of wooden

flotsam, a dream, a beautiful anomaly.
Everette Maddox wrote truly,
"a blue-green frog town
on lily pads." When it comes,
we huddle in centuries-old houses,
which stood before they ever named
the storms, too proud to run.

We know the highest ground
is nearest to the river, our levees
the oldest, highest, and best—
we hope the flood comes only to
Jefferson, St. Tammany, and unlucky
Plaquemines, where Mardi Gras Olympian
gods took their awful sacrifice
in 1927 with no hurricane,
merely an epic flood.

"The scientists say it will
all wash away," sang Gram
Parsons, kindred nomad spirit
who came to us in death.
But yet, no California fault line
Apocalypse, no Gulf Coast tsunami.
Still, computer models hum,
animated tidal surges dance
like a video game, experts preach
their secular damnation,
and oil men and nutria gnaw
at the remaining water land
between New Orleans and
the Atlantean legend.

Manfred Pollard

An Elegy for Everette Maddox

> I felt like one river joining another
> I felt like the Mississippi
> flowing into the Ohio
> Right where Jim & I
> passed Cairo in the fog
> Right where the book got good.
> —E. Maddox

I almost hear his mocking chortle—loud
into a wicked cough aloft the wind
inside his dark coat loss of eloquence
and war each night, lost sometimes twice a day.
At last he won the siege of alcohol,
surrendering each battlefield romance.

Maxine, I see a mountain mapped with smoke
and choked confederates of poetry,
who pose behind his ashen stand of friends,
a wreath for us and our day's finite rounds.
A Finn of humor's lost, less laughter rings
the bar for songs of mother's tumor—love.

He often praised low poetry that burns
and swore a life is greater than these wounds.
When "Adam's Curse" was Everette's favorite Yeats,
that hollow moon turned over rebel yells.
A captive beauty broke from its cold light
when Everette's poetry would rise again.

Some poems Everette wrote still flower at night
so black his ash is driven through the ink.

Yet even in the maw of death they lift
a glass to toast the friendship of his gift.
His voice of rotten teeth and rankest tongue,
could torch the hearts of strangers in a storm.

He was a teacher of the strength of strings,
the most uncommon ghost that some had known;
a nervous system linking writers in
New Orleans' oldest streetcar line of fire—
desiring deeply taught, not knowing what
it is that lies beyond Elysian Fields.

Past neon-nights and air-conditioned days,
green mercy drifts along beside his raft,
where one may read the meaning of his grace
—a shaded place to rest in kinder lights.
If love in ignorance may earn us praise,
then glory lets us stay so sick, so long.

JC Reilly

Para(mad)doxical

When rumpled tweed polished barstools, when
endless Sundays promised confluence of booze, smoke, poetry,
myth was born. Your myth, undiluted as the amber splash
in double old-fashioneds you'd grasp with hands transparently thin.
Slaying dragons—climbing Everest—maintaining an address—
such picayune matters compared to the crafting of lyrics
you'd stockpile in your paper sack, like fortunes
or miracles—though you'd always known a dearth of both.
Umpteen hidden loves, spontaneous overflows of powerful demons
proved your undoing, but how they seasoned mystique like cayenne.
Oh, everyone noticed. The clothes that engulfed you, the taut
skin of your face, the doorways you sheltered in, these
shouted decline like Reconstruction's heavy carpetbag—
until the South rose again in your laughter, your wit a Dixieland
medley playing long into the night. When you'd recite
poems or the impromptu lecture, the quickening you felt
overcame us as the River after days of cloudburst, a thrall
enough to briefly dim the immolation of your soul. But
to die a myth, an archetype? Only you could find that droll.

Randall Schroth

Thirteen Ways of Looking at a Blackboard

I
Among twenty-eight students,
The only moving thing
Was the chalk on the blackboard.

II
I was the instructor,
A geek
In front of three blackboards.

III
Outside whirled the autumn winds.
Inside, my tiny pantomime.

IV
A man and a woman
Are sometimes one.
A man and chalk and a blackboard
Are not.

V
I do not know which to prefer,
My lunch box,
Or the ham sandwich,
Having a job
Or just after.

VI
Icicles dripped in the window.
Beyond them, a gas station,
A '57 Chevy station wagon

Getting gassed up.
A Nomad
It drives away.
Where were we?

VII
O thin instructors,
What do you imagine that you know?
Do you not see the nifty shoes
On the feet
of the students about you?

VIII
I know southern accents
And lewd, inescapable administrators;
But I know, too,
That the blackboard is covered
With what I know.

IX
When the chalk flew to the back of the room,
It marked a connection
With one of many heads.

X
At the sight of a blackboard
Under fluorescent lights,
Anyone, in his sleep,
Would cry out sharply.

XI
Flying over Kansas,
Coach class, after spring break,
A fear pierced him,
In that he mistook
The shadow of the plane
For a blackboard.

XII
The chalk is moving,
The blackboard needs cleaning.

XIII
The clock stopped that afternoon.
Power lines were down.
It was snowing.
The blackboard sat
In the empty room.

Louie Skipper

From *Deaths That Travel with the Weather*

EVERETTE MADDOX ,
hair still parting on the right and your black beard

over-running the same brown tweed
and pipe, have you come

back to life looking professorial

to find if there is anywhere to go where respect comes with the
job?

Harvard? Hell?

You are no more invisible now
than when you lived the life of the mind.

I must tell you I no longer trust the Department of English
or even the dawn to release

some new beginning,
some fresh start of belonging. Or have you come
back in anger to scare your friends,

believing everyone
but you had gotten laid? I would like to look

around and find you at my side or help you to your home
on some unrelenting Monday like this
burdened with desire in the wind
tearing leaves across the college lawn. Or is home for you now
as it has always been,

everywhere you cannot find again?
　　Does autumn still fire you with an air of nostalgia
for pure youth? Remember the years with promise
in Tuscaloosa, those fierce colleagues you cursed

who charged headlong into careers?
What were they looking for?
From where you stand is it possible

for a man to live
　　　safely with his writing? Read to me again the only poem

I ever understood, the one that makes me
　　remember to follow, to listen and not to speak.

Teachers, friends,
maybe the dead live again in the lives they changed.
　　　Does the richness

　of language explain
　　　the best of ourselves only to cut

us out of the crowd with a heightened sense? I have been
struggling as much as ever for what refuses to be

　anything
other than the maples' crowded color staggering red to orange.
　　So I want you to tell me where you are, Rette
Sometimes I see you
　　in the moonlight out of style, come badly to the end, alone.

If death is just a way we have of getting there
　　I want you to climb into another shape on the other side.

You wanted happiness.

Your heart was suspect. At the last
    you drank Scotch by the fifth and slept in trash.

  Homeless,
     your face draws closer when I write,

still trying for the right words to find their way
    into your wish and mind that you were here.

Robert Stock

Walking with Angels

For Everette & Franz

Whoever you may be, however endowed,
you know the dangling strain that youth may bear
if you have walked with angels unaware,
what though they stepped out roundly, self-avowed,
and one has brought you safely through the crowd
(that makes a shambles of the thoroughfare)
into your solitude, a silence where
your awe can grip the leap from groin to cloud.
His healing stroke is at the desert well
most faithfully shown, for there you're given time
to feature yourself, then drop a stone below;
thus, out of discomposure, rounds propel
your face against the crumbling walls of lime,
and, when you're most alone, he lets you go.

Leon Stokesbury

The Royal Nonesuch

*Extempore Effusion upon the Death
of Everette Maddox (1944-1989)*

Given recent events,
it's easy to see why
that bilgewater-slick
New Orleans night
stink stays stuck
in the craw. Almost
midnight in The Maple
Leaf, and you, Big E.,
querulous for hours,
while black cascades
of rain made mighty sure
the never ending steam-
bath just kept roaring.
Across Oak Street, through
the front bar window,
the red and blue KINKO'S
flickered and
flashed, reflecting
in the street like rubies
and sapphires. Then up
through the mildew, up
through the smoke, up off
that sticky Dixie Beer
floor, you raised it
at last, dog-eared
and dirty, on high
for me to read. And
I was so smitten, so

enamored, by
the incredible original
aptness of the title
of that somewhat-soiled
manuscript version

of your 2nd collection,
I exclaimed, "Damn!
I'll swap you one
fifth of Chivas for
the use of this!" And,
to my surprise, you
whispered, "OK." Given
recent events, I wish
I had offered a big
beef filet. But even
back then, you were, by
far, the absolutely
thinnest person I
had seen: only man
to match poem and
body to perfection:
paring things down
to the barest bone.
Given recent events,
and in verification
of your claim
that black
steambath night back
in 1983, something
a bit like sapphires
and rubies gleaming
in the streets, and
with, perhaps, just
a touch of a hint
of intent toward late
reparations, let me
say, sad pal, skinny

feller, funny friend,
and as the record runs
down now, you are, no
doubt about it, and
irrevocably so,
the one and the only,
the late Dauphin.

Helen Toye

A New Coat for Everette

He would freeze in
his summer seersucker coat,
ever shaking into fall.

The Maple Leaf Bar cold, damp
after a rain washed the streets.
Puddles defied the Christmas spirit.

The bar towels to be taken for washing in the morning
acting as his pillow as he waited for closing time,
trying to keep his body from shaking,
stretched out on a bench.

Everette needs a warm coat, I thought,
a new coat, something warm and stylish.
We meandered several blocks to my home,
Everette carrying the towels
in a bag slung across his shoulder
while trying to skirt puddles.

He would bathe in the morning,
take his clothes and the bar towels
to the washerteria, slip my key
under the door when he left.
And I would go to work
even though it was a Saturday.

Nancy was having a Christmas party.
I went out for fifteen minutes to a shop
on St. Charles Avenue that advertised
a big Christmas sale. Up a flight of steps,

a salesman showed me the perfect coat:
a black felt coat with a gray stripe—
a magical new coat for Everette.

How many warm bodies have gathered since?
How many remarked on his ghostly resemblance
to the miniature doll in a Christmas display next door—
the black-bearded man in the sleigh
clothed in a black felt coat with a gray stripe
and a pretty girl on his arm?

Gail White

Partying with the Intelligentsia

Poets will drink you out of house and home,
no matter how much booze you've squirreled away,
and afterwards they simply won't go home

till fading darkness warns of coming day,
and then they burble "Goo'bye! Time to g'ome!"
Poets will drink you out of house and home.

Architects aren't much better, by the way,
and theater people have IQ's of foam.
At 3 AM they simply won't go home.

These artsy types want someone else to pay
for dinner, want to use your car, your comb.
Poets will drink you out of house and home,

leaving your living room in disarray,
swearing they find your house a pleasure dome.
Even at dawn they simply won't go home;

some have passed out, others regroup and bray
a chorus of "Wherever I may roam."
Poets will drink you out of house and home,
and afterwards they simply WON'T go home.

Carolyne Wright

On Learning That I'm Not C. D. Wright, Couple Walks Out of Maple Leaf Bar

The Dirty Dozen Brass Band was second-
lining on the p.a. system, a direct feed
from WWOZ's command post above Tipitina's

Uptown. At the Leaf, poets were gathering
in a slow swirl—Jimmy and Martha and Lee,
Bonnie and Maxine and Brother Blue

with his finger-popping soft shoe—
around Everette at the bar, swizzle stick
in his vermouth, in his white linen

suit jacket like a man who should have just
dismounted from a five-gaited Walking Horse,
a smooth ride between tobacco rows.

Pads in the shoulders to bulk him, conceal
rib slats ridged as a zydeco rub-board,
carcinoma sculpting its pulmonary tunnels.

And where was my man, James Willie?
Fingering a page of Walcott or Soyinka
in a corner under the Tiffany torchière

with the librarian poets from Loyola.
In spaghetti strap frocks and kitten heels,
spangled *bustiers* and plumage of paradise

flounced skirts, they fluttered close,
rhinestone crucifixes winking in their cleavage.

James Willie's head dipped with a warm

rumble of breath into the uncatalogued
space between them. I wouldn't confront him
later: who could change this need?

I lingered under the Maple Leaf shingle
for who knows what. *Feets don't fail me now*
the Dirty Dozen chortled in caterwaul

of cornets, tumbler of tubas in Everette's
trembling hand as the white-blond and bleached
blue-eyed couple sidled over and announced

they'd driven all the way from Little Rock
since dawn to meet me. *Who?* Jarvis
and Jolene. My would-be students from

Fayetteville. *Okay. But I'm from Seattle.*
I said. "You're not C.D.?"
I'm not. Their call my response, fast as a

scat attack and fade. *But I'll read good as any
stand-in!* "No deal," they wheedled on stiletto
moccasins, stepping deep into the ozone

daze of Carrollton, the Dozen played out
in afternoon's decay. Then James Willie
was behind me, Lee beaming at the crowd

from a lemon gel glow over the tiny
stage: *You're first.* Shook leaf, I stumbled
toward the podium on fail-safe feet.

Who else knew it would be
years before I stopped taking
No for an answer?

Ahmos Zu-Bolton II

Everette Maddox

Years after your death
I started to understand your poetry

After a desperate summer of rusty tragedy,
After sloe gin and walking these streets,
I started to understand what & why it means
To be half in and half out of New Orleans,
A jerk in the cosmic corner of some bar,
A liquid hero milking rumor's booze

you always played a gentle bukowski
and I played leroi jones

Years after your death
I picked up my copy of *Bar Scotch*
And read into the glass

The years run away like
Homeless poets, slow-motioned
& true. You left your footprints
on Maple Street;
And all the poets with panicky wings
Who stand where you stood,
Are the landlords of your sober words
And their leftover promises.

FICTION

Ellen Gilchrist

The Raintree Street Bar and Washerteria

There were four poets at the bar and the son of a poet tending bar and the Piano Prince of New Orleans playing ragtime in the next room. It was a good day at the Raintree Street Bar and Washerteria. It was a Wednesday afternoon and it was ninety-nine degrees in the shade and (because of that) there was no one in the bar but people other people could trust. All the rich ladies and Tulane students had found air-conditioned places to hang out in and people who needed the Raintree to keep their lives in order could lounge around the bar sipping beer and listening to the Piano Prince play "Such a Night" and "Junco Partner" and "I Walk on Gilded Splinters" while in the back room the washing machines and dryers did their accustomed work. It was June in New Orleans, Louisiana, and it was exactly as hot as it was supposed to be.

"Fuck a bunch of rich women chasing my ass all over town," the Most Famous Poet in New Orleans was saying to the Jazz Poet. "Fuck them calling me on the telephone. I can't even take a shit without the goddamn phone ringing off the hook. 'Finley, is that you? You don't sound like yourself, honey. Is something wrong?' Is something wrong, you goddamn bitch, you bet it's wrong. Leave me alone. Oh, please, for God's sake, leave me alone." The Most Famous Poet laid his head down on the bar and the Jazz Poet raised an eyebrow in the direction of the bartender.

"Come on, Finley," the bartender said. "Come lie down on the sofa in the office. You got to save yourself for the night. Jay-Jay's coming to sit in with the band and Johnny Vidacovich will be here. You don't want to use it up in the daytime, do you? Come lay down."

"Lie," the Most Famous Poet said. "Chickens lay." His head was almost to the edge of the bar, his right hand shoved his beer farther and farther down the bar. The phone beside the cash register was ringing. "Don't answer it," he continued. "I'm not here. Say

Finley isn't here. Finley is in Galway where he wants to be. Finley gone bye-bye. For God's sake, Charles Joseph, help me." Now he was all the way down and the Jazz Poet moved behind him and propped him up and held him to the bar.

"Who doesn't he want to talk to?" the Jazz Poet asked. "Who's he hiding from now?" The Jazz Poet had only wandered in to wash a load of clothes. He hadn't meant to get so deep into poetry on a Wednesday afternoon in June.

"The society lady painter. The one that does the cartoons of her friends."

"Oh, shit," the Jazz Poet said. "I remember her."

"She came in here last night all gussied up in black. She'd been to that Andy Warhol thing at the museum. Her mother was with her. Her mother's as bad as she is. Her mother was chasing ass all over the bar. They parked right out front and left the motor running. She's been stalking Finley for days. I guess he laid her. He shouldn't lay them if he doesn't want them coming after him."

"Christ," the Jazz Poet said. "Jesus Christ."

It was June of 1979. A hard time for poets in New Orleans. Every society woman in town who wasn't into tennis was into poetry. They were trying to be poets, but they didn't know how. Some of the ones who were into tennis were also into poetry. They were into poetry but they didn't know how to do it yet. They didn't know how to write the poems or what poets to talk about or how to get anyone to publish the poems they wrote in case they wrote them. There wasn't a big poetry hook-up yet. Of course, over at Tulane a real poet was teaching a poetry class but it met at inconvenient hours for society women just getting into poetry and besides you had to already know how to do poetry to get into it.

Society women are hard to keep out of something once they decide they want to be in, however, and they had discovered the Raintree Street Bar and Washerteria. One of them had even brought her maid over one day pretending their washing machine at home was broken. There she was, sitting at the bar drinking beer and pretending to be a poet and going back every now and then to make sure the maid wasn't bored.

The society women were being terribly frustrated by the world of poetry in nineteen hundred and seventy-nine and if there is one thing a society woman won't put up with it is being frustrated or bored.

"Finley started a poetry magazine with her," the bartender was explaining. "She got drunk one night and gave him a check for five thousand dollars to revive *The Ouachita Review.* Now she's making him do it."

"They asked me for some stuff," the Jazz Poet answered. "They said they'd pay five dollars a line. I gave them a poem. First American Non-exclusive Serial Rights only, of course. Well, it looks like he's out, Charles Joseph. You want to leave him here on the bar?"

"Move his beer. No point in having to clean that up."

Sandy George Wade made his way down Raintree Street from the streetcar stop on Carrollton Avenue, walking as fast ninety-nine degrees in the shade would allow him to walk, admiring the windows of the little old-fashioned shops, pawn shops, and shoe repair shops and an antiques store and a bakery. He had the address of the Raintree in his pocket. A poet named Francis Alter who came to teach at his reform school had given it to him a few months before. "Go by there," the poet had said. "There are good people there. People who will help you."

"Can I say I'm a friend of yours?"

"Sure. There are people there who know me. They know my work."

"Are you famous?"

"They'll know my work. Poets know other poets by their work. Go there if you get lonely in New Orleans. Keep this address. You might need it someday." The poet had folded up the piece of paper with the address of the Raintree on it and watched while Sandy put it in his pocket.

Sandy arrived at the door of the Raintree and looked inside and saw the Jazz Poet holding up the Most Famous Poet at the bar and heard the Piano Prince playing "High Blood Pressure." *I get highhhh blood pressure when I hear your name.* It looked like a good place to stop. It looked like a place where a man could begin to straighten something out. The Jazz Poet was wearing a clean white T-shirt and a panama hat. He looked like a poet should look and Sandy walked on down the bar and took a seat beside him and ordered a beer.

"Did any of you ever know Francis Alter?" he asked. "He told me I could find friends here if I used his name."

"Francis," the Jazz Poet said. "You know Francis?"

"I knew him down in Texas. I was in his class."

"He's the best. The absolute nonpareil. The very best. Look, we've got to get this guy to the office. You want to help?"

"Sure, I'll be glad to help. Who is he?"

"He's a great poet. The best in New Orleans."

Sandy and the Jazz Poet eased Finley off the stool and moved him toward the office, with the bartender leading the way. "Don't answer it," Finley kept calling out. "Tell her I'm not here."

"He's not here," the bartender said. "That's for sure."

"Finley in spirit land," the Jazz Poet added. "Hey, I could make a poem of that. Finley gone to spirit land where no rich lady bother him. Not make him read her dreadful poems. Not make him listen to her whine. No ladies call him on the phone. No magazines send him rejection slips. No blues in spirit land. Goddamn, Charles Joseph. Listen to this. Ain't No Blues in Spirit Land. What a riff."

"That's good," the bartender agreed. "That's really good, Dickie. Especially the last line."

"Where are we going?" Sandy asked. He was now the sole support of Finley. The other two were leaning against the walls talking. The four of them were wedged into a small hall between the bar and the washerteria. The air was thick with the exhaust from the dryers. The smell of panties cooking, Sandy decided. Little flowered panties getting cooked.

"Turn in that door," the bartender said. He took back his part of the burden, hooked his shoulder under Finley's arm, and began to drag him to the door. "Right in there, that's the office." Sandy pushed open the door and they entered a small neat room with a large sofa in the one corner.

"Right there," the bartender directed. "Ease him down. That's it. He'll be okay as soon as he gets some sleep."

"What's wrong with him?" Sandy said. "Who doesn't he want to call him?"

"He's in deep trouble," the bartender answered. "They put an article about him in the paper and now all the society women are after his ass. It happens. I told him not to let them interview him. My old man's a poet. I slept in a bed once with W. H. Auden. I know about this stuff."

"You slept with Auden?" the Jazz Poet said. "You never told me that."

"He was passed out in my bed, in Starkville, when he came to read, the last year before he died. He slept in his clothes. God, he was a lovely man."

"I envy you so much," the Jazz Poet said. "I would give anything to have had your childhood."

"It was nice," the bartender agreed. "I wouldn't trade it."

"Who's Auden?" Sandy asked. "Is he some friend of yours?"

"Let's go back to the bar," the Jazz Poet answered. "I want to hear about Francis. All my life I wanted to meet that man." He put his arm around Sandy's shoulder, and, with the bartender leading the way, they went back down the hall and out into the lofty beer- and cigarette-laden air of the Raintree bar. The sky had darkened. It was going to rain. The Piano Prince had just returned to the piano after taking a break to get a fix in the men's room. He smiled upon the world. He lifted his genius-laden fingers and dropped them

239

down on the piano and began to play his famous rendition of "Oh, Those Lonely, Lonely Nights."

"This poetry seems like a good deal," Sandy began. "I like the feel of it. I'd like to get in on some of it."

"It's about death, baby," the Jazz Poet answered. "But it's to keep the skull at bay. I wrote a poem about waiting in the welfare line that got me so much pussy I had to change my phone number. I just wrote down what everybody said while we waited to get our checks. That line used to stretch all the way down Camp Street from the old *Times-Picayune* Building past Lafayette Square to the Blood Bank. I met some characters in that line who were unforgettable and I made the longest poem in the world out of it and used to put it on down at this theater we had on Valencia Street. I had to beat them off with a stick when I'd do my welfare line poem. I'll do it for you someday."

"It's great," the bartender put in. "It's a great poem."

"But enough about me," the Jazz Poet added. He pushed his panama hat back from his brow and wiped his face with a pale orange and white bandanna, then tied the bandanna around his neck. He could see their reflection in the bar mirror. Charles Joseph's back in his ironed white shirt and the good-looking new kid and his own hat and bandanna and strong hawkish profile. "Tell me about Francis," he went on. "I'd give anything to know him. He's the best there is, the absolute best."

"I thought you said that guy was."

"He's the best there is down here. Francis is the best in the United States. He's a god."

"I'm going to go see him," Sandy said. "He said I could go up there to Arkansas and help him run some lines."

"I'll go with you. God, I'd love to go up there. Do you think he'd mind if I came along?"

Oh, those lonely, lonely nights. Oh, those lonely, lonely nights. In the adjoining room the Piano Prince was playing his heart out. He was in heaven, back in the arms of his honey juice and as soon as he finished here he'd be back in his bed with his monkey in his arms. *Monkey, monkey, monkey*, the Piano Prince sang to himself and laid down his heart into his hands. *Oh, those lonely, lonely nights. Oh, those lonely, lonely nights.*

"That guy is really good," Sandy said. "That guy is something else."

"Yeah, that's the Piano Prince. He's an addict. He plays to get his fix. He's the best. He's so popular now he doesn't come here often anymore. Oh, shit, look out there." He pointed out the window to where a big green Mercedes Benz was pulling up beside the curb. "That's the Lady Jane coming after Finley. Oh, yes, it's her and who the hell is that she's got with her?" A short busy-looking woman in a white tennis dress got out of the car and came in the door with a determined look on her face. Right behind her, in her wake, as it were, was a taller, thinner woman with long red hair. They moved like an armada into the bar and took up a determined position near the cash register. "Is Finley here?" the woman asked the bartender. "Tell me the truth, Charles Joseph. Have you seen him?"

"He was here a while ago," the bartender answered, "but now he's out."

"Well, I have to find him. Where did he go?" "What do you need Finley for?" the Jazz Poet put in." It's nice to see you, Janey. Who's this with you?" "Allison Carter, the painter. You know her work. I had that show for her, remember? Allison, this is Dickie Madison. Hayes Madison, Junior. His daddy's the district attorney. He's our Jazz Poet. You ought to hear him sometime. Have you seen Finley, Hayes? We really need to find him. It's about *The Ouachita*."

"He was in here a while ago. What's the problem?"

"We have to see the printer. The printer won't fix the typos. It's a mess. We took it to that place on Marengo and they promised they'd have it by last week and now it isn't finished and they won't fix the typos. Your poem looks great."

"She has a poetry magazine," the Jazz Poet explained to Sandy. "She revived an old one called *The Ouachita*. He knows Francis Alter, Jane. He's going up there to visit him."

"You know Francis Alter?" The woman turned her attention to Sandy. "Where did you know him?"

"He taught at a school I went to. He told me I could come and see him anytime I wanted to."

"What school?"

"Down in Texas. You wouldn't have heard of it. It's really small."

"Oh, okay. Well, if you see him tell him we'd really like to publish some of his stuff. What did you say your name was?"

"Sandy. Sandy Wade."

"This is Allison Carter, Sandy. She's a painter. She's great. She's going to do our cover. So, do you think Finley's coming back?"

"He might be back tonight," the bartender said. "He said he wanted to come hear the band. Johnny Vidacovich is going to sit in, and . . ."

"Tell him to call me," Jane said. "Tell him I'm looking for him. Look, could we have a Diet Coke? I really need something to drink." The bartender got two not particularly clean glasses down from a shelf and put some less clean ice in them with his not very clean hands and filled them from a hose that led God knows where, to some subterranean Diet Coke well. Lady Jane shuddered and reached in her purse and took out five dollars and laid it on the counter. She held the dirty germ-filled Diet Coke at a distance from her tennis dress.

"So," she said. "You know Francis Alter? That's amazing. I've been trying to meet him for years. I'd give anything to be in his class."

"Are you a poet too?" Sandy asked.

"Well, sort of. I mean, I haven't published anything yet but I'm learning. I've been so busy getting this magazine published I don't have time to write. Well, come on, Allison. Let's get out of here. Jesus, it's so hot in here. It's so hot everywhere. You really need some air conditioning in this place." She put the untouched drink down on the counter and left the change beside it and took her friend's arm and left the way she had come, in a hurry, and went out and into the car, which she had left running with the air conditioner on.

242

"Who was that?" Sandy asked.

"That's why Finley can't answer the telephone."

At nine o'clock that night they were all back at the bar. The band was filing in, beginning to warm up. The regular drummer was at the bar, drinking water and talking to the new bass player. Sandy had been home and showered and changed and put on his best white Mexican wedding shirt and his earring. The Jazz Poet had gone home and collected his lady, the ex-lesbian minimalist poet, Kathleen Danelle. Finley had sobered up and washed his face and hands and put on his painted Mirò tie. The Piano Prince had had another fix. The sun was all the way down behind the levee and now it was only ninety-two degrees in New Orleans, Louisiana, and the big fan that blew the air around the Raintree Street Bar and Washerteria could make some headway in its work to make the poets and other patrons more comfortable in their progress through the month of June, nineteen hundred and seventy-nine. The pinnacle year of poets in New Orleans. The year the ladies loved the poets. The year the poets got all the pussy and the preachers got none. Those were the days, the people from the Raintree would say later. Those were the years.

This night, the sixth of June, nineteen hundred and seventy-nine, was the beginning of the end for the poets of New Orleans, but they didn't know it yet. So far, only six people knew that Francis Alter was dead. A married lady named Crystal Weiss knew it and her husband, Manny, and their two children and their two best friends. They had known it since seven o'clock. They had all been out to eat to celebrate the remission of a terrible leukemia inside a child of their two best friends. A gala celebration at a famous steak house. They had feasted on steak and fried potatoes and buttered mushrooms and salad smothered in Roquefort dressing and several bottles of fine red wine. A nineteen fifty-nine Mouton Rothschild from Manny Weiss's legendary cellar. The Weisses had even let the children have a glass of wine. Drink up, they said to their children. Cancer is on the run. Man has triumphed once again.

After they had finished all the food and wine, they had gone to the Weisses' house to sit around the pool and celebrate some more. Then the phone rang. A chill of premonition went around the people at the pool. Something's wrong, everybody said. Something's happened.

Manny answered the phone. Francis is dead, the caller said. Francis shot himself.

It was unbelievable. Francis had just been in New Orleans visiting all of them, charming them to death with his beauty and poetry, charming their children, charming the sick boy, charming their parents and the people they invited to meet him, charming the maids and yardmen, charming the birds down from the trees. Then he had gone home to his meager poet's cottage and lain down upon a bed and shot himself through the heart. He had gone into a bedroom and lain down upon a bed and blown his heart to smithereens. He had decided to put an end to all his poetry and pain and the hard work it is to be alive. Besides, he believed that if he killed himself everyone would be sorry and not be able to forget him. He was right about that.

As soon as the phone call came all the people around the Weisses' pool felt guilty for being alive. The Weisses' best friends soon went home. The Weisses' children were sent to their bedrooms to watch their television sets. The Weisses started getting very drunk. Then Crystal Weiss decided it was time to drive down to the Raintree and tell the poets. "The poets should know," she told her husband. "You stay here with the kids. I'm going to tell the poets."

"You shouldn't drive," he said, halfheartedly.

"It doesn't matter. I'm not drunk."

"Okay," he said and let her go. As soon as she left for the Raintree he went downstairs to his darkroom and began to print a roll of film he had taken when Francis was visiting them. It was a film of a Martin Luther King parade they had gone to with the poets. It began with a series of photographs of Francis eating breakfast in their dining room, smiling and charming everyone in sight. Manny cut off a negative of Francis sitting at the breakfast table and began to make a print. It was pitch-black dark in the darkroom and the face of the dead poet floated up in the developer, eyes first, then nose, then chin. "My God," Manny cried out loud and fled from the room. "This is nuts. What am I doing mixed up with these crazy people?" He left the print in the developer and ran up the stairs and into his little four-year-old girl's room. He covered her with a blanket and took off her shoes and turned off her television set and kissed her on the head. Then he went into his fourteen-year-old stepson's room and sat down beside him on the bed. "What are you watching?" he asked.

"Nothing," the boy said. "Is Francis really dead? Francis is dead? He said he was going to take me fishing. He said we were going camping on the White River. He said he was coming back."

Crystal Weiss drove drunkenly in the direction of the Raintree. No one at the Raintree knew yet that Francis had killed himself. No one knew anything except that the night was young and Johnny Vidacovich was coming to sit in with the band and they had plans for one another. Finley's plan was to get the married lady to leave him alone. Hopefully, to give him five thousand more dollars for the magazine and still leave him alone. The Jazz Poet had two plans, one, to get Finley and the rich lady to do a special issue of the magazine featuring only his poetry and, two, to get Sandy to take him up to Arkansas to meet Francis Alter.

The bartender, Charles Joseph, had a plan to write a novel about the whole bunch of them, using their real names and then taking them out later so they couldn't sue him. Maybe also change the name of the street and get his dad to edit it since his dad was a sober man who worked hard and taught school as well as being a poet. His dad was extremely worried about Charles Joseph wasting his youth tending bar. He'd be glad to edit a novel Charles Joseph wrote so he'd have a chance to get rich and make something of himself. If I could get a million dollars for a book I'd be in high cotton, Charles Joseph was thinking. I'd go off to the islands and never come back. I'd drink all day and play cards and get all that island pussy. What a lovely deal. Charles Joseph rubbed his rag across the bar, fixed drinks, opened beers, rang up charges on the cash register, whistling to himself, lost in island dreams, singing along with the music on the juke box. *Iko, Iko . . . Iko, Iko, Ole. Laissez les bon temps roule. Oh, those lonely, lonely nights. Oh, those lonely, lonely nights.*

About nine-thirty the rich lady, Jane Monroe, and her girl-friend, Allison, and her mother, Big Jane, who was even richer than her daughter, came breezing in the door. They stopped at the cash register to talk to Charles Joseph. "I don't know whether to get a table on the dance floor or the other room," Jane asked. "What do you think?"

"The dance floor," Charles Joseph said. "Johnny Vidacovich is sitting in. It might be the last time he ever plays here."

"This is so exciting," Big Jane said. "This reminds me of the south of France."

"Get a table, Momma," Jane said. "I've got to talk to Finley." She had spied him at the end of the bar talking to Sandy.

"What do you guys want to drink?" Charles Joseph asked.

"A martini," Big Jan answered. "Make it a double." She smiled a curved smile through her third face-lift, wrinkled what was left of the skin around her eyes. "I love martinis. And load it up with olives."

"Coming up." Charles Joseph smiled back, thinking about her tons of money, thinking about the story he had heard about her dancing naked on the bar at Lu and Charlie's. "Now that would be something to see," he said out loud.

"What?" Big Jane asked. "I don't understand."

"I heard you were a great dancer," he said. "I heard you could dance like everything."

"We'll try it later," she answered. The smile had straightened back out. She moved in. "Come try me out." She took the martini he offered her. "You look like your daddy," she added. "I knew him when he was young."

"Go to the table, Momma," Lady Jane said. "I'm going to talk to Finley. Come on, Allison." She pulled her guest down to the end of the bar where Sandy was telling stories of the great poet.

"He's the most beautiful man I ever knew," Sandy was saying. "He makes everything seem important. He read us poems, Yeats, Rilke, Rimbaud."

"Oh, my God," Jane said. "I'd give anything to hear him read. He won't give readings. Tulane offered him two thousand dollars and he wouldn't come. And here he is, down in Texas, reading to a bunch of kids. Oh, God, that's just like poetry."

"He made poetry seem the most wonderful thing in the world. I'm going up there to see him. I'm going to help him run some lines."

"I'm going too," the Jazz Poet put in. "He's going to call and ask if I can come. I worship Francis Alter. I worship at his shrine."

"He steals from black people," Finley muttered. "He steals everything he writes from them."

"Oh, sure," Jane said. It was her chance to pay him back for all the times he had never called her up. "Oh, sure, you're not jealous or anything, are you, Finley? You're so great, of course. Why would you be?"

"What are you doing here, Jane?" he answered. "What do you want with me?"

Crystal Weiss came into the Raintree and stood beside the cash register for moment watching the dancers in the adjoining room. Big Jane was jitterbugging with a martini glass in her hand. The wife of the owner of a steamship line was dancing with a tall skinny poet who taught at UNO. A fat poet was seated at a table with glasses all around him looking wise and cynical. He was the Fat Cynical

247

Poet. Many people were afraid of him. Johnny Vidacovich had shown up and was playing the drums like all hell had broken loose. The Piano Prince was playing standing up. I hate to tell them, Crystal thought. I don't know if I want to be the one to spread this. Of course she was dying to be the one to tell, dying to be known as the first one who knew, dying to be remembered as the great poet's friend. She arranged her face into a mask of sadness and mystery and despair and walked down the bar to where Finley was sitting between Jane Monroe and Sandy. "Can I talk to you?" she said. "I have to tell you something private." Jane Monroe flinched. Sandy admired the blonde intruder's long white dress and long white hair. Finley got up off the stool and walked with Crystal into the hall.

"What's up?" he asked. "What's happened?"

"Francis is dead. He shot himself. It's true. It's really true. I talked to James and to Sam. They saw it. People were in the house. He did it with people in the house."

"Oh, God, oh, my God."

"I know. Oh, Finley. He's gone. Gone forever." She let Finley take her into his arms and then she began to cry. Then the terrible news spread around the bar and into the adjoining room and the Fat Cynical Poet stood up and shook his head back and forth and the bartender opened himself a beer and the band began to play "The Saint James Infirmary Blues" as slowly as they could play and all the dancers stopped and stood around and looked each other over. A death had come among them. A poet had died by his own hand, had given the lie to all the gaiety and pussy and beer and poetry and jazz.

"Such a night," the Piano Prince began to play. *Sweet confusion under the moonlight.*

Richard Katrovas

From *Mystic Pig: A Novel of New Orleans*

From the streetcar, past Lowerline, then Cherokee toward Broadway, Nat glimpsed his best friend, Bart Linsey, who was on his back in the grass of the neutral ground by the tracks. They'd been best friends through elementary, junior high, and high school, stayed in close touch through college when Bart went off to UVA but came home every holiday, and about a third of the way into Nat's first marriage. After that, he'd get in touch every couple of years, and reuniting was always a highlight. He'd not heard from Bart in six years, since Nat, Lou, and Marti (and Edie, though no one knew it yet) had had him over for Thanksgiving six years ago. Nat sometimes forgot that he had a best male friend, but the shock of seeing Bart passed out, filthy—even from a moving vehicle he could see the filth—and emaciated awoke a powerful feeling of fealty.

Even as he ran he realized he'd left his workout bag on the streetcar. He patted his ass to feel his wallet, which he sometimes threw in the bag before leaving the house, and was relieved it was there. As he stood above Bart, with whom he'd had so little contact over the past decade, he caught an ugly whiff of physical degradation, alcohol, and piss. His hair and skin were filthy. The stench of his long-lost best friend reached into Nat and coiled around what little of the redfish he'd been able to get down in his agitation at lunch. Bart had likely not bathed in weeks, and there were sores on his lips and forehead. He wore a nice Italian suit, Gucci shoes, and a Rolex.

Bart had always dreamed of being a famous writer, had written hundreds of stories and poems in his teens, and indeed had begun to publish in some fairly respected venues through his twenties. He'd thrived on the local literary scene, and through his thirties had been a local literary lion, publishing poems in *The New Yorker* and in a thin, handsome collection of verse every couple of years. From a wealthy shipping family, Bart had been Nat's only friend growing up who'd come from a family more financially secure than Nat's own, and even as they'd drifted apart, Nat had delighted a little in Bart's literary successes as they were trumpeted from time to time in the *Times-Picayune* Sunday Book Section. He'd always wished Bart well with his ambitions, even as other guys, like that idiot Frank Mancini, Roberto Mancini's third son and Nat's and Bart's classmate at Morgan Heights, howled with laughter every time Bart "the poet" was mentioned. Frank was always quick to point out that only girls and faggots read poetry. Bart, a large athletic kid, would simply good-naturedly knock the shit out of Frank and continue chatting about Whitman. A big hit with the girls, Bart had transcended adolescent prejudices so effortlessly he'd been universally admired, even by Frank and his gang. The only one of Nat's friends from the neighborhood who'd also attended Morgan Heights, Bart had often held forth so eloquently the teachers themselves seemed enthralled. He'd taken that same class from the remarkable little Boston gnome the year before Nat, and had been asked to choose and read aloud a poem at the school's memorial service. He'd read "Ode on a Grecian Urn" in a peculiarly ironic tone, hamming it up as one might have at the beginning of the course. Then he'd recited section six of *Song of Myself* with a joyful and optimistic passion appropriate to the poem, and to the life of a man in love with beauty. Every shocked kid had been healed a little by that performance.

Nat'd tried to read one of Bart's earlier, more successful books, *Checking In At the Entropy Hotel*, while browsing through the Maple Street Bookstore, and had stood for twenty minutes puzzling through it. He'd wanted to buy it, but he simply couldn't justify laying down $18.95 for something which, clearly, he found mildly torturous to read. It had seemed to be smart stuff, even a little witty when comprehensible. But like so much modern and contemporary literature, the poems seemed in code for which Nat had not been supplied the key.

This sick man, so obviously close to death, was his best buddy with whom Nat had played chess and talked abstractly about life the whole summer of his fourteenth year. Then they'd discovered drugs together. How many joints had they smoked together? How many tabs of acid had they dropped? How many girls had they both, on different occasions, of course, "hosed," "popped," "porked"? Nat touched Bart's neck as he'd seen done in movies and felt immediately silly; Bart was heaving breaths, even snoring a little, and Nat didn't really know what he was feeling for. He certainly didn't like touching his old friend, and reflexively wiped his hand on his pant leg.

"Bart," he said and then again, louder, "Bart."

A young, black voice from behind him said that the dude was really fucked up, and then asked how Nat knew him.

Nat asked the boy—a beautiful, small kid holding a bicycle that had a basket on the handlebars spilling the ends of a plastic bag—if he knew this man, and the boy said yes, Bart was a poet, and he was Bart's muse. Nat asked the boy his name, and he said Willie. Nat said Willie what, and the kid said Willie None-your-goddamned-business, then corrected himself, saying it was Mr Willie None-your-goddamned-business.

Ok, Mr Willie, Nat said, and told the boy that he and Bart used to be best friends, that they'd hung out together a lot. Nat then said, with a desperation that was surprising to himself, that he couldn't just leave Bart like that, to which Mr Willie None-your-goddamned-business said it looked to him like Bart'd left himself like that.

Nat pressed again to know how the boy knew Bart; Willie knew Bart was a poet, but Nat didn't get the second part, that the boy was Bart's muse. From his crouch over Bart, he stared hard into the child's eyes to see the truth. Nat was particularly worried about Bart's Rolex.

Willie said again that Bart was a poet, and that he, Willie, was his muse. Then Willie pointed at a large, white house and said that was where Bart lived. Nat recognized it as an old mansion that had recently been converted into expensive apartments.

Then the boy said that Bart gave him good money to buy him booze from over there, but now Bart had four big boxes of booze so he wouldn't be needing Willie for that anymore, or at least for a while.

Nat did not pursue the assertion that a child was being allowed to purchase liquor from a convenience store, but asked Willie where he lived. Willie answered by asking where he lived, to which Nat answered that he lived only a few blocks away, on Pine. Nat rose and formally introduced himself, extending his hand. Willie let his hand disappear, limp, in Nat's large white hand.

Then Nat asked if Bart lived with anyone, and Willie just stared down and asked Nat if Bart looked like he lived with anyone, and Nat felt ridiculous for having asked the question.

Nat stared down at the dying man; Bart had been one of his most important teachers, the way certain soul-quickened peers help focus the world in adolescence as numb adults may not. He simply couldn't leave Bart there. He asked Willie to help him, said he'd pay Willie for his help. Willie asked how much, and Nat said five bucks, and Willie pointed out that the dude was pretty stinky, and Nat said ten, and Willie said okay.

Nat managed to sit Bart up; Bart's eyes rolled back in his head at first, and Nat figured the best thing would simply be to call an ambulance, but realized he'd left his cell phone in his workout bag. He said shit under his breath, then got a couple of quarters out of his pocket and, holding them out to Willie, told him to go over to the payphone and call an ambulance.

"Am I tenured?" Bart blurted.

"What?" Nat said, and Willie said Bart meant dead, that he always said that when he meant dead.

"No, you're not tenured," Nat said earnestly, recalling that Bart had taught for several years at Loyola. Nat recalled, too, the title of Bart's most recent volume, *Teach Me How To Die*, favorably reviewed in the *Times-Picayune*.

"My mother died," Bart said.

"I'm sorry to hear that," Nat said, a bit startled by the non sequitur. Bart's mother, though stiffly patrician, had always been kind to Nat, seeing him as a positive influence on Bart, whom she had seemed to dislike as one might dislike an expensive heirloom.

"Why?" Bart asked, and it seemed he was expecting an answer, until he said, "excuse me," then turned his head and spewed a reddish torrent onto the grass as Willie moaned and turned away. "Died in her sleep," Bart continued. "She did not deserve to die in her sleep," he finished. The crimson bile dripped down his cheek. "I'd like to stare upon a large body of water as I die. Preferably the ocean, but the lake will do. Will you take me to Lake Pontchartrain? I fancied organ music a moment ago, but now I want to look at the lake."

"Why don't we get you home, clean you up, and call a cab? You need to be in a hospital," Nat said.

"Never!" Bart yelled, suddenly enlivened. "I'll never return to one of those foul places. People die there, you know," he said, but his gallows humor was lost on Nat, who sought the least filthy part of him to grasp and lift. Bart was startlingly light.

Cowboy-style, Nat had one of Bart's once-muscular, now frail arms over his own neck, and Willie served as a kind of walking stick, Bart's quivering hand lightly grasping Willie's skull for balance as Willie walked his bike. They got him across the tracks, the double left lane of St Charles, but nearly dropped him as they squeezed awkwardly through the low gate to the house. Hobbling up the porch steps Bart crashed to his knees, but recovered, under the circumstances, almost gracefully.

Once they'd wedged through the main entrance of Bart's building, which to Nat's surprise was unlocked, Willie led them down a sour hall to a door that was opened a crack.

As Nat gently dumped his rank cargo onto the sofa, he marveled at how relatively well kept the apartment was, in dramatic contrast to its occupant. The furniture was an odd though tasteful mixture of modern and art deco, with much fine wood that had been recently polished. Two broad bookshelves that reached almost to the twelve-foot ceiling were packed and orderly, and as Nat glanced at them, obviously alphabetized. "You need a bath, pal," Nat said.

"I need a drink," Bart corrected. "Willie, fetch me a bottle from the top case over there," Bart ordered, and Willie said he didn't fetch for anyone.

"Take a twenty out of the cookie jar, then, and bring me a bottle, my little friend."

"Who in God's name sells liquor to a child?" Nat blurted, and Willie said that his mama owned the store across the street, and she knew who the booze was for. Willie added that she often came over and helped Bart out.

"Help out how?" Nat inquired, and Willie said he should look around and ask himself if he thought Bart was keeping this place looking so nice.

"The cookie jar," Bart reminded Willie.

Willie reminded Nat that he owed Willie ten bucks. Nat peeled a ten from his clip. Then Willie headed for the kitchen.

"Cool it," Nat said. "This guy doesn't need any more booze. I'll make him some coffee and try to get some food in him." Nat wheeled into the kitchen and yanked open the fridge: a withered grapefruit, a small jar containing a few green olives suspended in a filmy liquid, two plastic bottles of Canada Dry tonic water, and an all-but-empty Hellmann's jar.

There was indeed a cookie jar. Nat lifted the round belly of the jolly brown bear: packed with twenties. Nat plucked one out. "Mr Willie, run across the street and get a quart of milk and some saltines. Keep the change."

Nat called Lou at the shop, told her he wouldn't be able to pick up Edie and wasn't sure if he'd be able to make the game with Marti tonight. He told her he'd run into Bart, and needed to help him with something. She was mildly upset he'd not be able to pick up Edie because some customers were lingering and she wasn't sure she'd be able to get them out in time to close the shop twenty minutes early, but she heard the edge in his voice, and didn't press; then he called Birdsong to remind her that several thousand Shriners were in town so she should probably order three or four extra butts from Benny, because those old boys suck down a few raw oysters as a concession to local color then go straight for the red meat.

"You're a busy fellow," Bart observed, his torso slumped forward and to the right, held up by the couch arm. His eyes were closed. Nat strode back into the kitchen and looked into the cupboard over the sink, and then the one over the immaculate electric stove—Nat guessed that it had never been turned on—and found an unopened jar of Community instant. It stood between a battered paperback of *Atlas Shrugged* and a huge jar of pickled pig's feet that at first glance Nat thought, startled, contained a fetus. The cupboards were otherwise empty, except for numerous roach motels. There was a pot on the sink; Nat put on some water to boil, and looked around for a cup. Next to the happy bear was a mug with PERFECTION SUCKS stenciled in black on its glossy vanilla surface, and numerous pencils and pens sticking out of it which Nat dumped on the counter. He rinsed the mug in the sink.

He put the strong brew on the coffee table in front of Bart, at first looking around for a coaster then feeling stupid for doing so.

"Lord," Bart breathed, his eyes still closed, his face propped by his left elbow so that the heel of his hand held his cheek, pushing it into his eye socket. "What is that foul aroma?"

"Drink it," Nat ordered, "then take your clothes off."

"But darling, we haven't even kissed," Bart quipped, not opening his eyes or moving. Nat began to assist Bart with his jacket and then his pants. Bart turned into a stinking rag doll. When Nat'd gotten him down to his sock (he'd only been wearing the left one) and unspeakably disgusting briefs, he trotted into the bathroom and started the hot water.

He let Bart stew languidly for awhile, checking often to be sure he'd not slipped under.

Three empty aspirin bottles lay on their sides in the medicine cabinet; one half-full stood upright. Nat sprinkled five or six into his palm. When Willie returned, Nat forced Bart to swallow the aspirins and wash them down with big swallows of the cold milk. Then, while Bart still sprawled in the tub, he forced him to eat some crackers and swallow some more milk. To Nat's mild astonishment, Bart kept it all down. Then Nat made him swallow the now-cool coffee, and even with this it all stayed down.

Nat reached in and drained almost all the filthy water, then ran some more up to Bart's chest. On his own initiative, Bart actually dug out with his long filthy nails a petrified sliver of soap that had eons ago molecularly bonded with the crusty chrome. He began to wash himself. Nat drained the tub twice more, and reminded his old friend to get his hair, which, awkwardly with the soap sliver, Bart did until Nat found an all-but-empty Head & Shoulders bottle, filled it with hot water, and anointed Bart's greasy head with the suds of the shampoo residue. Then he gingerly rubbed the suds in, then poured clean hot water over Bart's head with a bucket from under the sink. Bart's body resembled the photographs of ancient carcasses scooped from bogs, and Nat did not doubt that the man was dying.

As Bart, revived, began to dress himself in quite nice clothes that no longer fit him, Nat glanced out the front window. One of the smaller parades, a new one on a route that had never been tried before—skimming down St Charles from Carrollton before turning onto Nashville—would roll in a few hours; people were already milling about, staking out prime spots for families: coolers, ladders with jerrybuilt seats for the wee ones, lawn chairs, and blankets. Willie turned and pumped down Broadway.

"When did you come to this, Boo?" Nat asked gently, using his private name for his old friend. Nat had told him, after a long discussion about *Catcher In the Rye* one summer evening on Nat's porch, that Bart scared the living shit out of him sometimes. Bart had laughed, then ceased suddenly, made his eyes big and wild, and said in a voice so soft as to be barely audible, "Boo."

"Difficult to say," he replied. "I got on the ol' slippery slope about twenty years ago. Things went really bullshit just over a year ago." He fell back upon the sofa, closed his eyes.

"What happened?"

"What usually happens to destroy one's self-esteem and crush one's life?"

"A woman kicked your ass. You fell in love and got your heart stomped," Nat guessed.

"I was in love, old friend, and my heart got crushed. But it had nothing to do with a woman, except in some psychosexual sense. I mean, if one wishes to factor my warped affections for Mother into the nasty little equation, one may. I certainly don't."

Nat stared at him. Bart's head was pressed back against the wall over the sofa cushion. His eyes remained shut. He was so thin his once barrel chest was sunken. Not all the sores on this body, Nat suddenly realized, were the wounds of an unsteady drunk. His color was ghastly. Glancing at Bart when he was folded into the tub, Nat had assumed, with shivers, that he was witnessing the result of life wholly in the bottle. "You taking medication?" he finally asked? "AZT? Any of that stuff?"

No answer. Half a minute passed. Nat sat down. "You've got lots of money. You could've lived a long time."

"Money money money . . ." Bart breathed, eyes closed, tapping his finger on the arm of the couch as he chanted. "Money money everywhere and n'er a drop to drink," he mumbled. "I need a drink, Natty."

Katheryn Krotzer Laborde

From "The Ballad of Waltzing John"

On a broader scale I'm talking about Waltzing John Elliot. I remember the first time I saw him: it was a hot May night, a Saturday night, that first night at the Leaf. My second week in town. The smoke was heavy and the rockabilly band was blasting. John had his head on the bar; his hair was matted with sweat and dandruff. I thought he was a bum, but you said he was an artist. A poet. And, desperate for money, he had talked you into sponsoring the weekly poetry readings which started the next day. You had faith that a spiffed-up John and the hush of poetry on a Sunday afternoon would bring a touch of class to the Leaf. I remember the first reading well: it was the first time in my life I understood poetry.

He was so clean and confident I didn't recognize him. He walked straight up to the mike, book in hand, smiling at the ten or so of us gathered in the back, slouching as well as you can slouch in those cast iron chairs, propping our feet on those cast iron tables. He smiled, introduced himself, spoke in that puffed-up way he has—had—quoting this poet and that, and somehow charming the pants off every woman in the process. He was so relaxed, so striking in the warm spring light, oblivious to the sluggish whir of the ceiling fan above. And when he opened *Mad Man's Waltz* and read "Descent," I felt myself leaning toward him, watching his mouth as he read, aware only of his broad-bowed mouth and the mosaic of words that poured through it: some funny, many self-deprecating, but all addressed *To Fiona,* all based on the pain that seared his life so completely.

That first reading was before *we* were an item (before that time, our time, I watched you, memorized your every move, your silent laugh, your heavy language of hands). After the readings caught on, became fashionable even, you were impressed by the "brainy Joes" who flocked to the Leaf on a regular basis. I still remember the night you brought in that chessboard (John called it your idea of an intellectual face lift) because you asked me: *Well, Malou, do you think people will mind playing chess in the window?* I thought they might. All I could picture was sweaty people, sitting in a window that faced west on a hot afternoon, cursing the heat and each other. But I turned my vision to cooler seasons, evening tournaments, and I said what you wanted to hear. You led me from the bar and together we arranged that faded table, the mismatched chairs, sliding our shoulders to the music of the Tex-Mex band.

I caught John watching us that night—lining up those little pieces in the window, laughing because we didn't know the first thing about setting up a chessboard. He was shaking his head. It's funny to think I was in love with you at that point. I mean, *right now* I hate your guts, hated you the moment I saw you out with that girl, the one who works across the street from the Leaf (what's her name? Deenie? Jeanie? I walked into Kaldi's the Friday before last and saw you, saw her, all cozy in the corner. I saw your beady little eyes bulge out of their sockets and down her blouse).

Maybe I was never really in love with you to begin with. Maybe I just really needed someone in my life at the time, and I tried to force you into that role. Maybe the sex was enough. For a while. But I need more in my life than a weekend Romeo. John knew that.

God, I miss that shabby coat, the hunched shoulders, the shaggy beard, the most beautiful egg-blue eyes I've ever seen. I miss the way he wrote in frantic spurts on paper napkins. I can see him now: quoting Byron into a glass of Scotch, eyeing tight-assed college girls, napping and drooling on the bar. . . .

William S. Maddox

Summers

But there was another world, connected only accidentally to family, related to the world of Planton, Alabama, only in the sense that it was an escape from it. It existed in space (the Bowies' acre on the highway to Birmingham) and in time (the summers of the late fifties and early sixties) but mostly it existed in imagination, for what it really was was nothing at all. What it could be, to Jake and Eddie left alone by their parents and rarely visited by friends over summer vacation, was everything, whatever they could dream it to be. Their minds fed on each other's and what began as a thought, a whim, became a version of reality, an edifice, an image clear and emotionally charged, strong enough to last for decades.

They usually rolled out of the double bed with a built-in book-case Edward had made for a headboard about 7:30 on summer mornings. Their room was a small rectangle with space only for a bed, a chest of drawers on Eddie's side, and on Jake's side a small rolltop desk with pigeonholes, most of them empty, although one was stuffed with clipped-out Pogo cartoons from the *Birmingham News* that he liked to reread often, fascinated by Walt Kelly's tinkering with the language. There was a window at the head of the bed and the foot, and, after a space of about four feet, two small closets with curtains for doors. Each boy had his own closet and, although Joan hung up their clothes for them, she never bothered the litter that accumulated on the floor so that in time the flinging back of the curtain released an aroma of discarded toys, books, piles of papers, magazines, unidentifiable stuff, musty odors of the years. Off to the left of the bedroom was another small room where Edward had built desks for them, actually a set of planks nailed to two-by-fours on either side of the room, each jealously defined as Jake's or Eddie's and buried under more clutter: papers, scribblings and drawings, beginnings of stories handwritten or, after they got an old manual Royal machine that Edward brought home from work, typed, inky and usually smudged. Living among the papers were books, old magazines, and again toys in various stages of disrepair and neglect. At the end of the room was a four-by-four window that looked into the living room. Through the judicious placement of a mirror on the front living room wall, the window allowed Edward to sit in his chair on the right side of the living room and see straight through all the way into their bedroom.

The first steps of the day usually led into that living room where Joan had left the television on before returning to her room which she would leave only to make lunch and later to cook a late afternoon supper. The set was always on, tuned to the Today show, a collage overseen by Dave Garroway and including both Jack Lescoulie reading sports and Frank Blair droning the news once every half hour at the sleepy gawkers from the street who pressed their faces to the picture window that looked into the studio. The show was populated at other times by the simian star J. Fred Muggs, assorted other animals, singers, pianists, show business people, political figures and, once in a great while and to the boys' delight, a writer, never anyone they had heard of but a writer nonetheless. Jake and Eddie's world in the summers began with the idea of writers more than with writing, the idea of books even more than what was in them, the love affair with words printed on a page that began with both of them as soon as they could read a few lines. But even when there were no writers, they watched the Today show until it went off at eight. They loved the shots of the picture window because the people there, whether they held up funny signs or just stared blankly, whether they were tourists up early or locals on their way to work, were in New York City, a magical place so far from the Bowies' acre in central Alabama that it might have been in another solar system.

The living room was arranged simply and always the same, even though the particular items of furniture might vary from time to time. As they entered from their side of the house, the boys saw a chair beside Jake's window and then a low two-shelf bookcase Edward had built to house the encyclopedia bought at the grocery store one volume at a time. Across the front wall there was a window, then an old Zenith television sitting on a dark brown stand with the oval black-rimmed mirror hanging over it. Next to it was the front door which opened on to a small screened-in porch, and past the door in the corner an old black bookcase with glass doors, filled with the boys' books from the 1920s and a few classics, a gift from Edward's father before he died. Along the right wall there was always a sofa and in the corner of the room Edward's chair, a big overstuffed monstrosity that lived in the same spot throughout Jake's childhood. Next to Edward's chair was the door into the dining room, then a space heater, and finally Joan's chair in front of the window into the boys' room.

The bookcase contained the most important object in the entire house to the boys, in a sense the wellspring of the world they created: the encyclopedia. For once it was there, it became like a Bible to both of them, one that told them great truths about the world beyond Planton. They read the histories of nations, short biographies of world statesmen and geniuses. They scoured through the maps and virtually memorized the articles on major cities like New York, Paris, London. But most importantly, they found that scattered through these volumes were articles on major writers. Jake had loved reading and the feel and smell of books since he could first read one, just as Eddie had, but that love took on a new and romantic dimension after he stumbled across the biographies of the men themselves: William Faulkner, distinguished and silver-haired with arrogant mustache and labeled experimental and Gothic and Southern (like him!); Sinclair Lewis, dour and depressed with cigarette burning by the side of his face and wonderfully simple titles in italics; Jack London, windswept and rebellious in leather and aura of madness; Ernest Hemingway, looking younger than the pictures they sometimes saw on television or in *Life* magazine, with dark mustache and angry warm eyes that spoke of drinking bouts and egomania and exotic places like Paris and Havana and yet still tied somehow to the Michigans of the world, the Kansas City side of life (could it be that some of these people, these gods, came from places not unlike Planton?); even the plodding Theodore Dreiser, baldish and professorial, who scandalized with realism the regular-normal-America places of his youth; and John Dos Passos, with name from who knows where and face like any man not a god and his wildly experimental USA, a country not at all like Planton, Alabama. Then the more tragic, the ethereal, the pained and dying young: Scott Fitzgerald, successful and well-paid but always broke, often drunk, penning anthems of a time that died before it began but not only a writer and traveler and drinker like Hemingway but had set foot in Alabama! had walked on same earth and concrete as Alabama humans did on Friday nights while going shopping and their grandmother Emmaline, once a flapper of sorts herself, claimed to have met Zelda! (as did everyone else in Montgomery who was alive during that decade); and Thomas Wolfe, gangly in body and style and youthfully dead with brain exploded like one of his paragraphs but born in North Carolina (raised in small city? got away? got out? escaped? could not go home again?).

And then there were those from other lands (he could turn to the maps) like Marcel Proust, writer of the gigantic, the novel that never ends, dark and sickly and alone, glaring expectantly from France and from the grave at a child in Alabama; Franz Kafka, from another time and continent, hiding behind death and mystery and difficult frightening novels with emotionless titles, trying to say something to two boys helplessly trapped in the red clay hills. Did not that page in Volume JKL have something different about it, a lingering vapor from a musty bureaucrat's silent rebellion left to those of later eras he would not live to see? Did not that particular page, like those of Faulkner and the rest, emit some secret message that the preceding page and the one after did not? And there, buried away in the same JKL volume, a craggy man behind dense glasses and impenetrable gaze who went by the name James Joyce (most experimental-everyman-epic theme-streamofconsciousness-mostinfluential-bawdysomewhatscandalous-Liffeycrazed-pome-granatecomparing-bloompicking-Lover of the Language(s). Could his page, the pages of other writers, possibly be made of the same paper and print as those of mere statesmen and wars and species of plant and animal? Nonsense, he thought, and he was hooked.

They dreamed of other things as well, read about painters and painting and their bohemian life (Impressionists and rebellion in oil, then home-leavers for Tahitian escape and plodders into the earth) and for a while played with Edward's paints, created master-pieces of youthful idiocy (if Jackson Pollock can do it), then read of the great composers very Russian and very German, romantic and tragic (deaf, dead, drunk, poor, outcast) and pretended to be Beethoven by mussing their hair and staring wildly unable to hear Tchaikovsky by wrapping themselves in heavy winter coats even though it was in the 90s in July, and listened in the sweltering after-noons to the classical station out of Montgomery, talked of writing symphonies and living in Berlin or Vienna. But they always came back to the writers, the titles, the names, the photographs in the encyclopedia.

With their fifty cents a week allowance each of them saved for books which they ordered by mail from the Dexter Book Store on Dexter Avenue in Montgomery. They discovered the Modern Library; it became their guide and with books at $1.95 and Modern Library Giants at $2.95 plus postage, they could order several apiece every summer. In time they acquired a small library hidden away in a small rough house on the highway to Birmingham that no one that drove by, even if they were aware of the titles or knew the names of Faulkner, Proust, Lewis, Joyce, or Hemingway, could have imagined was there. Edward and Joan never encouraged them, never discouraged them, never asked what was in the books or inspected them, not even when *Ulysses* came and the boys raced from the mailbox by the highway, tearing the package open as they went, back to their bedroom and turned first to read what Molly Bloom yes had to say and they found words yes like bitch and whore and yes and breasts and yes naked.

When they left the house through the rectangular porch with tattered screens and green lizards hanging dumbly on the door, out to the ten-by-ten slab of cement that Edward called the patio, they first saw the cats lounging there with white matted fur and pink tongues hanging out, a lineage founded by Rhubarb, a big tabby, and White Kitty, a Persian given to them by Aunt Ellen. The brood grew over the years into an inbred mongrelized race that included Smokey, a gigantic long-haired black cat whose ebony fur appeared to rust in the summertime sun, turn reddish and hazy before their eyes as he sat in the high grass at dusk and jumped at grasshoppers as they lept suicidally through their evolutionarily-appointed rounds. Then there was Yellow, a big orange male who regularly practiced cat incest with his mother, producing various litters of runts and kittens who died and an occasional survivor like Beauregard, a tiny bluish-gray who never grew beyond his size at four months, had a slight limp, and had to be protected from the others, and a succession of other white cats, most of them female, all of whom were named White Kitty when they were small because then they were easily distinguished from their mother, but came in time to form a harem of litter-producers that all looked alike, bore the same name, and served the same function.

The cats were interesting to watch and talk about but they were not magic. And when the two boys looked beyond the cats, they saw only the ordinary: a slight rise between the house and the highway which was broken only by spotty browned Bermuda grass and a couple of stunted oaks and a smattering of other trees. Flower beds with petunias, geraniums, begonias, and sweet-williams lined the right side of the yard. A slat fence ran from the north side of the house to form a side yard where they sometimes kept a dog and which was home for the optimistic morning glory vine that smiled deepest blue flowers at the wooden swing in front of the side yard. Beyond the gravel driveway on the left side of the yard, two giant pines stood over a hundred feet high, then on the far edge of the rise lived a sickly chinaberry tree and a cedar which Edward adorned every holiday season with colored lights which he forgot to take down until June. Beyond those trees was a twenty foot stretch of gravel scattered across red clay between the rise and the shoulder of the highway that steamed and made bluish-gray mirages of haze in the summer sun. But there was no magic in the yard either. The magic was in the books inside and in the mind of Eddie, thin and nervous like his mother, blackhaired and blue-eyed with dark eyebrows and slim face, moody and petulant but driven by a desire to go somewhere, be something, learn more than anyone else had ever learned, find some place on the planet the romance and excitement that books and music promised. And it was in the mind of Jake, who looked like his brother plus twenty pounds, with the same hair and eyes, small nose and lips, but with cheeks puffy and red, arms flabby, stomach protruding, legs slow and heavy, who devoured every dream and idea his brother could provide and then searched for more in the books, in the music, in the old movies, Jake who never entirely believed he had been born in the right place.

They walked the acre all day and also the surrounding acres, overgrown with vines and kudzu, thick with pines and oaks, some stricken dead by lightening with uprooted bottoms of bug-filled pungent red earth, the ground carpeted with years of pine straw that rustled with unseen birds and reptiles. They walked for hours and talked of other places, cities, countries, pretended that their acre was a country all its own, named and renamed it, imagined the cats as the royal family, talked of writers and writing, painters and painting, musicians and music.

Now and then they talked about God even though Edward never forced any religious beliefs on them, only took them with him to church on Sunday mornings as any parent would do but did not take them back again on Sunday and Wednesday evenings. They decided that they believed in God, they had to believe in God, because of what they saw around them every day—the trees, the flowers, the cats, the sky—and what they felt inside when they dreamed of other places and other lives and, if for no other reason, because of the vastness of the planet and of history. But they could not bring themselves to believe the Jesus story they heard every Sunday. It was more than a little far-fetched but, more importantly, it was not necessary to believe it to believe in nature or writing or New York City or the eighteenth century. Once one of these discussions led naturally to the topic of death. Jake asked Eddie what he though it was like after you were dead and when Eddie answered, "Nothing, it's just dark," Jake felt empty inside and never brought it up again. But they never talked about their mother who over the years worked less with those flower beds in the summer and whose meals became simpler and more predictable every year and who left the acre very rarely now, then later left her room filled with cigarette smoke and tension less and less or about their father who was always at work or choking down a quick meal or asleep.

After Edward surprised them one day by bringing home an ancient Royal manual typewriter, black and heavy and permanent even though it had been discarded from the office at the gin shop, they began to write simple stories on it, took turns typing out one and two page tales, mostly dialogue, often dirty. Then after they ordered through the mail from an advertisement in *Time* magazine a book that contained plot summaries from one hundred great novels, they began to write parodies of the books as soon as they had devoured the plots. They did not write as themselves but pretended that each of the cats had taken on the personality of a writer or several writers. White Kitty, debauched and vaguely decadent as far as cats go, became Fitzgerald and Eddie wrote parodies of him under her name. Smokey, the moody and dark-souled cat of the dusk, became Faulkner-Dostoyevski and penned feline epics patterned after *The Sound and the Fury* and *The Brothers Karamazov*, although it was Jake who pounded the keys. Eddie crawled inside the imaginary but nonetheless bawdy personality of Rhubarb to become James Joyce and write the Ulyssean epic—it spanned ten typewritten pages—of a day in the life of Everycat. They shared the personage of Beauregard whose sickly nature paralleled Proust in Eddie's "Remembrance of Cats Past" but whose furtive paranoia drove him to write "The Catsle" with Jake's Kafkaesque help. Even the big lusty Yellow emerged on the page as Hemingway to write a short and crisp "The Tail Also Rises." They read the stories to each other repeatedly in the long summer afternoons and the stories became myths and the personalities were engraved in the faces of the whiskered and unsuspecting pseudo-authors. Jake and Eddie sat in the swing to read the stories; they laughed and forgot the heat, snickered at the dirty lines they barely understood and forgot their isolation, told and retold the stories of their characters wandering feline but human through the streets of Paris, New York, Dublin, or St. Petersburg and forgot the barren wooden house only a few feet away. They forgot the dusty shoulders of the sizzling homeless highway out front and the acres of nothingness around them, surrounded by the miles of county road and desperate inbred families who clustered around flickering television sets in the afternoon to watch game shows and soap operas while the two boys rewrote literature on a typewriter with a tail. They forgot the counties beyond Autauga that made up the state of Alabama, wooded, verdant, mountainous, redearthed and blueskyed but mean, barren of spirit, hating, living in a failed past and dreading the future, reeking of racism and ignorance and intolerance, nervously hostile to the world beyond that state line. Jake and Eddie sailed over that state line every morning and dreamed of never crossing it again.

Only twice during their childhood did their parents try to take them away from the acre by interrupting the summer routine with an attempt at a normal family vacation. Edward got two weeks off a year from the gin shop but usually used them to do extra sign-painting work or to make additions or repairs to the house. He disliked time off from work, had no use for vacations. Joan, faced with the prospect of having to leave the house, stay somewhere else a few days, and be around strangers, disliked the idea of a vacation as much as Edward but she became obsessed with the idea that the boys needed it because they kept to themselves too much during the summer. Edward resisted, complained that they could not afford it and that the car would not make any long trips but Joan persisted and Eddie jumped into the argument whenever he could. His friends took vacations with their parents and he wanted to be like his friends. Jake had only the vaguest notion of what a vacation was but was caught up in Eddie's enthusiasm and begged for it along with him.

In the summer of 1957, Edward gave in, and they drove down the state highway into Florida and then to the beach at Ft. Walton. They spent three days in a pastel-colored cheap motel on the beach. Joan could only stand the sun for a few minutes at a time because it made her stomach queasy. She could not find anything she could eat in the little cafes and hamburger joints they tried. Eddie got sunburned and complained that they had never taught him to swim. Edward hated every minute of it, was restless the whole time, spent most of the day in the room watching television, and never even took his shirt off outside.

As soon as they had checked in, Jake settled into a vinyl-covered chair and enjoyed the sweet-smelling air conditioning in the room, the neatly matched furniture, and the carpet under his feet. At first he wanted to stay in the room but after Eddie coaxed him outside and he caught his first view of the Gulf of Mexico he was transfixed. Everything he had yet seen on earth came to an end—the bend in the highway beyond his house, the acre where they lived, even the woods around their house stopped at one road or another. But this relentless rolling water in front of him had no end; it was his ability to see far enough that gave out before the Gulf did. They had to hound him to come inside to keep from getting sunburned. He splashed in the surf, picked up shells, and drew patterns in the sand, but his eyes always returned to that horizon, something so much larger and unlimited than he was that he felt not threatened but comforted. But Jake could not express what he felt to the others; the sense of peace and joy it brought remained inside him. On the evening of the third day, they drove home in exhausted silence; nobody mentioned a vacation next summer.

Two years later, Joan suggested another vacation because she never got to see her mother, who was getting too old to ride the bus from Montgomery to Planton. She did not get along well with her mother, who nagged her about her health, her nerves, and her poor eating habits, but she was still her mother. Joan wanted to spend more time with her because she did not expect her to be around for many more years. Edward surprised them all by suggesting a weekend vacation. They could drive to Montgomery, he explained, spend a weekend in a hotel downtown, Joan could visit Emmaline while the boys explored the city, and he would not have to miss any time from work.

They checked into the Whitney Hotel on Montgomery Street on Friday night. They walked through the lobby that was decorated with plush red carpet and waist-high brass planters with ferns and were shown to a double room by a bellboy who was at least fifty. Jake and Eddie pretended that they were not in Montgomery at all but were staying in a hotel in Manhattan, having miraculously both won the Pulitzer Prize for fiction that year. Their parents let them roam the hotel for an hour. They stalked the halls like detectives, trying to learn everything about hotels they could, as if a hotel was some mysterious private club that had to be penetrated in secret. When they saw a nameplate on a door and realized that some people actually lived in hotels, they were awestricken. They peered around corners at Negro maids pushing bundles of sheets in hampers but ran away before they could be seen. They marveled at room service leftovers lying decadent and discarded on the floor: wadded cloth napkins, unopened packages of crackers which they stole and ate, and a small drained half-pint of whiskey which they took into an alcove, smelled, and licked around the cap. They staggered playfully down the hall and laughed so hard that they could not stop, still giggled uncontrollably in the room and made their parents laugh even though Joan and Edward had no idea what was so funny.

The first night they saw Emmaline. She lived now with three other elderly ladies in an older home on the east side of town, surviving on her late husband's railroad pension and the proceeds of the sale of her rooming house. Her two rooms on the first floor were filled with heavy ancient furniture of cedar; the pieces dwarfed her as she moved past them, now bent and tiny with her dull gray hair bunned on her head, the little eyes darting madly but without the old fire, her lips and cheeks puckered around the false teeth which she removed later in the evening, but with an oval smear of rouge on each cheek just as she had worn it as a youngster. The adults talked for hours while Jake and Eddie squirmed, bored, on various items of furniture. They fell asleep on the bed next to their grandmother before the conversation ended and had to be carried to the car and then into the hotel.

On Saturday morning, Edward gave them enough money to see a movie at the house across the street, the same theater where he had met Joan almost two decades earlier, then a little more for snacks at the movie and hamburgers at a diner at the end of the block. He charged Eddie with responsibility for his younger brother and promised that if they stayed on the block for the day then the next day they could go around the corner and see Dexter Avenue by themselves. He then drove Joan back to her mother's, left her cab money back to the hotel, and disappeared for the day.

It was only one block in Montgomery, Alabama, but for Jake and Eddie, it might as well have been all the cities in the world. They walked up and down for hours, watched the taxicabs letting fares out at the hotel, followed street vendors selling newspapers, stared at men in suits and elegantly dressed women coming out of restaurants, and gawked with the same fascination at a no-legged beggar with face as confused and poorly formed as his cardboard sign. They lost themselves in the plush maroon seats of the theater, threw popcorn at each other, saw bits and pieces of the Disney movie on the screen, and were roundly shushed by everyone around them. Afterward they went to the diner at the end of the block and sat at the counter (Jake's chin barely cleared it) while a tolerant older waitress with her hair in a net brought them greasy square little hamburgers with onions cooked into them. They buried them in catsup and washed them down with cokes, slushy and cold and tasting of carbonation which the waitress refilled until they could drink no more. They stood outside until it was dark, admiring the neon signs that blinked into waking, then rushed upstairs to find Joan already in the room—she had had enough of Emmaline—but Edward not yet there. They stretched out on the bed and watched television with Joan on the other bed but fell asleep early. They woke up a little when Edward came in smelling of smelling they did not know was Miller High Life, but were too tired to listen to the hushed but bitter argument that began.

There was a queasy tension in the room the next morning as the four of them packed bags and took baths. They knew from the terse conversation that their father had gone to a bar and drank beer all day, that Joan was furious, that they would be glad to get home and disappear into the peaceful thickets surrounding their home while their parents fought. But they begged to be given the promised time on Dexter Avenue, persisted even through the strained talk of their parents. Finally, Edward gave them an hour, no more. They were down the elevator and around the corner in five minutes. They only glanced up the sloping avenue which was crowned by the state capitol, replica of the one in Washington but symbol of the Confederacy and its resistance, adorned with both the Alabama flag and the battle flag of the rebel troops. They sought another symbol and quickly located the Dexter Book Store about halfway down the block. It was only fifteen feet wide with a narrow door flanked by two small display windows with the latest bestsellers standing at attention for passersby. Eddie pushed on the brass handle and they were inside. The smell of newsprint greeted them from the stacks of Sunday papers just inside the front door. Along the walls were tightly packed shelves of glistening book covers. Almost every foot of space between those walls was occupied by ceiling-high shelves bursting with the smell of crisp printed paper, glue, and slick book jackets. The entire room, narrow and darker toward the back but bookstuffed there as well, had the same aroma that thrilled Jake when a new book came in the mail and he opened it deadcenter, spread the sticky pages apart and thrust his face deeply into the inner margins and inhaled. They walked reverently through the shelves until they came to a glass counter about halfway into the store. Behind it a bemused Jewish man about sixty with heavy eyelids and drooping lower lip stood watching them with his arms folded across his chest. Eddie walked up to the counter and explained that they were the ones from Planton, Birmingham Highway, Box 134, who ordered all the books.

"You?" he smiled. He let his arms down and smoothed the front of his rumpled gray suit. "You're Eddie Bowie? And Jake Bowie?" He laughed a long deep chuckle. "Well, I'll be damned. I'll be just damned." He looked at them for a moment, still smiling. "Well, you boys just look around. Just look around all you want to." He extended one arm toward the back of the store.

They each kept an eye on the big black and white clock with the relentless red second hand on the back wall of the store; they knew they had less than an hour. But they prowled through the store and tried to forget about going home to Planton. They found an entire set of shelves with nothing but Modern Library editions and forgot about the anticipated silent ride home and the endless questioning that would certainly keep them awake that night as Joan begged to understand why Edward had done something he had never done before, why he had sat in a dreary bar with a whining juke box and drank beer all day with only Hank Williams for company. They opened one thick hardbacked book after another and forgot about the lonely acre and the sad noble trees that stood uncomplaining and without rendering judgment on the family that lived there beneath them. Eddie found a volume of the complete works of Shelley and Keats and lost himself completely. Jake pulled every Faulkner book off the shelf he could find; he read the first two or three lines and glanced at the back cover of each one. Just as the clock neared the hour, he found a clean new copy of *The Sun Also Rises* and pulled it down. He smelled it, he held it at his side as if he was walking down the street with it, and as he opened it in the middle and spread the book apart, the pages crackled with the sounds of Paris.

Bill Roberts

From "Coming Up on the Wrong Side"

After months of avoiding the Live Oak and other spots that might thrust him before his undoer, Mike decided that he was ready to confront Dieter. Not for a fight, but maybe to buy him a beer as a way of putting it all behind him. He went to the Live Oak on his first day off and saw Scott Maddox drinking alone at the bar.

"Hey Scott, you ready for a refill?"

Scott tipped the glass toward him and looked into it like a seer reading tea leaves. He smiled. It was three in the afternoon. He was just waking up and in a congenial mood, drinking alone, puffing on his pipe.

Mike ordered a "Scott Special," which was bar scotch filled to the brim for only a dollar, and got himself a draft. Mike had reservations about buying Scott a drink, knowing that it was killing him. But all the regulars figured as well that if you took him off the scotch, he would probably go a lot quicker.

"So, how's the weekly poetry going?" Scott had run the Sunday poetry readings since being turned out to pasture from academia. He was a poet of comic genius, far superior to those institutional poets, those poets in residence. But coming from the piney woods of Alabama, from parents who never knew that the Depression had ended in 1941, had not taught him the finer points of endearing oneself to university deans and professors.

"We've got a wonderful fiction writer coming from Lake Charles, you'll like him." Scott promoted every writer. That's how he made his twenty dollars a week. "Why don't you come by? I haven't seen you for months."

"Yeah, I might. Say, you know Dieter, don't you?"

"Oh, yeah, there was a going-away party for him a little while ago. He up and married this high-class good-looker from Peru. He moved to Lima." He shook his head. "I was sorry to see him go. He used to buy me meals and I had a place to stay on cold nights when

274

I needed it. Now I don't know from day to day."

Mike felt as if he'd been abandoned after a bad joke had been played on him. He finished his beer and walked to the streetcar stop in a daze. He rode it through the evening up and down the same route until the driver was ready to retire it at one in the morning.

Vicki Salloum

From *Faulkner & Friends*

He woke with a heavy weight inside his head, his nose and fingers numb, and as he struggled to get to his feet he felt as if he would pass out, a lightness, dizziness, almost overpowering him. He coughed—a hacking cough—and as he lay there for a few moments more to gather strength, he heard the loud voices of a couple passing on the sidewalk, animated, ignoring him, their voices collapsing into murmurs as they casually drifted on. He opened one eye, measuring the day's brightness to estimate the time. Judging by his usual getting up habits and the brilliance of the sun, he figured it was perhaps a little before ten in the morning. He could feel the cutting winds, and his fingers, nearly frozen, caused him more concern than the pain inside his head. *I must get up,* he thought, *I need a drink.* He remembered he had no money and the bottles of the night before were empty. He forced himself to his feet: there was a task awaiting him.

He knew what day it was; he never forgot such things. He rubbed his hands together. Leaning heavily against the brick side of the gallery, shuffling forward until the bricks ended, he forced himself onto the sidewalk, walking in slow, mechanical strides, head bowed, looking like a wound-down robot, he made his way to Magazine Street where he would use the john at Friendly's Bar and splash water on his face then head for the shop, where there would be wine to drink before the task began, calming him, giving him courage, helping him get through it all, helping him talk to strangers about Joe Christmas and Lena Grove and the middle-aged spinster whose partly severed head had turned clean around.

He had an obligation, perhaps his last, certainly not his first, and he believed in discharging obligations though his actions in the past decade certainly refuted that. But then that was in the past when he was crippled and ill and he was better than that now. He believed people are capable of change and should be given a second chance. He was giving himself a second chance. If not, why bother to get up in the morning? And he would do his best, with all the resolve left in him.

Emma Rose Brewer sat in the second row, near enough to the moderator's chair so that she could see and hear everything. Dressed in her black and orange animal print cardigan, her matching long sleeved shell and black pull-on pants, Emma Rose was a bit early, the first to arrive as was her custom, and her plump thigh, lifted in an ambitious attempt to transcend the other but failing, returned to its original position as a paper plate filled with appetizers rested in her lap.

She popped a sausage bread square into her mouth and saw the man arrive. Her first impression was that he did not belong, someone would have to escort him out, a tramp on the street, the patina of failure as glaring as his seedy pants. It was not the quality of the clothes that stuck out, for he wore a wool shirt jacket, a turtleneck in smoky jade and cotton deck pants in black, but the condition of it that disgusted her, dirty, threadbare, looking as if it'd been slept in.

One could clearly see he was not in tip-top shape by the blood-shot eyes behind the wire-rimmed glasses and the look of exhaustion or illness, and a look that told her he definitely did not want to be here but was here to elude the cold, perhaps. And his face looking drained, the flesh sallow above his silvery beard. It was especially the condition of the clothing, the turtleneck ripped at the waist, the pants perhaps twenty years—that was repugnant to her, and she shuddered. Taken altogether, the shabby creature shuffling in with his sluggish gate and decrepitude was a disgrace that should be escorted out. *Some people have no pride, don't do anything to better their lives,* Emma Rose thought as her perused the man while popping a cheese ball in her mouth.

She saw him head for the table containing the bottles of wine, and nobody stopped him. She saw a woman embrace him, the woman who'd greeted her at the door, her arms enfolding him, pressing her cheek to his, in genuine and joyful welcome, then wrapping an arm around his back as if to hold him up as he lifted a glass and tried pouring the wine, hand shaking, and the woman taking the bottle from him and pouring it herself. *Someone she knows*, Emma Rose surmised. *Close friend from the past or dirt poor relative.*

She watched the others drift in for it was now past starting time. She recognized a few. Ever since she'd retired six months earlier from her librarian's job at the university, she'd seen several of the people now gathered here at past signings and readings and discussions about town: Margie Dawson in her green sweater and bright lipstick and tight pants, her curly red hair pinned up at the back; Ruby Jean Hodorowski in her beige dress and pumps, one of her former colleagues at the library. And there was the art patron Delphine Schlumbrecht and the socialite Megan Hulle and a few others she didn't recognize, an elderly man in faded jeans, trying to be hip with his long white hair tied in back and an artist-type— appropriately trendy—with a single earring and ponytail.

She saw the derelict glance about the room. He seemed shy, a little afraid, gulping down his wine and pouring himself another. He poured a third glass then brought it with him as he took his place in the moderator's chair. *Surely this is a mistake*, Emma Rose thought. *Someone will come get him, force him to surrender his seat, escort him to the back, to one of the chairs facing the moderator's way in the back, far enough away where he's not too close to me.* She was not in the best of moods, whether it was from loneliness or too much time on her hands, she was not sure, but she knew she couldn't tolerate a smelly bum sitting next to her today. Her nerves were shot, as they'd grown increasingly, ever since her supervisor had a talk with her that day six months ago, told her she was making mistakes and forgetting things and maybe she ought to think about early retirement—she'd been forced out to pasture after forty years of devoted work.

It had not been easy forgetting the humiliation of that meeting. It had not been easy trying to booster her spirits and belief in herself after being told she was half senile and not to be trusted with the tasks she'd performed for more than forty years. And for six months now all there was to do was come to events like this, where her companions were derelicts with bloodshot eyes and old men frantic to be young and dilettantes like Megan Hulle with nothing else on their calendars.

She tried daily to find a purpose in life, but no one wanted to hire her for even part-time work, a sixty-four-year-old woman, so she kept herself active by scouring the newspaper for lectures and readings and the occasional play but plays cost money so mostly she ended up at free events. She could at least contribute here; she'd read more books than anyone she knew and could match anyone word for word when it came to intellect. It may be that her short-term memory was shot but she still possessed a lifetime of knowledge. And the author she knew best was her beloved William Faulkner, though she was most familiar with *Sanctuary,* by far his best work. And the gall of her supervisor to imply she'd lost her faculties, relegating her to a life of idleness when she had so much to give the world. Not like the deadbeat in the moderator's chair (*why hadn't someone escorted him out?*), not working, not contributing, a good-for-nothing that fate had put here to spoil another day.

He sat motionless, languid, only moving once to set his glass down, and then he looked about nervously until his eyes locked on hers and, as if he saw in them everything—her contempt, misgivings, her vile ill will—he cast the most unhappy look she'd ever seen at the dog-eared paperback book he clung to.

"My name's Leo," he said softly, signaling for their attention. "Welcome to the shop. We'll be talking about *Light in August.* It's Faulkner's best, in my opinion."

"I don't agree with that."

The voice came from up close. Emma Rose was shocked to discover the voice was hers, the words shooting out seemingly without her permission. It didn't bother her that she disagreed, for she wasn't afraid to be contrary when the occasion called for it, but she wasn't normally contentious over trivial things and she'd never in her life blurted out a comment only to find out afterward it was hers. It was queer and, most alarming, she heard the ire and resentment in it.

279

The bum ignored her. "Who," he went on, "do you think is the most tragic character?"

"Lena Grove," Ruby Jean shouted after Megan Hulle whispered in her ear. Emma Rose hated Ruby Jean's loudness but knew it was due to her being half deaf. It was the most pathetic combination, Ruby Jean's hearing loss and her massive craving for attention, for Ruby Jean always liked to have the first and last word in every conversation but she never said anything worthwhile in Emma Rose's opinion. "Lena Grove!" Ruby Jean repeated, in case nobody heard the first time. "There's nothing more tragic than being abandoned and pregnant."

"She wasn't more tragic than the Rev. Hightower," the artist averred. "He was disgraced because of his wife's affair. He lost his congregation and completely withdrew."

"And he stunk, too," the old man added, delighted to see a smile on a face or two.

"Hightower became the object of rumors," the artist continued earnestly. "He withdrew from society and had no connection with anyone. It was like living a dead man's life."

"But he reentered the world of the living," the bum said to him. A little color reappeared on his cheeks as he seemed to regain his confidence. He searched the room for faces. "Does anyone know how he did that?"

There was silence. He continued. "He gave Joe Christmas an alibi for his whereabouts the night of the murder. It was his attempt to reenter the world of the living by helping another human being. Some people say that was his redemption."

"He helped a *murderer*," Emma Rose shrieked.

She heard the tone, vehement, hysterical. Where did it come from? It was like some spirit possessing her, playing tricks on her mind, and it would be fascinating if it weren't so disturbing, for the tone of voice was betraying her, a powerful agitation driven by an evil demon exploding from her mouth and she had no control.

A silence followed.

She listened, realizing no one was so much taken aback by what she said as by the frantic tone, shocking her as well, so much so that she squirmed and the paper plate shifted in her lap and a half-eaten spinach pie fell to the floor. She bent to pick it up, lost hold of the plate and it fell as well and she could hear Megan Hulle giggle and that infuriated her. Trying to pick up all the food crumbs, her face lifted toward the watching eyes, her own squinting in anger, her mouth shaped in an O as she shrilled, "Joe Christmas was a worthless scumbag *murderer.*"

"You don't have to be so overwrought," Megan stage whispered. Then Megan exploded in giggles, nervous and gleeful. She managed to suppress the giggles and then she said with strained patience. "There are those who see Joe Christmas as a victim of horrible oppression, Emma Rose, because he was part black, which makes him sympathetic, even a Christlike figure."

"But he slit Joanna's *throat,*" said Emma Rose, voice rising. "She cooked his food, gave him a place to sleep, had sex with him, then he goes and slits her throat. Doesn't anybody give a damn?"

The bum-moderator picked up his glass, put it to his lips and emptied it. He shut his eyes as if savoring the wine's comfort, then he looked at her and this time his eyes betrayed no emotion. "Christmas had no identity." It was if a dead man spoke. His voice was a monotone. "He had no idea who his parents were so he was a cipher to himself and everyone else. That was his tragedy."

"There're lots of folks in this world who don't know who their parents are," she said with contempt. "But that doesn't mean they're supposed to go around *killing* people." Her hands began to tremble. Her tone took on the injured quality of a child. "Why are you making excuses for him?"

"Certainly I'm not . . . no one's . . . " His voice began to falter. He shook his head in disbelief then lowered it and smiled. It was as if he found it amusing she could think he cared enough to give excuses. Slowly, feebly, he set down the glass. When he sat up, he turned to the paperback and leafed through the pages. "There is a scene here where he says . . . ," and he began to read, " . . . 'I have never broken out of the ring of what I have already done and cannot ever undo . . . '" He closed the book but did not lift his eyes from it. "Can't you pity that?"

"No," Emma Rose snapped. "You're making excuses . . . making excuses for a *murderer.*"

The bum looked exhausted. He glanced anxiously at the empty glass, tightened his hold on the paperback, squeezing it and wincing at the same time, and then it seemed as if a wave of despair had taken over, as if he were some prisoner chained in lifetime confinement inside some black and empty hole. Emma Rose couldn't help for one moment pitying him as she suddenly pitied her own life. And then his voice seemed far away—way off in Alabama or Mississippi, wherever Joe Christmas came from—as he spoke to no one in particular in words she strained to hear:

"I keep going over the part about him thinking it was loneliness he was running from and not himself and the street running on, catlike, and how one place was the same as another to him, but in none of them could he be quiet."

She could tell he had memorized the lines in a book of five hundred pages. He took off his glasses, rubbed his eyes, and she could saw the red in them and how he seemed oblivious to everything around him.

He suddenly looked at her intently, and she hadn't expected that. In a disembodied voice, he said, "Have you ever felt like that?"

Emma Rose paused. She said nothing for several moments and all eyes were upon her. His, too, did not waver.

Finally, she said, "Ever felt like what?"

Somebody behind her sighed. The bum showed no expression. He got up, made his way to the wine table. He filled a new glass to the brim and, with his back to all of them, downed it and poured another. She didn't even wait until he finished. She stood up, he still with his back to her, and shouted: "Look at you—that's your fifth or sixth glass of wine." Then with her hands on hips, said, "Maybe some of us here don't have anything to run away from. And maybe people like you are jealous of people like us. People who don't do anything but work hard all our lives and treat people decently and try to be honest. It's people like you who feel sorry for some cold-blooded, mulatto drifter who just because he's half black and doesn't know who his parents are thinks he can get away with slitting a girl's throat. Look at how you look."

She stretched out an arm and pointed. "Why you don't even have the decency to put on some nice clothes. *Look at you*. Why, one would suspect you've never done a day's work in your life. But no one respects hard work anymore, so you should get along just fine. Just don't patronize me because I don't have sympathy for your ne'er-do-well drifter—which is just what *you* are: a ne'er-do-well, deadbeat worthless bum of a drifter."

He did not turn. He bent forward toward the table and then his body collapsed, the wine bottles and glasses and hors oeuvres crashing to the floor along with the table . . . . Now was a good time to leave, Emma Rose thought, another notch in the belt of her own devastation.

JOURNALISM

Nancy Harris

"Last Blast on My Toy Trumpet": *American Waste,* The Incredible Shrinking Poems

Everette Maddox, homeless guru-poet of the Maple Leaf Bar (who died of esophageal cancer in Charity Hospital, February 13, 1989), spent the final years of his life wasting away like "a naturalistic stick" on the curbs, gutters, sidewalks, benches, grassy levees in the Carrollton section of New Orleans by the mouth of the Mississippi River. On a conscious level he feared death and voiced this fear to his friends, who did not want to accept that his obvious physical deterioration was seriously life-threatening. On another level—the soul or higher self—he knew that death was approaching. The poems ascended, in spite of themselves, from the gutters and curbs of the city he loved. His poetic eye was a periscope from this lowest of angles—a gaunt vision and shocking point of view that was pared down to the bone on the edge of premonition—of his own death, his own merging with the universal. *American Waste* is a paradoxical palimpsest of angels and gutters, spiritual love and ribald lust.

Like the character in the cult classic movie, *The Incredible Shrinking Man*, Everette, along with his language and poetic forms, contracted to the minimal and the menial, as in the first nine lines of "How I Start My Day":

> First I go through the line
> at K&B
> & get a pack of matches
> Next I go to Woolworth's
> & drink 3 cups of coffee
> & look longingly
> at the little bottles
> of pineapple juice
> on the shelf

Everette looking longingly at the "little bottles of pineapple juice" is heartbreaking, given his poverty, but he had chosen his priorities: matches and pipe tobacco, coffee, later glasses of bar scotch. That detail reflects the sparse choices his life had shrunk to, but also, like the toy-sized Incredible Shrinking Man terrified in his dollhouse, he began to realize that the instant between the opposites of contraction and expansion was the moment of merging with the cosmic, the small becoming the great. The final poem in *American Waste*, "Flowing on the Bench," senses this merging:

> As I was going to sleep
> on the iron bench
> in the back of the bar
> I felt all right
> I felt I was joining something
> Not the Kiwanis Club
> No
> I felt like one river joining another
> I felt like the Mississippi
> flowing into the Ohio
> Right where Jim & I
> passed Cairo in the fog
> Right where the book got good

This merging with the universal permeates the imagery of the book, miraculously accomplished by the lurid little mundane details of a minimalistic existence, much like the characters in Samuel Beckett's novels and plays. His foreboding premonition of his death is again eerily sensed in "Composed on the Back of a Dark Green Muddy Waters' Poster" with yet another allusion to Mark Twain:

> When I woke up on the batture
> & you were not only gone
> but had never been there
> & I heard the aluminum
> silence of the river
> I was scared—

287

it wasn't *metaphysical*
exactly
I just thought they were firing
cannons over the water
to make Huck's carcass rise

"The aluminum silence of the river" is an incredible image of *American Waste*, underlined by the irony that Everette's ashes would be released into the muddy waters of the Mississippi along with garbage and discarded beer bottles. I was haunted by the ending of Beckett's novel *Murphy*, where the main character in a parody of an 18th century picaresque novel, Murphy, dies in a fire and his ashes are accidentally dropped and spilled on the floor of the pub he had frequented, and are swept out the front door of the tavern along with other dust and waste. Unfortunately, I had loaned Everette my copy of *Murphy*, which mysteriously disappeared along with many of his books after his death, or I would quote this final passage from the novel, which uncannily mirrors Everette's absurdist shrinkage into the *American Waste*. As Ihab Hassan says of Samuel Beckett in *The Literature of Silence*, "Beckett reduces; he never simplifies."[1]

Everette flirts with existential despair, but he always returns to romantic idealism, as in "Home In Their Biblical Beds":

the very spiritual
bodies of women
flow away
in white dresses
in Poe & Rosetti
The most famous
flow-away being
Millet's "Ophelia"
in the basement
of the Tate Gallery
How come people
don't really flow away
but grind & groan & crackle
& waste into a naturalistic stick

like my mother did
at St. Jude's
in Montgomery
20 years ago

Again, the flowing away of the river, a symbol of death, resurfaces with the wasting death of his mother from cancer, paralleling his own death. While the poem "Heaven," dedicated to his mother and Rupert Brooke, is probably the finest and most accomplished poem in *American Waste* (too long to quote here in its entirety), in which his "Mother died of the/ late 20th Century/ where heaven was a hospital," I think that "Home In Their Biblical Beds" is central to the manuscript, especially to the theme of unrequited love and woman as the spiritual muse for the poet. The fact that "people/ don't really flow away/ but grind & groan & crackle/ and waste into a naturalistic stick" further attests to his awareness that romantic idealism is just a poetic device.

His vision, often gleaned from curb and sidewalk, in looking up at American society from an angle that is upsetting to many, puts the perspective on the level of animals, especially street dogs. A jolting juxtaposition of this "low life" animal lust and spiritual love is the poem "A Vision."

I was sitting on the curb
by Dante & Oak
& in my mind's eye
or vice-versa
the hitherto locked
& jewel-encrusted
iron gates of your vagina
swung open
It was King Solomon's
mines
& I was clinging like a bat
for dear life
to that golden wall

As in alchemy, the mystical "chymical marriage" arises out of the *prima materia*, the dung heap of matter, the scarab rolling the ball of dung to the sun. The quest for unrequited love was a game for Everette, that he played in his last poems dedicated to Suzy Malone. He knew the object of desire was unobtainable, yet he used Suzy as his muse, because he somehow knew this was his last chance to blow his "toy trumpet" and create the poems in *American Waste*. His ability to write again after years of silence was what helped him to cling "like a bat/ for dear life/ to that golden wall" of imagination in the magical realm of making poems. And yet, this mixture of the profane and the sublime does not result in the whole opus, *lapis philosophorum*, of *American Waste*. Thus the ordinary facts of an ordinary existence ("I got up & staggered/ down Oak Street/ to buy some matches," "Ordinary American Paranoid Revisited") and the (at first glance) sexist poems to a barmaid's teats are tincture in the alembic of life and love that raise the vision far, far above the curbs and gutters of Everette's homeless existence. The dark humor in "Me & The Dog & The Bone Of Love" reveals the poet's academic stance in the game of unrequited love:

> Well—I woke up on the sidewalk
> next to a dog—
> inadvertently I assure you—
> & the dog said
> "What's the problem pal?"
> & I said, "Unrequited love"
> & the dog said "Pretty?"
> & I said "Pretty as moonshine
> through a broken bottle"
> The dog said "Sounds serious—
> where's she at?"
> I said "Across the street"
> The dog said "Long way"
> & I said in my best graduate school idiom
> "An unbridgeable gulf"
> Dog said "Well—want a bone?"
> & I said "I got a bone on"

> The dog said "Naw man—I mean to gnaw on"
> & I said "Well dog—
> considering the encroachment
> of a solid black sky
> unrelieved by her smile
> don't mind if I do"

Over and over again the literal, physical point of view is horizontal, as in "Where I Had Been," which was "on my hands & knees/ gnawing at the sparkles/ on the sidewalk," conveying another stray dog image, while in "The Outbound Dog" he empathizes with the outcast mongrel:

> My friend Tony
> threw some Mardi Gras beads
> around a yaller dog's neck
> as was yanked to a trendy grey
> Volkswagen in front
> of the Maple Leaf Bar—
> & then receded
> leaving me slumped against the opposite wall—
> I was drunk
> I can't speak for the dog
> but I said "Dog
> the air wears thin
> hot wire that son of a bitch
> & high tail it
> for points elsewhere
> I think
> I can take care of myself"

This identification with the "outbound dog" and the advice to "high tail it/ for points elsewhere" reveal a desire to exit a "trendy" society whose material values could never co-exist in his sidewalk world of K&B, Woolworth's, Muddy Waters, Carrollton Station and the Maple Leaf bars. In spite of despair and cynicism, the irony and absurd humor display the self-awareness of a Beckett character or the anti-voices of Mr. Bones and Henry Pussycat in Berryman's *Dream Songs.*

In 1988, the year prior to his death, Everette gave a reading at the Maple Leaf Bar from many of the poems that comprise *American Waste.* He was in good humor and loved the fact that the poems were retrieved from a brown paper grocery bag, mostly inscribed on napkins, bar coasters, and other scraps of paper. However, most of the poems were meticulously recopied from their original form onto lined notebook paper in plain block capital print. He made several copies of some of the poems. Therefore I have to strongly disagree with much of the consensus at the publication of *American Waste* in 1993, four years after his death. Most opinions were that the poems were not his "best work" and were unfinished and unrevised, but that they were remarkable given the extent of his illness, alcoholism, and poverty. Bullshit! I was privileged to be one of the half dozen editors of the manuscript and also entered them from the paper bag "scraps" into my word processor, an extremely emotional experience. During this process, I was mostly struck by the sense of foreknowledge of his impending death and by the pervading sense of mystical union throughout the imagery in the poems. The poems are uneven, to be sure, but this intertwining of the trivial, the lusty, and the sacred weave a whole that is greater than its parts. The poem that wraps it all up, "What I Said To The Sky" coheres all the fragments:

> I reeled out of a 6-martini
> candlelit dinner
> & stood in the usual gutter
> clutching what was left
> of the 20th century
> & looked up into a sky
> the color of a bruise
> It looked like Mr Hyde
> in Classics Illustrated
> & I shook my fist
> at the God that had vacated years ago
> overdue on the moral rent

& said "I came up a romantic idealist
& life has made me a mean
cynical pessimistic piss-ant
fuck you & the clouds you rolled in on"
& some wise-ass passer-by said
"But what about Suzy"
& I said "Suzy
blew the last blast
on my toy trumpet
that's all"

That's all? The "last blast" on his "toy trumpet" is a book of life, "Les Très Riches Heures" of a poet in the ironic clutches of poverty and alienation at the close of a century he never felt at home in, a "romantic idealist" who was, in fact, homeless. The whole of *American Waste* is a soul-wrenching, mystical, and paradoxical tapestry that depicts a life illumined by the quest for love and harmony, interwoven with disappointment and discord. These poems contract to a bare essence of hope (Suzy) holding the human spirit in suspense to the very end. These poems are not "throw away" scraps and demented attempts to salvage his art from the curbs and gutters of alcoholism, homelessness, and illness. These poems bear witness that Everette exited this play of sound and fury with grandeur and elegance. *American Waste* is testimony of an uncompromising spirit that grasped the philosopher's stone at the moment of shrinking into nothingness, into all.

[i] Ihab Hassan. *The Literature of Silence: Henry Miller & Samuel Beckett.* New York: Knopf, 1967.

Richard Kilbourne

Poems Represent Bare Essentials of Maddox's Life, Art

Everette Maddox lived and died in New Orleans, his adopted home, a city he clung to in poverty and in sorrow. This book well represents as no other words could the bare essentials of his life and art. New Orleans and Louisiana, the South, are much the richer for this testament.

Bar Scotch is a book of poems, each of which falls under one of two rather vague general headings, a division that is delineated in the book. The first group might be denominated "alcohol" and what the demon drink symbolizes, including slow suicide. It is painfully apparent in these poems that alcohol is the most readily available medicine, the medium through which an intolerable reality can be filtered—or at least held—to a manageable level and translated into art.

By distancing the pain it is possible to give it meaning, bring into play a soaring gift for language. A poem in the book's second part, however, better informs this sensibility. "My whole life, the whole / effort of my life, has been directed / against that song—that bramble, / kudzu choking my heart, and my friends' hearts." The second part is about unrequited love, and many times the beloved is metaphorically the city of New Orleans itself. The voice in these poems is always skating on thin ice, drawing back from the edge of chaos.

The foundation on which the airy intelligence in these poems is grounded is as fragile as a reed, a leaning tower of Pisa balanced on a toothpick, an inverted image of the Eiffel Tower mirrored in a reflecting pond: ". . . I'd rather carve with flowers."

Maddox was very much a poet of the South. Lodged somewhere in the fissures of this reality one suspects the tragic is simply inherent, an imprecation for forgiveness that goes unanswered. No wonder he chose to finish his life in the most Southern of Southern cities, New Orleans.

His South, however, is some other place than the present; it is the South of eloquent and grand gestures. I suspect it is impossible to be a poet of the South in the present day: certainly Maddox mined the last gold from the deepest veins, often touching harsh bedrock. "I don't enjoy / listening to myself think."

The old South was simply intolerable: it required generations of neurotic artists, often alcoholic, to paste all of its myths together and then peer into its black heart. Its political and social realities are long gone, its eloquence and nuance are vague to the point of disappearing. What remains is its literature. Reading Maddox's poems I am reminded of Blanche Dubois covering the naked light bulb with a delicate paper lantern. It is amazing, too, how much the literature of the South has depended upon the kindness of alcohol.

Maddox's irony is very much a Southern characteristic. "When the present storm is on, isn't / the violent past the safest place to be?" His own epitaph might be these lines from his poem "Of Fashion": "Somewhere, Dover Beach / maybe, something fragile / and afraid is trying to last / forever." I would add, "Time that is intolerant . . . / Worships language and forgives / Everyone by whom it lives."

Errol Laborde

Everette Maddox—Poet

They tell the tale of Everette Maddox and the rose. Maddox was a person who seemed to be consumed with the notion of love: love of poetry, love of New Orleans, love of one of its neighborhoods—Carrollton—and love—real romantic, genteel sort of love—of women. Ever since his divorce in 1978 there were several women for whom he developed an affection, the affection of a poet. To one of these women in particular he would leave a single rose each Valentine's Day. Even after the woman had moved away, he would send her a flower, each year on that day of such sentiments. He did so even though the cost of love—the price of a rose and postage—was sometimes heavy for a man living on a poet's pay.

They tell of Maddox being the head of the class of the literary homeless. On nice nights when the stars could recharge the soul of a poet, he would sleep on benches near Riverbend or on bank steps. When the weather was bad, he had an invitation, and a key, to sleep in the cab of a friend's truck. Some pitied that, others sensed that that was the way he wanted it. "He literally couldn't open a can of tuna," one friend recalled. "He just refused to ever learn how." Nevertheless, he existed through the help of friends just as those friends existed because of this magnetic draw he seemed to have. Sometimes he needed financial help. One time in particular, a friend recalled, it was only a pittance he wanted as Valentine's Day approached. He had a basic human need to be met, that of postage—and a rose.

Even in other days when he had a home, there was a tinge of romance to it—the romance of literature. He had lived in the house on Prytania Street where F. Scott Fitzgerald had lived during his brief stay in New Orleans. Fitzgerald too had been in pursuit of romance, personified in his beloved Zelda. Fitzgerald's life may have been the one that Maddox might have most liked to live, that of the glamour and style of the Roaring Twenties. Maddox, a man without a home, was never a man without style. He always wore a coat and tie. Friends recalled that when Brooks Brothers opened in New Orleans he was there the second day. His passions, it turned out, included owning a sports coat with the Brooks Brothers name on the label.

All the better, it might be assumed, to officiate over his life's main public responsibility, the Sunday poetry reading at the Maple Leaf Bar. He was passionate about that, too, a friend recalled. "He always scrubbed up for that and he would put on whatever good clothes he had. He would be a real charmer."

More than being just his forum, the Maple Leaf was also his office, his desk being the bar counter. He liked a good drink and some will say that was one love affair that went too far. But others recall more poetic moments, the warm conversations from the perch of a bar stool, having a drink, speaking of both love and writing.

In retrospect, writing was probably his true love, albeit one that was fickle. There were dry spells in his productivity when the words did not come easily, and then there were times when such words flowed. *Bar Scotch,* his latest book, provides evidence of the good days. A pile of more recent poems, saved by a friend, provides hope for there one day being a follow-up. Words, of course, well-crafted and thoughtful words arranged by the poet have a durability of their own. Words of all types and arrangement fascinated him, as they would a man whose favorite books were *Ulysses* and *Huckleberry Finn.* Like Huck himself, Maddox was on a raft when all around him were in steamboats.

Last week his adventures ended. Maddox died February 13 in Charity Hospital of complications due to cancer. It fits the romance that characterized his life that on the next day a mailing addressed to him was received at the Maple Leaf. It was a Valentine's Day card from the woman—the one who had received the roses. There will be no roses any more. But there will forever be those who will sit around a good drink and speak of both love and writing and to have felt touched by the passions of a poet.

Susan Larson

Poets Do the Maple Leaf Rag

For some passersby, it's probably just another bar on Oak Street with particularly good music on weekends. For others, it's a place to go and have a beer and play chess. But for a few others, it's a literary landmark, the venue for one of the South's longest-running reading series; on any given Sunday afternoon, the Maple Leaf Bar belongs to poets and poetry.

Today at 3 PM, the Maple Leaf Bar will celebrate the tenth anniversary of its weekly prose and poetry readings, marking the occasion with an open-mike reading and by pouring champagne.

Since its inception in 1979, the reading series has boasted such participants as Ellen Gilchrist, Andrei Codrescu, and Ron Cuccia. But perhaps the name most associated with the series is that of poet Everette Maddox, who died last February.

Maxine Cassin, editor and publisher of the New Orleans Poetry Journal Press, remembers when painter Franz Heldner suggested to his friends Everette Maddox and Robert Stock that they begin a series of bar readings. The first two readers, she recalls, were Maddox and Stock, and she and Martha McFerren were the second. Photographer Clarence Laughlin also read one of his prose poems at the bar that summer.

"There were washers and dryers in the back," Cassin recalls. "And I remember one time in the middle of my reading when Everette said, 'Wait a second, I need to go put my clothes in the dryer.' It was really soapsuds and beer in those days. It was hot and muggy, and the smells from Christiana's Seafood Market next door weren't always pleasant."

Reading series are usually intangible bits of history, but the Maple Leaf activities have produced an anthology, *The Maple Leaf Rag*, published by Cassin's New Orleans Poetry Journal Press in 1980. Contributors included Yorke Corbin, Ralph Adamo, Peter Cooley, Ron Cuccia, Tom Dent, Ellen Gilchrist, William (Kit)

Hathaway, Martha McFerren, Raeburn Miller, Sue Owen, and Katherine Soniat, among others.

Another offshoot of the reading series is Pirogue Publishing, headed by Bill Roberts and Hank Staples. Pirogue has published Julie Kane's *Body and Soul,* Roberts' *Stories on the Drift,* and Everette Maddox's *Bar Scotch.* The company will publish Nancy Harris's *The Ape Woman Story* later this year.

Peter Cooley, who read at the Maple Leaf last Saturday, said, "That was a special experience for me, particularly since I was reading with my daughter, Nicole. Poetic work is done in such isolation that to have the kind of intelligent, receptive audience that turns out for these readings is really a gift."

The growing reputation of the series has been a key to its success. Many nationally known poets, who would ordinarily receive substantial remuneration for reading, have read at the Maple Leaf gratis, simply because it is part of a poet's itinerary in New Orleans.

Like any activity involving creative egos, the Maple Leaf series has had its moments of high drama, such as the time one poet knocked another's front teeth out or the time Happy Hooker Xaviera Hollander entered the bar looking for Everette Maddox, who had just died. The dog days of August inspired an annual "Dull Reading"; on one such occasion, someone read all of the verbiage on a fire extinguisher. As poet Richard Katrovas puts it, "Poetry readings are generally among the oddest examples of human behavior, and over the years the readings at the Maple Leaf have been among the most delightfully odd gatherings I've ever witnessed."

Bartenders and regulars have also gotten involved. One bartender, Bill Petre, was moved to perform a dramatic reading of "A Child's Christmas in Wales" during the holidays. The bar's owners, Carl Brown and John Parsons, have also been very supportive of the series.

Admission to today's reading is free. For information, call 866-9359.

Susan Larson

The Poetry's on the House: The Maple Leaf Bar Toasts 15 Years of Sunday Readings

The Maple Leaf Rag 15th Anniversary Anthology. Edited by Ralph Adamo, Maxine Cassin, Nancy Harris, J. Patrick Travis, with an introduction by Nancy Harris. Portals Publishing. $15.

Chances are, if you ask someone where to hear good music in New Orleans, you'll get a dozen different answers. If you want to know where to hear good poetry, the list is considerably shorter, but one thing's certain. The Maple Leaf Bar, that Carrollton land-mark, will be near the top of any short list of poetic destinations. A new book, *The Maple Leaf Rag 15th Anniversary Anthology,* cele-brates the place and the people who have performed their work there over the last decade and a half.

Poet Nancy Harris, who has run the reading series for the past five years following the death of founder Everette Maddox in 1989, provides a scene-setting introduction, taking readers to the 15th Annual Mardi Gras Poetry Extravaganza earlier this year. She chronicles the endurance of the reading series through hard times, especially the deaths of founders Maddox and poet Bob Stock, as well as through good times, marked by the publication of the *Maple Leaf Rag,* the first anniversary anthology. She also recalls books written by readers in the series and publishing companies begun by others. Harris's introduction gives the neophyte a fascinating little slice of New Orleans literary history as well as a glimpse into her own growth as a poet.

The poems are the work of more than one hundred writers who have read at the Maple Leaf. Some are well-known writers with other publications to their credit, writers such as Ralph Adamo, John Biguenet, Thomas Bonner, Maxine Cassin, Peter Cooley, Joel Dailey, John Gery, Lee Meitzen Grue, Julie Kane, William Matthews, Martha McFerren, Vassar Miller, Kay Murphy, Sue Owen, John Sinclair, Katherine Soniat, Leon Stokesbury, Glen

Swetman, Elizabeth Thomas, Helen Toye, Tom Whalen, and Janet Wondra, to name a few. Most contributors are regional writers, though many have moved on, but the list of contributors includes a number of prize-winning poets from around the country.

As one might expect, this anthology is suffused with the spirit of a particular place, New Orleans and its environs, in a particular time, over the last fifteen years, with all the sad sweet impossible hopes that are attached to poetry and people. Poet Tony Bland writes a "Poem from Horn Island," Thomas Bonner writes of playing "Ball at the Barracks by the Mississippi," Katherine A. Nelson-Born describes "An Epiphany in Mississippi," while Andrew Fox is "Hanging on the Fence By the Po' Blues Festival." Lee Meitzen Grue, long a stalwart of the New Orleans poetry scene, writes of "Li'l Queenie: Changes." Julie Kane, in "The Maple Leaf Bar," wants "to understand the place,/ to play with words like Booker played."

In many ways this collection could serve as a commonplace book of life in New Orleans. Christine Dumaine Leche describes the sustenance of food in "Bread" and "Manuel's Hot Tamales." Sharon Olinka, in "The Past, Waving," visits both Mandina's and Kate Chopin's house, while Elliot Richman, in "Doin' My Wash On Magazine Street in August," takes us to "the grungiest laundromat in New Orleans/ somewhere way down Magazine/ where the dryers operate on Heisenberg's/ Uncertainty Principle." The poet robbo recalls neighborhood life in "Stoop," while Katherine Soniat describes "Storyville, November 12, 1917: Midnight." John Sinclair and Beverly Rainbolt both draw on Mardi Gras for inspiration, while Elizabeth Thomas offers "Visions of Doom at Canal Villere."

Many poems are inspired by or dedicated to the late Everette Maddox. One of the best is William Harmon's "Free Refills," which remembers a time when Maddox said he "felt the/ most beautiful/ words in English/ were *Free Refills*," a moment in the life of a man Harmon calls the "greatest Montgomery romantic since Zelda, and/ a gentleman/ of courtly chivalry and enterprise to boot." Manfred Pollard, in "An Elegy for Everette Maddox," describes how "His voice of rotten teeth and rankest tongue/ could torch the hearts of strangers in a storm."

Other poems, such as Julie Kane's "The Maple Leaf Bar," remember the late pianist James Booker, as does David Love Lewis's "For James Booker the Third": "We pretended to know you,/ pretended to understand/ your droning anger./ Mad as Hell we could have said,/ Difficult to Know is what/ we came out with."

Nancy Harris, in "My Dog Comes to the Word 'Death,'" describes the dilemma of those left behind: "now, many of my best friends are in heaven/ & many of them are here./ Which way do I turn for comfort?"

Countless poets, many more than the hundred or so represented in this book, have turned for comfort to the Maple Leaf, which Harris describes as "my church and my salvation on Sunday afternoons." This anthology is a worthy hymn of praise to all who, all too often, must work at difficult jobs and save their most heartfelt efforts for the higher calling of poetry on Sunday afternoons.

Spike Perkins

Southern Poetic Voice Rises Again

I will admit being biased on the subject of Everette Maddox as we are in a sense colleagues: both affiliated with the Maple Leaf Bar in uptown New Orleans. For three and a half years I have performed music at the Maple Leaf, and Maddox has held his weekly poetry readings there for nearly a decade.

You might remember the Maple Leaf from the nightclub scene in the movie *Angel Heart*. It is a long, smoke-filled tunnel with pressed tin walls and ceiling, where blasts of zydeco accordion ricochet over the heads of dancing, sweating revelers all the way down to escape into the patio in back. It is frequented by local intellectuals, off-duty musicians, hip foreign tourists, drunks, and occasional politicians.

These are the environs of Everette Maddox and the setting for many of the poems in his new book, *Bar Scotch*. No doubt the subject matter will invite comparisons to Charles Bukowski, but Maddox's work is enriched by a stronger grounding in the literary tradition. Some of this belies the poet's academic past, but his command of this literary element never allows it to compromise the emotional power of the poems. Maddox doesn't shy away from vulgarity when it's effective, but uses it much more sparingly than Bukowski.

Both writers share a down-and-out Bohemian ideal where perpetual drunkenness is accepted, and wealth and responsibility are ridiculed. In the poem "The Jerk," for example, the executive protagonist makes a discovery about his ailing pickup truck:

> . . . "it
> only had a old $100 bill
> caught in the carburetor,
> which me and Bubba
> straightway dislodged."

When it comes to women, however, Maddox and Bukowski part

company. Where Bukowski is macho and contemptuous (though hilariously funny) and usually gets the girl anyway, Maddox is romantic and courtly, even in his most lustful moments, and usually strikes out. But he counters his rejections with a wistful humor:

> I realize I've earned
> eighteen lousy bucks, you
> still don't love me, and
> the witless River is
> flowing the same old way.

Loneliness figures prominently in the poems, but always humor keeps them from lapsing into self-pity. A bottle of bar scotch becomes the key to a private world:

> They don't think I have any fun:
> they don't know I carry a hip flask
> and talk, far into the night, to the rats.

Alcohol can be the catalyst for alienation as well as fellowship, but the poet faces even hangovers with an insatiable wit:

> That must have been
> the night the booze
> miscarried, and I got
> numbed outside but
> personally locked in
> with the Loveless Terrors;
> that's what I meant
> by snarling over my sweet
> roll: "Reach me my whip
> and chair in here, and
> don't forget the pistol."

There is also an answer to well-meaning friends who might suggest he drinks too much:

It's on purpose. I'm
drinking myself to
death. Melodrama!
That's why . . .
. . . Because it
never occurred to
me that the end of
the world would be so
dull.

But this is not a one-sided collection of poems. There are also arresting vignettes of New Orleans and the Alabama of Maddox's youth. He has succeeded in capturing on paper the most elusive and paradoxical aspects of the New Orleans ambience. For this is a city which is both the most sensual and the most spiritual in America, where antique Creole elegance and third-world funkiness not only coexist, they complement each other. The poem "New Orleans" echoes some of my own feelings on first seeing the city from the air, as well as some of my private ruminations on the effect of the city on its artists.

Also worthy of mention are Maddox's sonnets—the book contains six. He makes use of the form effortlessly, with a tone that is both natural and conversational. Of contemporary poets, perhaps only John Berryman has achieved this as successfully.

The publication of *Bar Scotch* marks something of a renaissance for Everette Maddox. There is an earlier collection, *The Everette Maddox Song Book*; he has been widely published in reviews and quarterlies throughout the United States and Europe, and his work has even been included in a few anthologies, but he hasn't made much noise on the literary scene for a number of years. This is truly an occasion to celebrate the return of a rich and unique poetic voice and to hope he achieves even wider recognition in the future.

Everette Maddox Bibliography

Authored Books

Maddox, Everette. *The Thirteen Original Poems.* New Orleans: Xavier University English Department, 1975.

—. *The Everette Maddox Song Book.* New Orleans: The New Orleans Poetry Journal Press, 1982.

—. *Bar Scotch.* New Orleans: Pirogue Publishing, 1988.

—. *American Waste.* Intro. by Ralph Adamo. New Orleans: Portals Press, 1993.

—. *Rette's Last Stand.* Intro. by Rodney Jones. Mobile: The Tensaw Press, 2004.

Edited Books

Cassin, Maxine, Yorke Corbin, and Everette Maddox. *The Maple Leaf Rag: An Anthology of New Orleans Poetry.* New Orleans: The New Orleans Poetry Journal Press, 1980.

Manuscript Collections

Williams Research Center of The Historic New Orleans Collection. 10 Chartres Street, New Orleans, Louisiana 70130

Xavier University Archives and Special Collections. Xavier University Library, Xavier University of Louisiana. 1 Drexel Drive, New Orleans, Louisiana 70125z

Contributors' Notes

Ralph Adamo's books include *Waterblind: New and Selected Poems* (Portals Press, 2002). He edited the Fall/Winter 1994 issue of the *New Orleans Review* containing a retrospective on Maddox's life and work.

Randolph Bates teaches nonfiction writing at the University of New Orleans. His publications include *Rings: On the Life and Family of a Southern Fighter* (Farrar, Straus & Giroux, 1989) and work in *Grand Street, Ploughshares, Prairie Schooner,* the *Los Angeles Times,* and the *Boston Globe.*

Grace Bauer is the author of *The Women at the Well* (Portals Press, 1996) and *Beholding Eye* (WordTech Press, 2006). A resident of New Orleans from 1974 to 1984, she now teaches at the University of Nebraska at Lincoln.

Stan Bemis is a native of California and a visual artist as well as a writer. He performs prison ministry work at Louisiana's Angola State Penitentiary.

Thomas Bonner, Jr., Kellogg Professor of English at Xavier University of Louisiana has books on Kate Chopin, William Faulkner, and Edgar Allan Poe. With Robert E. Skinner, he has edited *Above Ground: Fiction About Life and Death by New Southern Writers* (Xavier Review Press, 1993) and *Immortelles: Poems of Life and Death by New Southern Writers* (XRP, 1995).

Steve Brooks is an Austin-based singer-songwriter. His website is http://www.stevebrooks.net.

George Burton III lives in Shreveport, Louisiana. Another of his poems about the Maple Leaf Bar can be found in *The Maple Leaf Rag 15th Anniversary Anthology* (Portals Press, 1994).

Maxine Cassin is the author of *Against the Clock: New and Neglected Poems* (Portals Press, 2003). As co-founder and editor of the New Orleans Poetry Journal Press, she published Everette Maddox's first poetry book, *The Everette Maddox Song Book* (1982).

Christopher Chambers got his MFA degree from the University of Alabama at Tuscaloosa and, like Everette Maddox, drifted down to New Orleans. He teaches creative writing and screenwriting at Loyola University and edits the *New Orleans Review*. His work can be found in *French Quarter Fiction, Knoxville Bound,* and *Best American Mystery Stories 2003.*

Carlos Colon has published more than 1100 poems in locations ranging from the "Let the Good Times Roll" mural in his hometown of Shreveport to a display outside a temple on Sado Island in Japan.

Peter Cooley is a Professor of English and Director of Creative Writing at Tulane University in New Orleans. His eighth volume of poetry, *Divine Margins,* is forthcoming from Carnegie Mellon Press.

Joel Dailey lives close to the racetrack in New Orleans. His most recent collections are *Nutria Bounce* (Open 24 Hours, 2005) and *Lower 48* (Lavender Ink, 1999).

Ken Fontenot works for the Texas state government in Austin. A poetry book review contributor to the *Concho River Review,* he has new poems forthcoming in *American Poetry Review (APR).*

Louis Gallo is a Professor of English at Radford University in Virginia. His poems, stories, and essays can be found in such journals as *Glimmer Train, Kansas Quarterly, Missouri Review,* and *Modern Fiction Studies.*

Ellen Gilchrist's many honors include a National Book Award for fiction. She lives in Fayetteville, Arkansas. Her most recent books are *Nora Jane: A Life in Stories* (Back Bay Books, 2005) and *The Writing Life* (University Press of Mississippi, 2005).

Michael Greene and his wife, poet Beverly Rainbolt, were recently invited to hold a month-long writers-in-residency appointment at Plymouth's College of St. Mark and St. John in England.

R. S. Gwynn is a Professor of English at Lamar University in Beaumont, Texas. The recipient of the 2004 Michael Braude Award from the Academy of Arts and Letters, he is the author of *No Word of Farewell: New and Selected Poems, 1970-2000* (Story Line Press, 2001).

William Harmon is the James Gordon Hanes Professor in the Humanities at the University of North Carolina at Chapel Hill. A past winner of the Poetry Society of America's William Carlos Williams Award, he is the editor of *Classic Writings on Poetry* (Columbia University Press, 2005) and *A Handbook to Literature* (Prentice Hall, 10th ed. 2005).

Nancy Harris has been keeping the Maple Leaf Bar poetry readings going since the death of Everette Maddox in 1989. Her books of poetry include *The Ape Woman Story* (Pirogue Publishing, 1989) and *Mirror Wars* (Portals Press, 1999).

Karen Head is the Writing Program Coordinator at the Georgia Institute of Technology. Her first poetry book is *Shadow Boxes: Poems and Prose Poems* (All Nations Press, 2003).

Harry de la Houssaye has a Ph.D. in creative writing from the University of Houston. His poems have appeared in the *New Orleans Review, The Maple Leaf Rag 15th Anniversary Anthology,* and elsewhere.

Rodney Jones is the author of eight books of poetry including *Transparent Gestures* (Mariner Books, 1989), which won the National Book Critics Circle Award for poetry, and *Elegy for the Southern Drawl* (Mariner Books, 2001), which was a finalist for the Pulitzer Prize.

Julie Kane teaches at Northwestern State University in Natchitoches, Louisiana. Her most recent poetry collection, *Rhythm & Booze* (University of Illinois Press, 2003), was a National Poetry Series winner and a finalist for the 2005 Poets' Prize.

Fred Kasten's friendship with Everette Maddox began when both were students at the University of Alabama at Tuscaloosa. He is now the Program Director of public radio station WWNO-FM in New Orleans.

Richard Katrovas is the author of six poetry collections, a short story collection, two memoirs, and a novel. He is also the founding academic director of the Prague Summer Program in creative writing.

Richard Kilbourne resides in Clinton, Louisiana, where he practices law. His fourth book of legal and financial history is forthcoming in 2006 from Pickering & Chatto in London.

David Kunian has written and produced radio documentaries on James Booker, Michael Ward, Earl King, Guitar Slim, James Black, and the Dew Drop Inn, in addition to Everette Maddox.

Errol Laborde is the editor of *New Orleans Magazine* and the producer of the weekly "Informed Sources" news roundtable show on WYES-TV in New Orleans.

Katheryn Krotzer Laborde has published work in *Poets & Writers, Xavier Review, Mochila Review,* and *Desire.* Recently she was a finalist for the *Glimmer Train* Short-Story Award for New Writers.

Susan Larson has been the book editor of the New Orleans *Times-Picayune* since 1988. She is also the author of *The Booklover's Guide to New Orleans* (Louisiana State University Press, 1999).

William Lavender directs the Low Residency MFA Program at the University of New Orleans. His most recent poetry collection is *While Sleeping* (Chax Press, 2004). He is also the editor of *Another South: Experimental Writing in the South* (University of Alabama Press, 2003).

Doug MacCash is the art critic for the New Orleans *Times-Picayune*. He was one of the small band of journalists who stayed behind in the city to file news reports during Hurricane Katrina and its aftermath.

William S. Maddox (1949-1998), Everette's younger brother, was the author of the novel *Scattiato* (Portals Press, 1996) and co-author of the political science book *Beyond Liberal and Conservative* (Cato Institute, 1984). He taught political science at the University of Central Florida and the University of New Orleans.

William Matthews (1942-1997) published eleven books of poetry during his lifetime, including the National Book Critics Circle Award winner *Time & Money* (Mariner Books, 1996). He served as president of both the Poetry Society of America and the Association of Writers and Writing Programs (AWP).

Martha McFerren's four poetry collections include *Women in Cars* (Helicon Nine Editions, 1992) and *Contours for Ritual* (Louisiana State University Press, 1988). Journals in which she has published include *Poetry,* the *Georgia Review,* and the *Southern Review.*

Christopher Munford is the author of *Sermons in Stone* (Birch Brook Press, 1993) and the chapbook *River Night* (Sub Rosa Press, 1989). During the early 1980s he worked as a journalist in south Louisiana.

Kay Murphy is an Associate Professor of English at the University of New Orleans. The author of two poetry collections including *Belief Blues* (Portals Press, 1998), she has published poems, stories, and essays in journals including *Poetry, College English,* and *Fiction International.*

Sharon Olinka lives in New York City and is a frequent contributor to the *American Book Review.* Her second book of poetry is *The Good City* (Marsh Hawk Press, 2006).

Spike Perkins has resided in New Orleans since 1982, where he works as a musician and free-lance writer. He wrote the cult hit song

"Pitbull" with Coco Robicheaux, and he appears on Robicheaux's *Spiritland* CD.

Manfred Pollard is a visual artist as well as a writer. His photographs of Everette Maddox and of Maddox's funeral appeared in the Fall/Winter 1994 Maddox tribute issue of the *New Orleans Review.*

JC Reilly has published poems in *Plains Song Review, Rive Gauche,* and *Into the Teeth of the Wind.*

William Roberts, a native of Long Island, New York, has lived in south Louisiana since 1976. Together with Hank Staples he founded Pirogue Publishing, which published Everette Maddox's second book, *Bar Scotch* (1988).

Vicki Salloum's fiction piece is an excerpt from the second chapter of her novel-in-progress, *Faulkner & Friends.* Her short stories have been included in the anthologies *When I Am An Old Woman I Shall Wear Purple* (Papier-Maché Press, 1991), *Pass/Fail: 32 Stories About Teaching* (Red Sky Books, 2002), and *Voices from the Couch* (America House, 2002).

Randall Schroth taught at the University of New Orleans from 1981 to 1983 and read at the Maple Leaf; he now lives in Boulder, Colorado. New Orleans figures in the title of his 1985 chapbook, *Camels of the Vieux Carré.*

Louie Skipper is an Episcopal priest in Birmingham, Alabama. His poetry collections include *The Fourth Watch of the Night* (Swan Scythe Press, 2001) and *Deaths That Travel with the Weather* (Orchises Press, 1992).

Robert Stock (1923-1981) lived with his family in Brazil, Costa Rica, Mexico, New York City, and San Francisco prior to settling in New Orleans and becoming a Maple Leaf regular. His *Selected Poems (1947-1980)* was published by Crane & Hopper in 1994.

Leon Stokesbury teaches at Georgia State University. He is the author of *Autumn Rhythm: New and Selected Poems* (University of Arkansas Press, 1996) and the editor of *The Made Thing: An Anthology of Contemporary Southern Poetry* (University of Arkansas Press, 2nd ed. 2000).

Helen Toye has published her work in *Pudding House,* the *New Orleans Review,* and *Sunday at Four.* A native and longtime resident of New Orleans, she relocated to Memphis following Hurricane Katrina.

Gail White is the author of *The Price of Everything* (Mellen Poetry Press, 2001) and the editor of *Kiss and Part: Laughing at the End of Romance and Other Entanglements* (Doggerel Daze, 2005). She lives in Breaux Bridge, Louisiana.

Carolyne Wright is the author of eight books and chapbooks of poetry including *Seasons of Mangoes and Brainfire* (Eastern Washington University Press/Lynx House Books, 2nd ed. 2005), which won the Blue Lynx Prize, the Oklahoma Book Award in Poetry, and the American Book Award from the Before Columbus Foundation.

Ahmos Zu-Bolton II (1946-2005) was a poet, folklorist, storyteller, editor, and publisher. A former writer-in-residence at the University of Missouri at Columbia, he published five books of poetry including *1946: A Poem* (Ishmael Reed Publishing Company, 2002).

Acknowledgments

Ralph Adamo: "Introduction to *American Waste*," from Everette Maddox, *American Waste* (Portals Press), © 1993 by William Maddox. "Notes Toward an Elegy" and "Poem Ending Everette" from *Waterblind: New and Selected Poems* (Portals Press), © 2002 by Ralph Adamo. Reprinted by permission of the author.

Grace Bauer: "Three: for James Booker on St. Patrick's Eve," from *The Journal* (1996). "On Finding a Note to Everette Maddox in My Library Book, New Orleans, 1979," from *The Maple Leaf Rag* (New Orleans Poetry Journal Press), © 1980 New Orleans Poetry Journal Press. "Second Lining at My Own Jazz Funeral," from *Shenandoah* (1990). Reprinted by permission of the author.

Stan Bemis: "The Goddamned Absence," from *The Maple Leaf Rag* 15th *Anniversary Anthology* (Portals Press), © 1994 by Portals Press. Reprinted by permission of the author.

Steve Brooks: "Dead Poets Society," from *Purgatory Road* (Frog Records, 1995), words and music © 1991 by Steve Brooks. Reprinted by permission of the author.

George Burton III: "Sonnet for Everette Maddox," from *Sunday at Four* (2002). Reprinted by permission of the author.

Carlos Colon: "One More Way of Looking at a Possum," from *Sunday at Four* (1997). Reprinted by permission of the author.

Peter Cooley: "Some Kind of Resurrection," from *The Hawaii Review* (1997). Reprinted by permission of the author.

Ken Fontenot: "Poem Ending with Resolutions, Half-Baked" and "Winter and the Moon Tugs at the Mind," from *All My Animals and Stars* (Slough Press), © 1988 by Ken Fontenot. Reprinted by permission of the author.

Louis Gallo: "Yeah," from *The Maple Leaf Rag 15th Anniversary Anthology* (Portals Press), © 1994 by Portals Press. Reprinted by permission of the author.

Ellen Gilchrist: "The Raintree Street Bar and Washerteria," from *The Age of Miracles* (Little, Brown), © 1995 by Ellen Gilchrist. Reprinted by permission of Don Congdon Associates, Inc.

William Harmon: "Free Refills," from *The Maple Leaf Rag 15th Anniversary Anthology* (Portals Press), © 1994 by Portals Press. Reprinted by permission of the author.

Nancy Harris, "Introduction to the 15th Anniversary Edition of *The Maple Leaf Rag*," from *The Maple Leaf Rag 15th Anniversary Anthology* (Portals Press), © 1994 by Portals Press. "Memento Mori" and "My Dog Comes to the Word 'Death,'" from *Mirror Wars* (Portals Press), © 1999 by Nancy Harris. "Unemployed in Fall #2," from *Shards* (Umpteen Press), © 2002 by Nancy Harris. Reprinted by permission of the author.

Rodney Jones: "Some Notes on Everette Maddox," from the *New Orleans Review* (1994). Reprinted by permission of the author. "Elegy for a Bad Example," from *Elegy for the Southern Drawl: Poems by Rodney Jones* (Houghton Mifflin), © 1999 by Rodney Jones. Reprinted by permission of Houghton Mifflin Company. All rights reserved.

Julie Kane: "The Bartender's Hair," "Everything But Blue," "The Maple Leaf Bar," and "Mapleworld; or, Six Flags Over the Maple Leaf," from *Rhythm & Booze* (University of Illinois Press), © 2003 by Julie Kane. Used with permission of the University of Illinois Press.

Richard Katrovas: "From *Mystic Pig: A Novel of New Orleans*," from *Mystic Pig: A Novel of New Orleans* (Smallmouth Press), © 2001 by Richard Katrovas. Reprinted by permission of the author.

Katheryn Krotzer Laborde: "From 'The Ballad of Waltzing John,'" from "The Ballad of Waltzing John," *Xavier Review* (1992). Reprinted by permission of the author.

Errol Laborde: "Everette Maddox—Poet," from *Gambit Weekly* (2 February 1989). Reprinted by permission of the author.

Susan Larson: "Poets Do the Maple Leaf Rag," from *The Times-Picayune* (11 June 1989). "The Poetry's on the House: The Maple Leaf Bar Toasts 15 Years of Sunday Readings," from *The Times-Picayune* (15 June 1994). © 2005 The Times-Picayune Publishing Co. All rights reserved. Used with permission of the *Times-Picayune.*

William Lavender: "'Living Water': Notes for an Essay on Everette Maddox," from the *New Orleans Review* (1994). Reprinted by permission of the author.

Doug MacCash: "On the Manuscript of *American Waste.*" Reprinted by permission of The Historic New Orleans Collection.

Everette Maddox: "Thirteen Ways of Being Looked at by a Possum," from *The Everette Maddox Song Book* (New Orleans Poetry Journal Press), © 1982 by Everette Maddox. Reprinted by permission of the New Orleans Poetry Journal Press.

William Matthews: "Dignity from Head to Toe," from the *New Orleans Review* (1994). Reprinted by permission of Sebastian Matthews.

Martha McFerren: "Southern Gothic," from *Women In Cars* (Helicon Nine Editions), © 1992 by Martha McFerren. Reprinted by permission of Helicon Nine Editions and the author.

Christopher Munford: "The Day After Easter in New Orleans," from *Sermons in Stone* (Birch Brook Press), © 1993 by Christopher Munford.

Kay Murphy: "Oh, Everette, There Is No Reason Why," from *Belief Blues* (Portals Press), © 1998 by Kay Murphy. Reprinted by permission of the author.

Sharon Olinka: "Bird of Death," from *A Face Not My Own* (West End Press), © 1995 by Sharon Olinka. Reprinted by permission of the author.

Spike Perkins: "Streets of New Orleans," from *The Maple Leaf Rag 15th Anniversary Anthology* (Portals Press), © 1994 by Portals Press. "Southern Poetic Voice Rises Again," from *Papyrus*. Reprinted by permission of the author.

Manfred Pollard: "An Elegy for Everette Maddox," from *The New Orleans Art Review* (1992) and *The Maple Leaf Rag 15th Anniversary Anthology* (Portals Press), © 1994 by Portals Press. Reprinted by permission of the author.

Bill Roberts: "From 'Coming Up on the Wrong Side,'" from "Coming Up on the Wrong Side," *Stories on the Drift* (Pirogue Publishing), © 1988 by Bill Roberts. Reprinted by permission of the author.

Randall Schroth: "Everette Maddox," from *Rolling Stock* (1990). "Thirteen Ways of Looking at a Blackboard," from *Northwest Shorthand* (Pink Dog Press), © 1989 by Randall Schroth. Reprinted by permission of the author.

Louie Skipper: "From 'Deaths That Travel with the Weather,'" from *Deaths That Travel with the Weather* (Orchises Press), © 1992 by Louie Skipper. Reprinted by permission of the author.

Robert Stock: "Walking with Angels," from *Selected Poems (1947-1980)* (Crane & Hopper), © 1994 by Harriette Stock.

Leon Stokesbury: "The Royal Nonesuch," from *Autumn Rhythm: New and Selected Poems* (University of Arkansas Press), © 1996 by Leon Stokesbury. Reprinted by permission of the University of Arkansas Press.

Gail White: "Partying with the Intelligentsia," from *Light Quarterly* (1999) and *The Price of Everything* (Mellen Poetry Press), © 2001 by Gail White. Reprinted by permission of the author.

Ahmos Zu-Bolton II: "Everette Maddox," from *Ain't No Spring Chicken* (Voice Foundation, Inc.), © 1998 by Ahmos Zu-Bolton II. Reprinted by permission of Amber Zu-Bolton.